S0-BAP-609

The No. 1 Price Guide to
M.I.HUMMEL®

Figurines,
Plates,
More...

**by renowned expert
ROBERT L. MILLER**

- accurate prices
- easy-to-use
- pocket size

1983/PORTFOLIO PRESS
Huntington, New York 11743

*This book is dedicated to my wife Ruth,
who made it all possible*

We solicit your questions, suggestions, opinions
and criticisms. If we can be of help in making your
collecting more complete and enjoyable, or if you
just want to say "hello"—call or write:

Robert L. Miller
112 Woodland Drive
Eaton, Ohio 45320
1-513-456-3735

The No. 1 Price Guide to
M.I. HUMMEL
Second Edition/First Printing

*Copyright © 1983 Portfolio Press Corporation. All rights
reserved. No part of this publication may be reproduced,
stored in a retrieval system, or transmitted in any form or
by any means, electronic, mechanical, photocopying,
recording or otherwise, without the prior permission of
the copyright owner or the publishers. Published in Huntington, New York and simultaneously in Toronto, Canada
and in London, England. Printed in the U.S.A.*

Library of Congress Catalog Card Number
83-060850
ISBN 0-942620-06-2

Introduction

This price guide is designed to meet the growing needs of dealers and insurance underwriters, as well as the collector-enthusiast. It is primarily intended as an aid in identifying, dating and pricing both current and older "M.I. Hummel" figurines, along with plates, bells, lamps, and other related "M.I. Hummel" items produced through the years by W. Goebel Porzellanfabrik of Rodental, West Germany.

This new, revised edition contains over 400 photographs and over 3,000 prices, plus reliable, pertinent information on size and color variations, and restyling or structural changes that have evolved to the present date. The inclusion of *all known* data, along with photographs, makes this the only complete and accurate price guide ever to be published. Since the author has had free access to the Goebel factory archives and the total cooperation of the Goebel company officials, the authenticity of the material contained in this price guide cannot be questioned. In addition, the author has worked with and studied "M.I. Hummel" figurines and other items of Hummel art continuously for the past 18 years. The publication of this book has been approved by W. Goebel Porzellanfabrik, the sole manufacturers of the "M.I. Hummel" figurines, plates, and bells.

The format of this guide provides a flexible bracket or price range, rather than one arbitrary price for each item. It is extremely difficult to assign an exact value for each figurine since many factors can affect this valuation. Prices do vary from one section of the country to another—and even sales within a given area may be at different figures. General economic conditions prevailing at the time of sale can affect valuations too. Exact values on older specimens of Hummel figurines are impossible to ascertain, because so many factors must be taken into consideration. In such instances, the rarity of the piece, its general condition (whether mint, restored, damaged), its color, its authenticity, and finally, its appeal to the collector, must be considered.

Certain figurines have always been more appreciated than others—hence they are more in demand and thus command higher prices proportionately. The same is true of ashtrays and holy water fonts, which have never been as popular as the figurines themselves. They, of course, usually sell at lower prices.

The price ranges quoted in this book reflect the current retail prices as opposed to wholesale or dealer prices. Thus a person selling a certain item cannot expect to receive the top bracket price in most instances. It is more likely he may receive a figure somewhere between the low and high quoted. Some dealers use the price ranges in this guide as a "bench mark," and offer the seller a percentage of either the high or the low figure. Again the rarity of the piece enters into the actual value determination. After reading the above, you may question the worth of any price guide in the first place. However, the author firmly believes the astronomical growth in Hummel collecting over the past few years dictates the necessity for such a yardstick of values. More and more collectors, novices and veterans alike, have been asking, "What should I expect to pay for this or that figurine?" "What should I sell my figurines for?" "What should I insure my collection for?" These questions are answered intelligently in this up-to-date list of values. The easy-to-read format provides simple and understandable information which reflects prices on today's market.

The author, having years of experience in buying and selling "M.I. Hummel" figurines and related items, would be the first to admit that there are wide fluctuations or variations in market prices today. It would be foolhardy and misleading to think that this or any other price guide could assign exact values for each and every Hummel piece. What has been provided in this guide is an accurate and reasonable range or "norm" so that the collector, dealer, or insurance agent can intelligently place a true valuation on each item. When it comes to a matter of worth, you must remember: it is "what the buyer is willing to pay, and the seller is willing to accept" that really sets the price. It takes *two* to strike a bargain!

—*Robert L. Miller*

The Remarkable Story of Sister M.I. Hummel

Children are children the world over. Impish or shy, saucy or quiet, mischievous or thoughtful...language differences don't matter, nor do variances in national custom. The innocence of childhood produces a universality that is loved and understood everywhere. This is perhaps the key to the remarkable and enduring popularity of the wonderful creations of Sister Maria Innocentia Hummel.

Berta Hummel was born in the town of Massing in Lower Bavaria, Germany, on May 21, 1909, one of six children of Adolph and Viktoria Hummel. Although a closely knit family, the children were not carbon copies of one another. While her older sisters were industriously helping their mother with household chores, Berta was busy drawing, making costumes for her dolls, and putting on theatricals for family and friends.

War broke out when she was only six. Her father was drafted into the army and the family was left without his guiding influence. Berta, whose artistic talents he had always encouraged, began to show signs of willfulness and lack of discipline, often taxing the patience of her teachers. Fortunately, her creativity was to be recognized early; due to the efforts of one of her teachers, she was enrolled at a fine religious boarding school at Simbach, near Massing, the Institute of English Sisters.

It was here that she first received artistic direction. Her flair for scenic and costume design fostered just for fun in the family's backyard, now began to emerge as a genuine talent. Soon she was designing for school productions. In four years, she progressed from only sketching the friends of her childhood and illustrating folk tales to painting landscapes in watercolor.

The religious training at the school

proved to be good discipline, and her development into a young lady and a promising artist was a delight to behold.

In 1927, when she was 18, Berta's proud father went with her to Munich where she was enrolled in the Academy of Fine Arts. To be on some familiar ground in otherwise strange territory, she took up residence outside the Academy in a dormitory run by a religious order.

The Academy, a prestigious center of design and applied arts, provided her with still more extensive training. Soon she began to paint in oils, and her experience with costumes was now expanded to include weaving of fabrics and designing clothing.

She was soon under the wing of a leading artist and teacher, who hoped she would remain at the Academy after graduation as his assistant. But a conflict was developing within Berta. Although she was gaining a great knowledge of art, its history, its scope and an exciting awareness of what travel and study in other cities, perhaps even other lands, might offer a young student, she was still the simple Bavarian girl from a warm, loving family, and her ties to her background were strong. Her feelings of religion were profound, and through a warm friendship at the dormitory with two Franciscan nuns who were also studying at the Academy, became even more important.

Her wonderful sense of fun never left her, and to the delight of her fellow students (and often the chagrin of the Mother Superior) she would play pranks at the residence. But more than anything, she was a gentle, emotional person, deeply affected by people and events.

In 1929, Hitler's National Socialist Party was on the rise in Munich, making specific promises of employment within the party. It offered an economic stability in depression years for sympathizers among the students of the Academy. But the militarism and politics of the Nazis were counter to Berta's sensitivities, and she turned with even greater need to the quiet, withdrawn life of her two religious friends.

With graduation drawing near, the pressures were becoming stronger for her to make a decision. On the one hand were her professors, eager for her to remain with them and continue her promising development. But on the other hand, with the frightening political atmosphere growing, there was the draw of fulfillment to be found behind the cloistered walls of a convent where she could continue her art while serving humanity through her devotion to God.

By the time of graduation in March 1931, she had made her decision. On April 22, she entered the convent of Siessen at Saulgau, and two years later was ordained Sister Maria Innocentia of the Sisters of the Third Order of St. Francis.

While a novice, she had taught art to children in kindergarten, and by late 1933 had so developed that she exhibited her work in a nearby town. Franz Goebel, fourth-generation head of W. Goebel, first became aware of her in 1934, and sought permission from her and the convent to translate her sketches of sparkling children and serene religious figures into three-dimensional form. This marked the beginning of a relationship between Sister Maria Innocentia, the convent and W. Goebel that continues to endure, long years after her death.

But dark clouds were hovering everywhere, and soon the sisters began to live in dread, for the Nazi government was determined to close the convent. In late 1940, the convent became a repatriation center for German nationals from other countries, and a small group of nuns, Sister Maria Innocentia included, remained to care for them.

It was a time of great deprivation. No longer able to remain in her spacious studio because of the terribly overcrowded conditions, Sister Maria Innocentia lived in a small, damp, basement room. Food and fuel were scarce, and she became terribly weakened by a lung infection. True to her dominant spirit, however, she tried to continue to work.

By November 1944 she was so ill that she was admitted to a sanitarium for treatment, where her illness was finally diagnosed as chronic tuberculosis. In April 1945, the war ended and, feeling somewhat strengthened, Sister Maria Innocentia returned to the convent to help with the enormous task of rebuilding. Her spirit as ever was strong, but her physical condition had deteriorated so that she was forced to enter another sanitarium the following November, leaving it in late 1946 to return to her beloved convent.

On November 6, 1946, at the hour of noon, the chapel bells rang out in solemn proclamation of the death of Sister Maria Innocentia at the age of 37.

A young life, full of spirit and love, came to a tragic end. But the youthful, loving spirit lives on in the pert faces of the Hummel children and the gentle bearing of the madonnas that are with us in ceramic. If we look at them a certain way, we can almost hear them breathe!

History and Explanation of Marks and Symbols

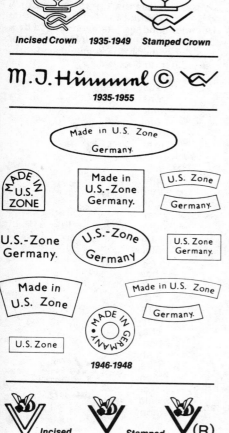

Incised Crown   **1935-1949**   **Stamped Crown**

M.I. Hümmel © ⌣

1935-1955

Made in U.S. Zone Germany.

MADE IN U.S. ZONE

Made in U.S.-Zone Germany.

U.S. Zone / Germany.

U.S.-Zone Germany.

U.S.-Zone Germany

U.S. Zone Germany.

Made in U.S. Zone

MADE IN GERMANY

Made in U.S. Zone

Germany.

U.S. Zone

1946-1948

Incised   **Stamped**   **(R)**

© W. Goebel

Full Bee   © **W. GOEBEL**

1950-1955

The "wide-crown-WG" trademark was used on the first "M.I. Hummel" figurines produced in 1935. On the earliest figurines it was incised on the bottom of the base along with the "M.I. Hummel" signature on the top or side of the base. Between 1935 and 1955, the company occasionally used a ©⌣ mark on the side or top of the base of some models. It is seen occasionally to the right of the "M.I. Hummel" signature. The "crown" appears either incised or stamped. When both are used on the same piece it is known as a "double crown" mark.

From 1946 through 1948 it was necessary to add the stamped words "Made in the U.S. Zone Germany." This mark was used within various types of frames or without a frame, underglazed or stamped over the glaze in black ink.

In 1950, four years after Sister M.I. Hummel's death, Goebel wished in some way to pay tribute to her fine artistry. They radically changed the trademark, instituting the use of a bee flying high with a "V." (Hummel means "bumble bee" in German, and the "V" stands for "Verkaufsgesellschaft" or distribution company.) This mark, known as the full bee trademark, was used until 1955 and appeared—sometimes both incised and underglazed—in black or blue and occasionally in green or magenta. In addition, the stamp "Germany" and later "West Germany" appeared. An (R) appearing beside the trademark stands for "Registered."

Sometimes the molds were produced with a lightly incised circle on the bottom of the base in which the trademark was centered. It has no significance other than as a target for the location of the decal. Some current production figurines still have this incised circle even though it is no longer used for that purpose.

Always searching for a mark that would blend esthetics with professionalism, the company continued to modify the trademark; in 1956, the company—still using the bee inside the "V"—made the bee smaller, with its wing tips parallel with the top of the "V." In 1957, the bee remained, although once again rising slightly above the "V." In 1958, the bee was smaller still and it flew deep within the "V," reflecting the changing trends of modern design. The year 1959 saw the beginning of stylization and the wings of the bee became sharply angular.

In 1960, the completely stylized bee with "V" mark came into use, appearing with "W. Germany." It was used in one form or another until 1979. In addition to its appearance with "W. Germany" to the right (1960-1963), it appeared above the "W. Germany" (1960-1972), and to the left of the "three line mark" (mid-1960's to 1972). The three line mark was used intermittently and sometimes concurrently with the small, stylized 1960-1972 mark. It was the most prominent trademark in use prior to the "Goebel bee" trademark.

It became apparent that the public was equating the "V and Bee" mark only with "M.I. Hummel" items, not realizing that the mark included the full scope of Goebel products. It was decided to experiment further with marks. In 1972, satisfied that it now had a mark designating a quality Goebel product, the company began using a printed "Goebel" with the stylized bee poised between the letters "b" and "e."

Since 1976, the Goebel trademark on Hummel figurines has been affixed by a decal on top of the glaze. It is possible for two figurines on the primary market to have differing decals.

Small Bee
1956

High Bee
1957

Baby Bee
1958

V Bee
1959

Early Stylized
(Incised Circle)
1957-1960

Germany
West Germany
Western Germany
GERMANY

Western
Germany
© W. Goebel
Copr. W. Goebel

1935-1955

W. Germany
1960-1963

W. Germany
1960-1972

© by
W. Goebel
W. Germany
1964-1972

In 1979, the stylized bee was dropped and only the name *Goebel* appears. The year of production will be on the base next to the initials of the chief decorator. These changes will be incorporated into production as existing stocks of figurines are exhausted.

The above information is a concise documentation of all W. Goebel trademarks authorized for use on "M.I. Hummel" figurines. In searching for accurate documentation on all W. Goebel trademarks used in conjunction with "M.I. Hummel" figurines, the author made a thorough investigation of the W. Goebel archives and queried the world's leading collectors. But it is always possible that a few rare and undocumented variations may exist.

Evolution of Geobel Bee Trademark in use since 1972

1979 Current Trademark

The Collection

Here is the revised and fully-authorized documentation of the complete collection of "M.I. Hummel" figurines, plates, plaques and all other art objects. This is the most definitive listing and photographic collection ever assembled. This list, compiled from the W. Goebel production journal in Rodental, West Germany, constitutes a record of all "M.I. Hummel" figurine identification numbers run in ascending order from 1 to 968. English and German names of the figurines, as well as their sizes, notes, and most models, will be found in the special annotated listing.

All sizes are approximate and depend upon exact method of measurement. Minor variations occur frequently and therefore should not be considered significant.

"M.I. Hummel" figurine identification numbers and their corresponding figurines are divided into five distinct categories:

Open Edition (OE): Pieces currently in W. Goebel's production program.

Closed Edition (CE): Pieces formerly in W. Goebel production program but no longer produced.

Open Number (ON): An identification number, which in W. Goebel's numerical identification system has not yet been used, but which may be used to identify new "M.I. Hummel" figurines as they are released in the future.

Closed Number (CN): An identification number in W. Goebel's numerical identification system that was used to identify a design or sample models for possible production, but then for various reasons never authorized for release.

Possible Future Edition (PFE): Pieces that have been designed and approved for production and possible release in future years.

Many collectors are interested in the trademarks that were used on "M.I. HUMMEL" figurines; therefore, we have used the numbering system of:

❶ =
Crown

❷ =
Full Bee

❸ =
Stylized

❹ = © by W. Goebel W. Germany
Three Line

❺ = Goebel
Goebel Bee

❻ = Goebel®
Current

to identify each mark that a particular figure can be found with. There will be some exceptions to this rule. We will list only the marks that were in general circulation of each figurine. For instance, HUM 347 Adventure Bound will be listed as only 4, 5 and 6 trademarks, as it was first sold in the U.S. market in 1971. We have, however, in our collection, an early sample model with a "full bee" trademark. This would be extremely rare, and would not be listed. Some early figurines will be found with no trademark at all. This fact does not lessen their value to any great extent, but does make it more difficult to determine their age. When figurines vary greatly in size, we will use the "bracket" system, showing the smallest to the largest size, i.e. 5½" to 6". Your measurement may vary depending on what means you use to measure. To properly measure a figurine, you should place it on a flat surface, then stand a ruler beside it. Place another ruler or straight object horizontally touching the highest point of the figurine and the perpendicular ruler. You will then have an accurate measurement.

Decoration-designations for "M.I. Hummel" figurines

All "M.I. Hummel" figurines are handpainted according to "M.I. Hummel's" original design. The decoration techniques had to be numbered because the factory uses so many.

The "M.I. Hummel" decor is done in painting method number eleven. A stroke-eleven (/11) is added to the model number following the size indicator in the factory's literature and price lists. *It does not, however, appear incised on the base.* In this book we only refer to incised numbers.

Decor. No.	Marked	Description
11	/11	all matte-finish colors in a rich variety of pastels inspired by rural surroundings
11 blue	/11 blue	madonna with dark blue cloak; rest of figurine in pastels
13	/13	ivory decoration in pastels
6 blue	/6 blue	madonna with pastel blue cloak; rest of figurine in matching pastels
6 red	/6 red	madonna with light red cloak; rest of figurine in matching pastels
83	/83	matte-finish shading on bisque body
H	/H	brown matte decor, very rare —not made after 1955
W	/W	white overglaze

Alphabetical Listing

The following is a listing of all "M.I. Hummel" Figurines and other related items. A valuable cross-reference to use alone or in conjunction with The Collection.

ANNIVERSARY PLATES

NAME	HUM No.
1980, Pair of girls from Ring Around the Rosie (Spring Dance)	281

ANNUAL BELLS

NAME	HUM No.
Annual Bell 1978, Let's Sing	700
Annual Bell 1979, Farewell	701
Annual Bell 1980, Thoughtful	702
Annual Bell 1981, In Tune	703
Annual Bell 1982, She Loves Me	704
Annual Bell 1983, Knit One	705
Annual Bell 1984, Mountaineer	706

ANNUAL PLATES

NAME	HUM No.
Annual plate 1971, Heavenly Angel	264
Annual plate 1972, Hear Ye, Hear Ye	265
Annual plate 1973, Globe Trotter	266
Annual plate 1974, Goose Girl	267
Annual plate 1975, Ride into Christmas	268
Annual plate 1976, Apple Tree Girl	269
Annual plate 1977, Apple Tree Boy	270
Annual plate 1978, Happy Pastime	271
Annual plate 1979, Singing Lesson	272
Annual plate 1980, School Girl	273
Annual plate 1981, Umbrella Boy	274
Annual plate 1982, Umbrella Girl	275
Annual plate 1983, Postman	276
Annual plate 1984, Little Helper	277
Annual plate 1985, Chick Girl	278
Annual plate 1986, Playmates	279

ASHTRAYS

NAME	HUM No.
Boy with Bird	166
Happy Pastime	62
Joyful	33
Joyful (without rest for cigarette)	216 (CN)
Let's Sing	114
Singing Lesson	34

BOOKENDS

NAME	HUM No.
Apple Tree Girl & Apple Tree Boy	252A & B
Book Worm, Boy and Girl	14A & B
Doll Mother & Prayer before Battle	76A & B
Eventide & Adoration (without shrine)	90A & B
Farm Boy & Goose Girl	60A & B
Good Friends & She Loves Me, She Loves Me Not!	251A & B
Joyful and Let's Sing	120
Little Goat Herder & Feeding Time	250A & B
Playmates & Chick Girl	61A & B
Puppy Love and Serenade with dog	122
Wayside Harmony and Just Resting	121

CANDLEHOLDERS

NAME	HUM No.
Angel Duet	193
Angel Lights	241
Angelic Sleep	25
Begging his Share (before 1964)	9
Birthday Cake (A Birthday Wish)	338
Boy with horse	117
Candlelight	192
Girl with Fir Tree	116
Girl with Nosegay	115
Heavenly Song	113
Herald Angels	37
Joyous News	27/I
Joyous News, Angel with Accordion	39
Joyous News,	

NAME	HUM No.

PLAQUES

Ba-Bee Ring	30A & B
Being Punished	326
Child in Bed, Wall Plaque	137
Flitting Butterfly	139
Little Fiddler	93
Little Fiddler (Wood Frame)	107
Madonna and Child (in relief)	249
Madonna Plaque	48
Madonna Plaque (Metal Frame)	222
Merry Christmas	323
Merry Wanderer	92
Merry Wanderer (Wood Frame)	106
Merry Wanderer (in relief)	263
M.I. Hummel Store Plaque (in English)	187
M.I. Hummel Display Plaque (redesigned from older model)	187A
M.I. Hummel Store Plaque (Schmid)	210
M.I. Hummel Store Plaque (in English, Oeslau)	211
M.I. Hummel Store Plaque (in French)	208
M.I. Hummel Store Plaque (in German)	205
M.I. Hummel Store Plaque (in Spanish)	213
M.I. Hummel Store Plaque (in Swedish)	209
Quartet	134
Retreat to Safety	126
Searching Angel	310
Smiling Through, Goebel Collectors' Club Plaque	690
Standing Boy	168
Star Gazer	237
Swaying Lullaby	165
The Mail Is Here	140
Tiny Baby in Crib	138
Tuneful Goodnight (Happy Bugler)	180
Vacation Time	125
Wall picture with sitting woman and child	156

NAME	HUM No.

TABLE LAMPS

Apple Tree Boy	230
Apple Tree Girl	229
Birthday Serenade	231
Birthday Serenade	234
Culprits	44A
Farewell	103
Good Friends	228
Happy Days	232
Happy Days	235
Just Resting	225
Just Resting	II/112
Out of Danger	44B
She Loves Me, She Loves Me Not	227
Shrine	100
To Market	223
To Market	101
Volunteers	102
Eventide	104
Wayside Harmony	224
Wayside Harmony	II/111

WALL VASES

Boy and Girl	360A
Boy	360B
Girl	360C

Old   New

HUM 1
Puppy Love
First modeled by master sculptor Arthur Moeller in 1935. A very few early models were made with the head tilted at a different angle and without tie. This old style is considered extremely rare and would command a premium of over $1,000. Always featured with a black hat. In old catalog listed as the "Little Violinist."

☐ 1	5 to 5¼"	(OE)	❶	$300-350
☐ 1	5 to 5¼"	(OE)	❷	$200-250
☐ 1	5 to 5¼"	(OE)	❸	$125-150
☐ 1	5 to 5¼"	(OE)	❹	$85-100
☐ 1	5 to 5¼"	(OE)	❺	$80-85
☐ 1	5 to 5¼"	(OE)	❻	$77.50

HUM 2
Little Fiddler
Also modeled by master sculptor Arthur Moeller in 1935, this figurine differs from the boy in "Puppy Love" in the fact that it always has a brown hat with an orange hat band. There are many size variations and all sizes have now been restyled with the new textured finish. Old name: "Violinist" or "The Wandering Fiddler." Same as HUM 4 except for the color of hat. Sometimes incised 2/3 instead of 2/III.

☐ 2/0	5¾ to 6½"	(OE)	❶	$350-425
☐ 2/0	5¾ to 6½"	(OE)	❷	$200-250
☐ 2/0	5¾ to 6½"	(OE)	❸	$125-150

☐ 2/0	5¾ to 6½"	(OE)	❹	$100-125
☐ 2/0	5¾ to 6½"	(OE)	❺	$95-100
☐ 2/0	5¾ to 6½"	(OE)	❻	$94.50
☐ 2/I	7½"	(OE)	❶	$500-750
☐ 2/I	7½"	(OE)	❷	$400-500
☐ 2/I	7½"	(OE)	❸	$200-300
☐ 2/I	7½"	(OE)	❹	$200-225
☐ 2/I	7½"	(OE)	❺	$185-200
☐ 2/I	7½"	(OE)	❻	$185
☐ 2/II	10¾"	(OE)	❶	$1750-2000
☐ 2/II	10¾"	(OE)	❷	$1200-1500
☐ 2/II	10¾"	(OE)	❸	$800-1000
☐ 2/II	10¾"	(OE)	❹	$700-800
☐ 2/II	10¾"	(OE)	❺	$630-700
☐ 2/II	10¾"	(OE)	❻	$630
☐ 2/III	12¼"	(OE)	❶	$2500-3000
☐ 2/III	12¼"	(OE)	❷	$1750-2000
☐ 2/III	12¼"	(OE)	❸	$1250-1500
☐ 2/III	12¼"	(OE)	❹	$750-850
☐ 2/III	12¼"	(OE)	❺	$680-750
☐ 2/III	12¼"	(OE)	❻	$680

3/I

HUM 3
Book Worm

This figurine was modeled by master sculptor Arthur Moeller in 1935. Old name: "Little Book Worm." Size 3/I has only one flower on page, while sizes 3/II and 3/III have two flowers on page. Sometimes incised 3/2 instead of 3/II and 3/3 instead of 3/III but does not affect the value as Arabic or Roman size indicators were used interchangeably for no basic reason. Same design was used for HUM 8. Book Worm was restyled by master sculptor Gerhard Skrobek in 1980 with the new textured finish.

☐ 3/I	5½"	(OE)	❶	$500-700
☐ 3/I	5½"	(OE)	❷	$300-400
☐ 3/I	5½"	(OE)	❸	$200-250
☐ 3/I	5½"	(OE)	❹	$150-200
☐ 3/I	5½"	(OE)	❺	$140-155
☐ 3/I	5½"	(OE)	❻	$140

☐ 3/II	. . . . . 8"	. . . . (OE)	. . . . ❶	$1250-1500
☐ 3/II	. . . . . 8"	. . . . (OE)	. . . . ❷	$1000-1250
☐ 3/II	. . . . . 8"	. . . . (OE)	. . . . ❸	$800-900
☐ 3/II	. . . . . 8"	. . . . (OE)	. . . . ❹	$700-800
☐ 3/II	. . . . . 8"	. . . . (OE)	. . . . ❺	$630-700
☐ 3/II	. . . . . 8"	. . . . (OE)	. . . . ❻	$630
☐ 3/III	. . . . . 9 to 9½"	. . . . . (OE)	. . . . ❶	$2500-3000
☐ 3/III	. . . . . 9 to 9½"	. . . . . (OE)	. . . . ❷	$1500-2000
☐ 3/III	. . . . . 9 to 9½"	. . . . . (OE)	. . . . ❸	$850-1000
☐ 3/III	. . . . . 9 to 9½"	. . . . . (OE)	. . . . ❹	$750-850
☐ 3/III	. . . . . 9 to 9½"	. . . . . (OE)	. . . . ❺	$680-750
☐ 3/III	. . . . . 9 to 9½"	. . . . . (OE)	. . . . ❻	$680

Notice great variations in sizes

HUM 4   Little Fiddler

Same as HUM 2 except it has black hat. Many size variations. Old name: "Violinist" or "The Wandering Fiddler." First modeled by master sculptor Arthur Moeller in 1935 but current production models have been restyled with the new textured finish. One of several figurines that make up the Hummel orchestra.

☐ 4	. . . . 4¾ to 5¾"	. . . (OE)	. . . . ❶	$300-325
☐ 4	. . . . 4¾ to 5¾"	. . . (OE)	. . . . ❷	$150-175
☐ 4	. . . . 4¾ to 5¾"	. . . (OE)	. . . . ❸	$100-125
☐ 4	. . . . 4¾ to 5¾"	. . . (OE)	. . . . ❹	$80-90
☐ 4	. . . . 4¾ to 5¾"	. . . (OE)	. . . . ❺	$75-80
☐ 4	. . . . 4¾ to 5¾"	. . . (OE)	. . . . ❻	$72

Newer model

HUM 5
Strolling Along
Originally modeled by master sculptor Arthur Moeller in 1935. Older models have eyes that glance off to one side. Newer models look straight ahead. Color of dog will vary.

☐ 5	4¾ to 5¾"	(OE)	❶	$300-325
☐ 5	4¾ to 5¾"	(OE)	❷	$150-175
☐ 5	4¾ to 5¾"	(OE)	❸	$100-125
☐ 5	4¾ to 5¾"	(OE)	❹	$80-90
☐ 5	4¾ to 5¾"	(OE)	❺	$75-80
☐ 5	4¾ to 5¾"	(OE)	❻	$72

Old style   *New style*

HUM 6
Sensitive Hunter
Modeled by master sculptor Arthur Moeller in 1935. Was originally called "The Timid Hunter." The lederhosen straps on older models of size 6. or 6/0 are parallel in back. Newer models have crossed-strap suspenders. All other sizes have crossed straps in all time periods. Sometimes incised 6/2 instead of 6/II. All sizes were restyled in 1981 and now have a more natural-looking *brown* rabbit instead of the original *orange*-colored rabbit. Some variations in the position of the ears of the rabbit in older models.

New style 6/O   Old style 6/O

☐ 6/0	4¾"	(OE)	❶	$250-325
☐ 6/0	4¾"	(OE)	❷	$150-200
☐ 6/0	4¾"	(OE)	❸	$125-150
☐ 6/0	4¾"	(OE)	❹	$80-90
☐ 6/0	4¾"	(OE)	❺	$75-80
☐ 6/0	4¾"	(OE)	❻	$72
☐ 6/I	5½ to 6"	(OE)	❶	$750-1000
☐ 6/I	5½ to 6"	(OE)	❷	$350-500
☐ 6/I	5½ to 6"	(OE)	❸	$150-175
☐ 6/I	5½"	(OE)	❹	$105-125
☐ 6/I	5½"	(OE)	❺	$95-105
☐ 6/I	5½"	(OE)	❻	$94.50
☐ 6/II	7 to 7½"	(OE)	❶	$1000-1500
☐ 6/II	7 to 7½"	(OE)	❷	$500-750
☐ 6/II	7 to 7½"	(OE)	❸	$300-350
☐ 6/II	7 to 7½"	(OE)	❹	$200-250
☐ 6/II	7 to 7½"	(OE)	❺	$175-200
☐ 6/II	7 to 7½"	(OE)	❻	$175
☐ 6.	5"	(CE)	❶	$400-500

7/I "double base" variation

HUM 7 Merry Wanderer

Can be found in more size variations than any other figurine. A six-foot model was placed in front of the Goebel factory in Rodental in 1971 to commemorate Goebel's 100th anniversary and in 1978 a ten-foot model was unveiled in front of the headquarters of the Goebel Collectors' Club in Tarrytown, New York. First modeled by master sculptor Arthur Moeller in 1935. Was restyled by master sculptor Gerhard Skrobek in size 7/II with the new textured finish in 1972, with an incised copyright date. Size 7/III was restyled in 1978 but without an incised copyright date. Older models of size 7/I have what collectors call a "double base" or "Stair step" base. All sizes and all time periods of HUM 7 usually have only five buttons on vest. Sometimes incised 7/2 instead of 7/II. The 32-inch model (HUM 7/X) was first sold in the U.S. market in 1976.

☐ 7/0 . . . . . . 6 to 6¼" . . . . . (OE) . . . . ❶ $350-500
☐ 7/0 . . . . . . 6 to 6¼" . . . . . (OE) . . . . ❷ $200-275
☐ 7/0 . . . . . . 6 to 6¼" . . . . . (OE) . . . . ❸ $135-180
☐ 7/0 . . . . . . 6 to 6¼" . . . . . (OE) . . . . ❹ $120-135
☐ 7/0 . . . . . . 6 to 6¼" . . . . . (OE) . . . . ❺ $100-110
☐ 7/0 . . . . . . 6 to 6¼" . . . . . (OE) . . . . ❻ $100
☐ 7/I . . . . . . 7 to 8" . . . . (OE) . . . . ❶ $750-1000
☐ 7/I . . . . . . 7 to 8" . . . . (OE) . . . . ❷ $750-850
☐ 7/I . . . . . . 7 to 8" . . . . (OE) . . . . ❸ $275-750
☐ 7/I . . . . . . 7 to 8" . . . . (OE) . . . . ❹ $225-275
☐ 7/I . . . . . . 7 to 8" . . . . (OE) . . . . ❺ $185-200
☐ 7/I . . . . . . 7 to 8" . . . . (OE) . . . . ❻ $185
☐ 7/II . . . . . . 9½ to 10¼" . . (OE) . . . . ❶ $1500-2000
☐ 7/II . . . . . . 9½ to 10¼" . . (OE) . . . . ❷ $1000-1500

☐ 7/II	9½ to 10¼"	(OE)	❸	$800-1000
☐ 7/II	9½ to 10¼"	(OE)	❹	$700-800
☐ 7/II	9½ to 10¼"	(OE)	❺	$630-700
☐ 7/II	9½ to 10¼"	(OE)	❻	$630
☐ 7/III	11 to 12"	(OE)	❶	$2500-3000
☐ 7/III	11 to 12"	(OE)	❷	$1500-2000
☐ 7/III	11 to 12"	(OE)	❸	$850-1000
☐ 7/III	11 to 12"	(OE)	❹	$750-850
☐ 7/III	11 to 12"	(OE)	❺	$680-750
☐ 7/III	11 to 12"	(OE)	❻	$680
☐ 7/X	32"	(OE)	❺	$7500-13,000
☐ 7/X	32"	(OE)	❻	$13,000 (list price)

HUM 8
Book Worm
Same as HUM 3 except smaller in size. Has only one flower on page. Old name: "Little Book Worm." Factory records indicate that this figurine was modeled by master sculptor Reinhold Unger in 1935.

☐ 8	4 to 4½"	(OE)	❶	$350-400
☐ 8	4 to 4½"	(OE)	❷	$200-250
☐ 8	4 to 4½"	(OE)	❸	$125-150
☐ 8	4 to 4½"	(OE)	❹	$100-125
☐ 8	4 to 4½"	(OE)	❺	$90-100
☐ 8	4 to 4½"	(OE)	❻	$88

New style   **Old style**

HUM 9
Begging His Share
There is much size variation in this figurine. Originally modeled by master sculptor Arthur Moeller in 1935 as a candleholder. Restyled in 1964, reduced slightly in size and made with a solid cake rather than with a hole for a candle. Can be found in trademark 3 with or without hole for candle. Called "Congratulatory Visit" in some old catalogues. Very early models have brightly colored striped socks.

☐ 9 .... 5¼ to 6" ..... (OE).... ❶ $400-500
☐ 9 .... 5¼ to 6" ..... (OE).... ❷ $300-350
☐ 9 .... 5¼ to 6" ..... (OE).... ❸ $150-175
☐ 9 .... 5¼ to 6" ..... (OE).... ❹ $100-125
☐ 9 .... 5¼ to 6" ..... (OE).... ❺ $90-100
☐ 9 .... 5¼ to 6" ..... (OE).... ❼ $88

Old 10/3   **New 10/III**   **Old 10/I**   **New 10/I**

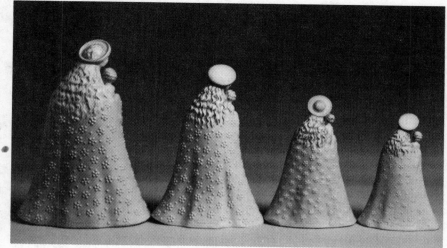

Note variation in halo

HUM 10   Flower Madonna

First created in 1935 by master sculptor Reinhold Unger according to the original drawing of Sister M.I. Hummel. In 1956 the mold was renewed (restyled) by Theo R. Menzenbach and made approximately 2 inches smaller. The halo was changed at that time from the open style to the flat style. It has been produced in white overglaze, pastel blue cloak, brown cloak, ivory cloak and pastel yellow. Only the pastel blue and the white overglaze are currently produced. The older color variations will usually range from $1,000 to $3,000 depending on color, condition and other variations. Old catalogues list it as large as 14 inches. Some earlier models appear with only the number 10 (no size designator). Also called "Sitting Madonna with Child" or "Virgin With Flowers" in old catalogues. Sometimes incised 10/3 instead of 10/III. In the spring of 1982 the large size (10/III), in both pastel blue and white overglaze, was listed as a "temporary withdrawal" by Goebel, possibly to be reinstated at a later date.

			Color	White
☐ 10/I	.9 to 9½"	(CE) ... ❶	$350-500	☐ $300-400
☐ 10/I	.9 to 9½"	(CE) ... ❷	$250-400	☐ $150-300
☐ 10/III	12 to 13"	(CE) ... ❶	$500-850	☐ $250-500
☐ 10/III	12 to 13"	(CE) ... ❷	$400-750	☐ $150-400
☐ 10/I	.7¾ to 8¼"	(OE) ... ❸	$160-200	☐ $90-125
☐ 10/I	.7¾ to 8¼"	(OE) ... ❹	$140-160	☐ $80-90
☐ 10/I	.7¾ to 8¼"	(OE) ... ❺	$130-140	☐ $70-80
☐ 10/I	.7¾ to 8¼"	(OE) ... ❻	$130	☐ $70
☐ 10/III	11 to 11½"	(OE) ... ❸	$350-400	☐ $200-250
☐ 10/III	11 to 11½"	(OE) ... ❹	$335-350	☐ $185-200
☐ 10/III	11 to 11½"	(OE) ... ❺	$315-335	☐ $175-185
☐ 10/III	11 to 11½"	(OE) ... ❻	$315	☐ $175

HUM 11
Merry Wanderer
Same style as HUM 7. Also modeled by master sculptor Arthur Moeller in 1935. Most models of "Merry Wanderer" have five buttons on vest. Some models in size 11 2/0 have six or seven buttons, and usually command a slight premium.

☐ 11	4¾"	(CE)	❶	$400-500
☐ 11 2/0	4¼ to 4½"	(OE)	❶	$300-350
☐ 11 2/0	4¼ to 4½"	(OE)	❷	$125-150
☐ 11 2/0	4¼ to 4½"	(OE)	❸	$75-100
☐ 11 2/0	4¼ to 4½"	(OE)	❹	$60-75
☐ 11 2/0	4¼ to 4½"	(OE)	❺	$55-60
☐ 11 2/0	4¼ to 4½"	(OE)	❻	$55
☐ 11/0	4¾ to 5"	(OE)	❶	$400-500
☐ 11/0	4¾ to 5"	(OE)	❷	$150-200
☐ 11/0	4¾ to 5"	(OE)	❸	$100-125
☐ 11/0	4¾ to 5"	(OE)	❹	$75-100
☐ 11/0	4¾ to 5"	(OE)	❺	$72-75
☐ 11/0	4¾ to 5"	(OE)	❻	$72

HUM 12
Chimney Sweep
Originally modeled by master sculptor Arthur Moeller in 1935, but has been re-styled several times through the years. There is much size variation in both sizes. Old name: "Smoky" or "Good Luck."

☐ 12 2/0	4 to 4¼"	(OE)	❷	$75-100
☐ 12 2/0	4 to 4¼"	(OE)	❸	$50-70
☐ 12 2/0	4 to 4¼"	(OE)	❹	$40-50
☐ 12 2/0	4 to 4¼"	(OE)	❺	$39-40
☐ 12 2/0	4 to 4¼"	(OE)	❻	$39
☐ 12/I	5½ to 6½"	(OE)	❶	$300-350
☐ 12/I	5½ to 6½"	(OE)	❷	$200-250
☐ 12/I	5½ to 6½"	(OE)	❸	$100-125
☐ 12/I	5½ to 6½"	(OE)	❹	$75-100
☐ 12/I	5½ to 6½"	(OE)	❺	$72-75
☐ 12/I	5½ to 6½"	(OE)	❻	$72
☐ 12.	6 to 6¼"	(CE)	❶	$300-350
☐ 12.	6 to 6¼"	(CE)	❷	$200-250

13/II New   *13/2 Old*

HUM 13
Meditation

First modeled by master sculptor Reinhold Unger in 1935 in two sizes: 13/0 and 13/2. Size 13/2 was originally styled with flowers in the back half of basket, but in 1978 was restyled by master sculptor Gerhard Skrobek with no flowers in basket. Large size (13/V) was modeled by Theo R. Menzenbach in 1957 with a full basket of flowers. The small size (13/2/0) was modeled by master sculptor Gerhard Skrobek in 1962. Three variations in hair ribbons were used through the years in the 13/0 size: the early crown mark figurines usually had a very short pigtail with only a red painted band for the ribbon; the early full bee trademark examples were made with a longer pigtail but no ribbon or bows at all; the later models were made with the longer pigtails and a little red bow or ribbon on each pigtail. All "Meditations" made since the early 1950's would be of this last style. A 1962 copyright date appears on newer models of size 13/2/0. Also called "The Little Messenger." Sometimes 13/2 instead of 13/II and 13/5 instead of 13/V.

☐ 13 2/0	4¼"	(OE)	❷	$125-150
☐ 13 2/0	4¼"	(OE)	❸	$75-100
☐ 13 2/0	4¼"	(OE)	❹	$60-75
☐ 13 2/0	4¼"	(OE)	❺	$55-60
☐ 13 2/0	4¼"	(OE)	❻	$55
☐ 13/0	5 to 6"	(OE)	❶	$300-350
☐ 13/0	5 to 6"	(OE)	❷	$200-250
☐ 13/0	5 to 6"	(OE)	❸	$100-150
☐ 13/0	5 to 6"	(OE)	❹	$85-100
☐ 13/0	5 to 6"	(OE)	❺	$78-85
☐ 13/0	5 to 6"	(OE)	❻	$77.50
☐ 13.	7 to 7¼"	(CE)	❶	$2500-3000
☐ 13/II	7 to 7¼"	(CE)	❶	$2500-3000
☐ 13/II	7 to 7¼"	(CE)	❷	$2000-2500
☐ 13/II	7 to 7¼"	(CE)	❸	$1750-2000
☐ 13/II	7 to 7¼"	(OE)	❺	$200-225
☐ 13/II	7 to 7¼"	(OE)	❻	$200
☐ 13/V	13¼ to 14"	(OE)	❷	$2000-2500
☐ 13/V	13¼ to 14"	(OE)	❸	$1000-1500
☐ 13/V	13¼ to 14"	(OE)	❹	$750-1000
☐ 13/V	13¼ to 14"	(OE)	❺	$680-750
☐ 13/V	13¼ to 14"	(OE)	❻	$680

14/B   14/A

HUM 14   Book Worm, Bookends, Boy and Girl

These figurines are weighted with sand through a hole on the bottom and closed with a cork or plastic plug. Sometimes sealed with a paper sticker and inscription "75 Years Goebel." The girl is the same as HUM 3 and HUM 8 except that the pictures on book are black and white rather than in color. Modeled by master sculptor Reinhold Unger in 1935. The boy was made only as part of bookend set and not normally sold separately. This policy, however, has now been changed and the boy can now be purchased alone and unweighted. This was done mainly to satisfy collectors who desired a figurine to match the 1980 Annual Bell that had a motif similar to the bookend boy.

☐ 14 A & B .. 5½" .... (OE).... ❶ $500-750
☐ 14 A & B .. 5½" .... (OE).... ❷ $300-500
☐ 14 A & B .. 5½" .... (OE).... ❸ $250-300
☐ 14 A & B .. 5½" .... (OE).... ❹ $210-250
☐ 14 A & B .. 5½" .... (OE).... ❺ $190-210
☐ 14 A & B .. 5½" .... (OE).... ❻ $190
☐ 14 A ...... 5½" .... (OE).... ❺ $95-105
☐ 14 A ...... 5½" .... (OE).... ❻ $95

Old model   **New model**

HUM 15
Hear Ye, Hear Ye
Old name: "Night Watchman." There are some variations in color of mittens. Right hand shows fingers on older models. Originally modeled by master sculptor Arthur Moeller in 1935. Older models usually incised 15/2 instead of 15/II.

☐ 15/0 ...... 5 to 5¼" ..... (OE) .... ❶ $350-400
☐ 15/0 ...... 5 to 5¼" ..... (OE) .... ❷ $200-250
☐ 15/0 ...... 5 to 5¼" ..... (OE) .... ❸ $125-150
☐ 15/0 ...... 5 to 5¼" ..... (OE) .... ❹ $100-125
☐ 15/0 ...... 5 to 5¼" ..... (OE) .... ❺ $90-100
☐ 15/0 ...... 5 to 5¼" ..... (OE) .... ❻ $88
☐ 15/I ...... 6 to 6¼" ..... (OE) .... ❶ $400-500
☐ 15/I ...... 6 to 6¼" ..... (OE) .... ❷ $250-300
☐ 15/I ...... 6 to 6¼" ..... (OE) .... ❸ $150-175
☐ 15/I ...... 6 to 6¼" ..... (OE) .... ❹ $120-135
☐ 15/I ...... 6 to 6¼" ..... (OE) .... ❺ $100-110
☐ 15/I ...... 6 to 6¼" ..... (OE) .... ❻ $100
☐ 15/II ...... 7 to 7½" ..... (OE) .... ❶ $750-1000
☐ 15/II ...... 7 to 7½" ..... (OE) .... ❷ $500-750
☐ 15/II ...... 7 to 7½" ..... (OE) .... ❸ $300-375
☐ 15/II ...... 7 to 7½" ..... (OE) .... ❹ $225-275
☐ 15/II ...... 7 to 7½" ..... (OE) .... ❺ $185-200
☐ 15/II ...... 7 to 7½" ..... (OE) .... ❻ $185

HUM 16
Little Hiker
This figurine was originally modeled by master sculptor Arthur Moeller in 1935. The old name of "Happy-Go-Lucky" was used in early catalogues. Slight changes can be noticed when comparing older models with new. Many old crown trademark pieces have a high gloss finish.

☐ 16 2/0	3¾ to 4¼"	(OE)	❶	$125-200
☐ 16 2/0	3¾ to 4¼"	(OE)	❷	$80-125
☐ 16 2/0	3¾ to 4¼"	(OE)	❸	$60-80
☐ 16 2/0	3¾ to 4¼"	(OE)	❹	$50-60
☐ 16 2/0	3¾ to 4¼"	(OE)	❺	$44-50
☐ 16 2/0	3¾ to 4¼"	(OE)	❻	$44
☐ 16.	5½ to 5¾"	(CE)	❶	$300-350
☐ 16.	5½ to 5¾"	(CE)	❷	$200-275
☐ 16/I	5½ to 6"	(OE)	❶	$250-300
☐ 16/I	5½ to 6"	(OE)	❷	$150-225
☐ 16/I	5½ to 6"	(OE)	❸	$100-140
☐ 16/I	5½ to 6"	(OE)	❹	$85-100
☐ 16/I	5½ to 6"	(OE)	❺	$78-85
☐ 16/I	5½ to 6"	(OE)	❻	$77.50

Current production on left

HUM 17
Congratulations

First modeled by master sculptor Reinhold Unger in 1935. Called "I Congratulate" in old catalogues. Older models do not have socks. Restyled in 1971 by master sculptor Gerhard Skrobek, who added socks, new hair and textured finish. Larger size (17/2) is no longer produced and considered extremely rare. Early crown mark pieces are marked 17 with either a zero or a 2 directly underneath. Old catalogue dated 1955 lists size of 3¾", which is believed to be in error. Crown and some full bee pieces have the handle of the horn pointing to the back. Since the large size is a closed edition (CE) and will not be produced again in the future, the size designator on the remaining size will eventually be eliminated, according to factory information, and will be incised 17 only.

☐ 17/0	5½ to 6"	(CE)	❶	$250-300
☐ 17/0	5½ to 6"	(CE)	❷	$150-200
☐ 17/0	5½ to 6"	(CE)	❸	$125-150
☐ 17/0	5½ to 6"	(CE)	❹	$100-125
☐ 17/0	6"	(OE)	❺	$66-75
☐ 17/0	6"	(OE)	❻	$66
☐ 17/2	7¾ to 8¼"	(CE)	❶	$5000-6000
☐ 17/2	7¾ to 8¼"	(CE)	❷	$4000-5000
☐ 17/2	7¾ to 8¼"	(CE)	❸	$3000-4000

Early models larger than newer models

HUM 18   Christ Child

Early models measure 3¾″ x 6½″. Old name: "Christmas Night." At one time this piece was sold in Belgium in the white overglaze finish and would now be considered extremely rare. These white pieces usually bring about double the price of a colored piece. Originally modeled by master sculptor Reinhold Unger in 1935.

☐ 18 . . . . 3¾ x 6½″ . . . (OE) . . . . ❶ $200-250
☐ 18 . . . . 3¾ x 6½″ . . . (OE) . . . . ❷ $100-150
☐ 18 . . . . 3¾ x 6½″ . . . (OE) . . . . ❸ $75-100
☐ 18 . . . . 3¼ x 6″ . . . . . (OE) . . . . ❹ $60-75
☐ 18 . . . . 3¼ x 6″ . . . . . (OE) . . . . ❺ $55-60
☐ 18 . . . . 3¼ x 6″ . . . . . (OE) . . . . ❻ $52.50

HUM 19   Prayer Before Battle on Big Round Tray (CN)

Factory book of models indicates: "Big round tray with praying child (with flag and trumpet) standing at wooden (toy) horse. Prayer Before Battle, modeled by A. Moeller —June 20, 1935." An additional note states that this item was not accepted by the Convent at Siessen. No known examples.

☐ 19 . . . . (CN) . . . ❶ . . . $5000 +

HUM 20
Prayer Before Battle

Created in 1935 by master sculptor Arthur Moeller. Only slight variations between old and new models. Some color variations, but most noticeable difference is in size. Newer models are smaller.

☐ 20 . . . . 4 to 4½″ . . . . . (OE) . . . . ❶ $300-350
☐ 20 . . . . 4 to 4½″ . . . . . (OE) . . . . ❷ $150-200
☐ 20 . . . . 4 to 4½″ . . . . . (OE) . . . . ❸ $125-150
☐ 20 . . . . 4 to 4½″ . . . . . (OE) . . . . ❹ $80-100
☐ 20 . . . . 4 to 4½″ . . . . . (OE) . . . . ❺ $75-80
☐ 20 . . . . 4 to 4½″ . . . . . (OE) . . . . ❻ $72

HUM 21
Heavenly Angel

Only figurine to have "½" size designator. Much variation in size. Old name: "Little Guardian" or "Celestial Messenger." First modeled by master sculptor Reinhold Unger in 1935. Sometimes incised 21/2 instead of 21/II. According to factory information, this figurine was also sold in white overglaze at one time. "Heavenly Angel" motif was used for the first annual plate in 1971 (HUM 264).

☐ 21/0	4 to 4¾"	(OE)	❶	$150-200
☐ 21/0	4 to 4¾"	(OE)	❷	$100-125
☐ 21/0	4 to 4¾"	(OE)	❸	$60-75
☐ 21/0	4 to 4¾"	(OE)	❹	$50-55
☐ 21/0	4 to 4¾"	(OE)	❺	$42-50
☐ 21/0	4 to 4¾"	(OE)	❻	$42
☐ 21/0½	5¾ to 6½"	(OE)	❶	$300-325
☐ 21/0½	5¾ to 6½"	(OE)	❷	$175-225
☐ 21/0½	5¾ to 6½"	(OE)	❸	$125-150
☐ 21/0½	5¾ to 6½"	(OE)	❹	$80-90
☐ 21/0½	5¾ to 6½"	(OE)	❺	$75-80
☐ 21/0½	5¾ to 6½"	(OE)	❻	$73.50
☐ 21/I	6¾ to 7¼"	(OE)	❶	$350-400
☐ 21/I	6¾ to 7¼"	(OE)	❷	$200-250
☐ 21/I	6¾ to 7¼"	(OE)	❸	$150-175
☐ 21/I	6¾ to 7¼"	(OE)	❹	$100-110
☐ 21/I	6¾ to 7¼"	(OE)	❺	$88-100
☐ 21/I	6¾ to 7¼"	(OE)	❻	$88
☐ 21/II	8½ to 8¾"	(OE)	❶	$1000-1250
☐ 21/II	8½ to 8¾"	(OE)	❷	$500-750
☐ 21/II	8½ to 8¾"	(OE)	❸	$250-350
☐ 21/II	8½ to 8¾"	(OE)	❹	$200-250
☐ 21/II	8½ to 8¾"	(OE)	❺	$184-200
☐ 21/II	8½ to 8¾"	(OE)	❻	$184

22/I   **22**

HUM 22
Holy Water Font, Angel With Birds
First modeled by master sculptor Reinhold Unger in 1935. Old name: "Sitting Angel." Variations in size, color and design of bowl are found on older models.

☐ 22.	...... 3⅛ to 4½"	... (CE)	.... ❶	.... $150-200
☐ 22/0	...... 3 x 4"	.... (OE)	.... ❶	.... $100-150
☐ 22/0	...... 3 x 4"	.... (OE)	.... ❷	.... $75-100
☐ 22/0	...... 3 x 4"	.... (OE)	.... ❸	.... $35-50
☐ 22/0	...... 3 x 4"	.... (OE)	.... ❹	.... $25-35
☐ 22/0	...... 3 x 4"	.... (OE)	.... ❺	.... $18-20
☐ 22/0	...... 3 x 4"	.... (OE)	.... ❻	.... $17.50
☐ 22/I	...... 3½ to 4⅞"	... (OE)	.... ❶	.... $300-500
☐ 22/I	...... 3½ to 4⅞"	... (OE)	.... ❷	.... $250-300
☐ 22/I	...... 3½ to 4⅞"	... (OE)	.... ❸	.... $200-250

HUM 23
Adoration
This ever popular design was modeled by master sculptor Reinhold Unger in 1935. Size 23/I was restyled in 1978, with new textured finish, by current master modeler Gerhard Skrobek. Older models can be found with either Arabic (24/3) or Roman (24/III) three. Both sizes were sold in white overglaze at one time in Belgium and would be considered extremely rare today. Old name: "Ave Maria." Most older models have rounded corners on the base of the large size while newer models are more square. Early double crown-marked, large size found without size designator—23 only. Early crown-marked, small size usually found without flowers on base.

☐ 23/I ...... 6¼ to 7" ..... (OE).... ❶	$600-700
☐ 23/I ...... 6¼ to 7" ..... (OE).... ❷	$350-425
☐ 23/I ...... 6¼ to 7" ..... (OE).... ❸	$200-275
☐ 23/I ...... 6¼ to 7" ..... (OE).... ❹	$170-200
☐ 23/I ...... 6¼ to 7" ..... (OE).... ❺	$155-170
☐ 23/I ...... 6¼ to 7" ..... (OE).... ❻	$155
☐ 23 ...... 8¾ to 9" ..... (CE).... ❶	$750-1000
☐ 23/III .... 8¾ to 9" ..... (OE).... ❶	$750-1000
☐ 23/III .... 8¾ to 9" ..... (OE).... ❷	$500-750
☐ 23/III .... 8¾ to 9" ..... (OE).... ❸	$300-375
☐ 23/III .... 8¾ to 9" ..... (OE).... ❹	$250-275
☐ 23/III .... 8¾ to 9" ..... (OE).... ❺	$220-250
☐ 23/III .... 8¾ to 9" ..... (OE).... ❻	$220

24/III   24/I

HUM 24   Lullaby, Candleholder

Records show that this figurine was first modeled in 1935. Both Arthur Moeller and Reinhold Unger are given credit—possibly one created the small size while the other the large size. Variations are found in size and construction of socket for candle on size 24/I. Old name: "Cradle Song." Also made without hole for candle—see HUM 262. Size 24/III had been considered rare but is once again in current production. Sometimes incised 24/3 instead of 24/III. In the spring of 1982 the large size (24/III) was listed by Goebel as "temporary withdrawal," to be possibly reinstated at a future date.

☐ 24/I ...... 3½ x 5 to 5½" . (OE).... ❶	$300-350
☐ 24/I ...... 3½ x 5 to 5½" . (OE).... ❷	$200-250

☐ 24/I	......	3½ x 5 to 5½"	. (OE)	....	❸	....	$100-150
☐ 24/I	......	3½ x 5 to 5½"	. (OE)	....	❹	....	$90-100
☐ 24/I	......	3½ x 5 to 5½"	. (OE)	....	❺	....	$77-85
☐ 24/I	......	3½ x 5 to 5½"	. (OE)	....	❻	....	$77
☐ 24/III	....	6¼ x 8¾"	.... (OE)	....	❶	....	$1000-1500
☐ 24/III	....	6¼ x 8¾"	.... (OE)	....	❷	....	$750-1000
☐ 24/III	....	6¼ x 8¾"	.... (OE)	....	❸	....	$350-500
☐ 24/III	....	6¼ x 8¾"	.... (OE)	....	❹	....	$325-350
☐ 24/III	....	6¼ x 8¾"	.... (OE)	....	❺	....	$285-325
☐ 24/III	....	6¼ x 8¾"	.... (OE)	....	❻	....	$285

HUM 25
Angelic Sleep, Candleholder

Records indicate that this figurine was first modeled in 1935 and that both Arthur Moeller and Reinhold Unger were involved with the design. At one time this figurine was sold in Belgium in the white overglaze finish and would now be considered extremely rare. Listed as "Angel's Joy" in some old catalogues. In some old, as well as new catalogues and price lists shown as 25/I in error. Made in only one size and incised 25 only.

☐ 25	....	3½ x 5 to 5½"	. (OE)	....	❶	....	$300-375
☐ 25	....	3½ x 5 to 5½"	. (OE)	....	❷	....	$150-225
☐ 25	....	3½ x 5 to 5½"	. (OE)	....	❸	....	$125-150
☐ 25	....	3½ x 5 to 5½"	. (OE)	....	❹	....	$85-95
☐ 25	....	3½ x 5 to 5½"	. (OE)	....	❺	....	$80-85
☐ 25	....	3½ x 5 to 5½"	. (OE)	....	❻	....	$80

26/O   26/I

HUM 26
Holy Water Font, Child Jesus
Originally modeled by master sculptor Reinhold Unger in 1935. The normal color for the gown is a dark red but is occasionally found in a light blue color. All that I have ever seen with the blue gown were in the small (26/0) size and with the small stylized (TM 3) trademark. Old crown mark and full bee pieces in both sizes usually have scalloped edge on bowl of font.

☐ 26/0	2¾ x 5¼"	(OE)	❶	$100-150
☐ 26/0	2¾ x 5¼"	(OE)	❷	$75-100
☐ 26/0	2¾ x 5¼"	(OE)	❸	$35-50
☐ 26/0	2¾ x 5¼"	(OE)	❹	$25-35
☐ 26/0	2¾ x 5¼"	(OE)	❺	$18-20
☐ 26/0	2¾ x 5¼"	(OE)	❻	$17.50
☐ 26	3 x 5¾"	(CE)	❶	$300-500
☐ 26/I	3¼ x 6"	(OE)	❶	$300-500
☐ 26/I	3¼ x 6"	(OE)	❷	$250-300
☐ 26/I	3¼ x 6"	(OE)	❸	$200-250

27/I   27/3

HUM 27 Joyous News

This figurine was made in two sizes. The small size as a candleholder while the large size as plain figurine. Both were modeled by master sculptor Reinhold Unger in 1935. 27/I is so similar to III/40/I that it is extremely difficult to tell the difference unless they are clearly marked. The small size "Joyous News" candleholder (27/I) is no longer produced and is considered extremely rare. Usually found only in crown trademark. Can be found with the candleholder on the front side or on the back side. Some models designed to hold .6 cm size candles while others designed to hold 1 cm size candles. The large size "Joyous News" is rare in the older trademarks: TM I, TM 2 and TM 3 but was reinstated in 1978 using the original molds, and the original number 27/3 (Arabic 3). In 1979 when it was restyled with the new textured finish the number was changed to 27/III (Roman III). Both 27/3 (old mold) and 27/III (new mold) can be found in TM 5.

☐ 27/I	2¾"	(CE)	❶	$300-500
☐ 27/I	2¾"	(CE)	❷	$250-400
☐ 27/3	4¼ x 4¾"	(CE)	❶	$1500-2000
☐ 27/3	4¼ x 4¾"	(CE)	❷	$1000-1500
☐ 27/3	4¼ x 4¾"	(CE)	❸	$750-1000
☐ 27/3	4¼ x 4¾"	(CE)	❺	$95-250
☐ 27/III	4¼ x 4¾"	(OE)	❻	$94.50

HUM 28
Wayside Devotion

First modeled by master sculptor Reinhold Unger in 1935. Old name: "The Little Shepherd" or "Evensong." According to factory information, this figurine was also sold in white overglaze finish at one time. Sometimes incised 28/2 instead of 28/II or 28/3 instead of 28/III. Also found without a size designator on the large size —incised 28 only. The small size 28/II was restyled by Gerhard Skrobek in the early 1970's. Made without the shrine (see HUM 99) and named "Eventide."

☐ 28/II	7 to 7½"	(OE)	❶	$600-750
☐ 28/II	7 to 7½"	(OE)	❷	$300-450
☐ 28/II	7 to 7½"	(OE)	❸	$225-300
☐ 28/II	7 to 7½"	(OE)	❹	$180-225
☐ 28/II	7 to 7½"	(OE)	❺	$165-180
☐ 28/II	7 to 7½"	(OE)	❻	$165
☐ 28	8¾"	(CE)	❶	$750-1000

```
☐ 28/III ..... 8¾" ........ (OE)....❶.... $650-900
☐ 28/III ..... 8¾" ........ (OE)....❷.... $500-650
☐ 28/III ..... 8¾" ........ (OE)....❸.... $300-400
☐ 28/III ..:.. 8¾" ........'.... (OE)....❹.... $255-300
☐ 28/III ..... 8¾" ........ (OE)....❺.... $231-255
☐ 28/III ..... 8¾" ........ (OE)....❻.... $231
```

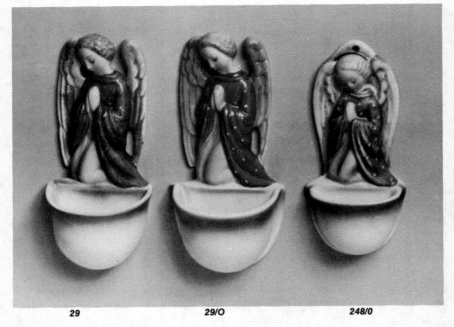

29   29/O   248/0

HUM 29   Holy Water Font, Guardian Angel
(CE) Closed Edition. Modeled by master sculptor Reinhold Unger in 1935 in two sizes.
Because of the fragile wing design, it was discontinued in 1958 and replaced with a
new design by Gerhard Skrobek and given the new model number HUM 248.

```
☐ 29 ...... 2½ x 5¾" ... (CE)....❶.... $1300-1500
☐ 29/0 ..... 2⅞ x 6" ...... (CE)....❶.... $1300-1500
☐ 29/0 ..... 2⅞ x 6" ...... (CE)....❷.... $1000-1250
☐ 29/0 ..... 2⅞ x 6" ...... (CE)....❸.... $950-1000
☐ 29/I ..... 3 x 6⅜" ...... (CE)....❶.... $1500-2000
☐ 29/I ..... 3 x 6⅜" ...... (CE)....❷.... $1500-1750
```

30/O A   30/I A

30/O B   30/I B

30/O A   30/O B

HUM 30
Ba-Bee-Ring

Old name: "Hummel Rings." Originally modeled in 1935 by master sculptor Reinhold Unger. There is some size variation between old and new pieces. Early red color rings are extremely rare. Now produced in tan color only. The girl, 30 B always has orange color hair ribbon, except on red color rings, then it is blue. Although now made in only one size, current production models still have incised "0" size designator. Factory representatives state that this "will possibly disappear sometime in the future." Priced by the set of two.

☐ 30/0 A&B . . 4¾" × 5" . . . (OE). . . . ❶ $300-500
☐ 30/0 A&B . . 4¾" × 5" . . . (OE). . . . ❷ $150-300
☐ 30/0 A&B . . 4¾" × 5" . . . (OE). . . . ❸ $125-150
☐ 30/0 A&B . . 4¾" × 5" . . . (OE). . . . ❹ $100-125
☐ 30/0 A&B . . 4¾" × 5" . . . (OE). . . . ❺ $90-100
☐ 30/0 A&B . . 4¾" × 5" . . . (OE). . . . ❻ $90
☐ 30/I A&B . . 5¼" × 6" . . . (CE). . . . ❶ $1500-3000
☐ 30/0 A&B . . Red Rings . . . (CE). . . . ❶ . . . . $5000 +

Note black child on left

HUM 31   Silent Night with Black Child/Advent Group with Candle (CE)
Only known and verified example of this figurine with black child is in the Robert L. Miller collection. Similar to HUM 54 except embossed earring and bare feet of black child. Modeled in 1935 by master sculptor Arthur Moeller but not produced in quantity. HUM 31 was also produced and sold with all white children and is also considered extremely rare. HUM 31 was still *listed* in old German price lists as late as 1956. That does not necessarily mean that it was produced and sold at that time. It could possibly have been listed in error since so very, very few have ever been located. According to factory representatives, a few HUM 54 were produced with a black child, but wearing shoes instead of bare feet. Several of these have been located and one is now in our collection.

☐ 31 . . . . 3½ × 5" . . . . (CE). . . . ❶ . . . . $3000-5000 (White children)
☐ 31 . . . . 3½ × 5" . . . . (CE). . . . ❶ . . . . $5000 +   (Black child)

32/0   32/0   32/I

HUM 32   Little Gabriel

There are many size variations in this figurine that was first modeled by master sculptor Reinhold Unger in 1935. Called "Joyous News" in some old catalogues. Newer models have no size designator since it is now produced in only the small size. The large size is found incised 32/I or 32 only and is considered extremely rare. "Little Gabriel" was restyled in 1982 with several changes—arms are now apart, angle of the wings is longer and the incised "M.I. Hummel" signature is on the top of the base rather than on the side, as in the past.

☐ 32/0 . . . . . . 5 to 5½" . . . . . (CE) . . . . ❶ $250-300
☐ 32/0 . . . . . . 5 to 5½" . . . . . (CE) . . . . ❷ $150-175
☐ 32/0 . . . . . . 5 to 5½" . . . . . (CE) . . . . ❸ $75-100
☐ 32/0 . . . . . . 5 to 5½" . . . . . (CE) . . . . ❹ $70-75
☐ 32/0 . . . . . . 5" . . . . (CE) . . . . ❺ $60-70
☐ 32 . . . . 5" . . . . (CE) . . . . ❺ $55-60
☐ 32 . . . . 5" . . . . (OE) . . . . ❻ $55
☐ 32/I . . . . . . 5¾ to 6" . . . . . (CE) . . . . ❶ $1250-1500
☐ 32/I . . . . . . 5¾ to 6" . . . . . (CE) . . . . ❷ $1000-1250
☐ 32/I . . . . . . 5¾ to 6" . . . . . (CE) . . . . ❸ $750-1000
☐ 32 . . . . 5¾ to 6" . . . . . (CE) . . . . ❶ $1250-1500
☐ 32 . . . . 5¾ to 6" . . . . . (CE) . . . . ❷ $1000-1250

New   *Old*

HUM 33 Ashtray, Joyful
First modeled by master sculptor Reinhold Unger in 1935. Older models have slightly different construction of ashtray.

☐ 33 . . . . 3½ × 6" . . . . (OE). . . . ❶ $200-300
☐ 33 . . . . 3½ × 6" . . . . (OE). . . . ❷ $125-175
☐ 33 . . . . 3½ × 6" . . . . (OE). . . . ❸ $90-120
☐ 33 . . . . 3½ × 6" . . . . (OE). . . . ❹ $75-90
☐ 33 . . . . 3½ × 6" . . . . (OE). . . . ❺ $65-70
☐ 33 . . . . 3½ × 6" . . . . (OE). . . . ❻ $65

HUM 34   Ashtray, Singing Lesson
First modeled by master sculptor Arthur Moeller in 1935. Slight variation in colors of older models. Several variations in construction on bottom of ashtray.

☐ 34 . . . . 3½ × 6¼ " . . . (OE) . . . . ❶ $250-350
☐ 34 . . . . 3½ × 6¼ " . . . (OE) . . . . ❷ $150-200
☐ 34 . . . . 3½ × 6¼ " . . . (OE) . . . . ❸ $100-140
☐ 34 . . . . 3½ × 6¼ " . . . (OE) . . . . ❹ $90-100
☐ 34 . . . . 3½ × 6¼ " . . . (OE) . . . . ❺ $80-90
☐ 34 . . . . 3½ × 6¼ " . . . (OE) . . . . ❻ $80

35/I   35/O

HUM 35
Holy Water Font, The Good Shepherd
First modeled by master sculptor Reinhold Unger in 1935. There are slight variations in size as well as variations in the construction of the bowl of font. Also found in the large size without a size designator—incised 35 only.

☐ 35/0 . . . . . . 2½ × 4¾" . . . (OE). . . . ❶ $100-150
☐ 35/0 . . . . . . 2½ × 4¾" . . . (OE). . . . ❷ $50-75
☐ 35/0 . . . . . . 2½ × 4¾" . . . (OE). . . . ❸ $30-35
☐ 35/0 . . . . . . 2½ × 4¾" . . . (OE). . . . ❹ $20-25
☐ 35/0 . . . . . . 2½ × 4¾" . . . (OE). . . . ❺ $18-20
☐ 35/0 . . . . . . 2½ × 4¾" . . . (OE). . . . ❻ $17.50
☐ 35/I . . . . . . 2¾ × 5¾" . . . (OE). . . . ❶ $200-350
☐ 35/I . . . . . . 2¾ × 5¾" . . . (OE). . . . ❷ $200-300
☐ 35/I . . . . . . 2¾ × 5¾" . . . (OE). . . . ❸ $100-150
☐ 35 . . . . 2¾ × 5¾" . . . (CE). . . . ❶ $200-350

36/I   36/O

HUM 36
Holy Water Font, Child with Flowers
First modeled by master sculptor Reinhold Unger in 1935. There are slight variations in size, color and in the construction of the bowl of the font. Also called "Flower Angel" or "Angel with Flowers."

☐ 36/0 . . . . . . 3¼ × 4¼" . . . (OE). . . . ❶ $100-150
☐ 36/0 . . . . . . 3¼ × 4¼" . . . (OE). . . . ❷ $50-75
☐ 36/0 . . . . . . 3¼ × 4¼" . . . (OE). . . . ❸ $30-35
☐ 36/0 . . . . . . 3¼ × 4¼" . . . (OE). . . . ❹ $20-25
☐ 36/0 . . . . . . 3¼ × 4¼" . . . (OE). . . . ❺ $18-20

New model   **Old model**

HUM 37   Herald Angels, Candleholder

Many variations through the years. On older models the candleholder is much taller than on the newer ones. The order of placement of the angels may vary on the older models. Current production pieces have a half-inch wider base. Originally modeled in 1935 by master sculptor Reinhold Unger.

38/O   *39/O*   *40/O*

HUM 38
Angel, Joyous News with Lute,
Candleholder

HUM 39
Angel, Joyous News with Accordion,
Candleholder

HUM 40
Angel, Joyous News with Trumpet,
Candleholder
Roman numerals to the left of the HUM number indicate the size of the candle

that fits into the figurine. Size I is .6 cm, size III is 1 cm. (Note: Not all figurines which hold candles are photographed with candles in this book, but they are usually sold with candles.) Also called "Little Heavenly Angel" in old catalogues. Also known as "Angel Trio" candleholders. Candleholders are always on right side of angel. These three figurines were originally modeled in 1935 by master sculptor Reinhold Unger. Very early pieces do not have a size designator—incised 38. 39. 40. only.

☐ 1/38/0	2 to 2½"	(OE)	❶	$100-125
☐ 1/38/0	2 to 2½"	(OE)	❷	$50-75
☐ 1/38/0	2 to 2½"	(OE)	❸	$35-50
☐ 1/38/0	2 to 2½"	(OE)	❹	$30-35
☐ 1/38/0	2 to 2½"	(OE)	❺	$25-30
☐ 1/38/0	2 to 2½"	(OE)	❻	$23
☐ III/38/0	2 to 2½"	(OE)	❶	$100-125
☐ III/38/0	2 to 2½"	(OE)	❷	$50-75
☐ III/38/0	2 to 2½"	(OE)	❸	$35-50
☐ III/38/0	2 to 2½"	(OE)	❹	$30-35
☐ III/38/0	2 to 2½"	(OE)	❺	$25-30
☐ III/38/0	2 to 2½"	(OE)	❻	$23
☐ III/38/I	2½ to 2¾"	(OE)	❶	$200-250
☐ III/38/I	2½ to 2¾"	(OE)	❷	$150-200
☐ III/38/I	2½ to 2¾"	(OE)	❸	$125-150
☐ 1/39/0	2 to 2½"	(OE)	❶	$100-125
☐ 1/39/0	2 to 2½"	(OE)	❷	$50-75
☐ 1/39/0	2 to 2½"	(OE)	❸	$35-50

□ 1/39/0 .... 2 to 2½" ..... (OE) .... ❹ $30-35
□ 1/39/0 .... 2 to 2½" ..... (OE) .... ❺ $25-30
□ 1/39/0 .... 2 to 2½" ..... (OE) .... ❻ 23
□ III/39/0 .... 2 to 2½" ..... (OE) .... ❶ $100-125
□ III/39/0 .... 2 to 2½" ..... (OE) .... ❷ $50-75
□ III/39/0 .... 2 to 2½" ..... (OE) .... ❸ $35-50
□ III/39/0 .... 2 to 2½" ..... (OE) .... ❹ $30-35
□ III/39/0 .... 2 to 2½" ..... (OE) .... ❺ $25-30
□ III/39/0 .... 2 to 2½" ..... (OE) .... ❻ $23
□ III/39/1 .... 2½ to 2¾" ... (OE) .... ❶ $200-250
□ III/39/1 .... 2½ to 2¾" ... (OE) .... ❷ $150-200
□ III/39/1 .... 2½ to 2¾" ... (OE) .... ❸ $125-150

□ 1/40/0 .... 2 to 2½" ..... (OE) .... ❶ $100-125
□ 1/40/0 .... 2 to 2½" ..... (OE) .... ❷ $50-75
□ 1/40/0 .... 2 to 2½" ..... (OE) .... ❹ $30-35
□ 1/40/0 .... 2 to 2½" ..... (OE) .... ❺ $25-30
□ 1/40/0 .... 2 to 2½" ..... (OE) .... ❻ 23
□ III/40/0 .... 2 to 2½" ..... (OE) .... ❶ $100-125
□ III/40/0 .... 2 to 2½" ... (OE) .... ❷ $50-75
□ III/40/0 .... 2 to 2½" ..... (OE) .... ❸ $35-50
□ III/40/0 .... 2 to 2½" ..... (OE) .... ❹ $30-35
□ III/40/0 .... 2 to 2½" ..... (OE) .... ❺ $25-30
□ III/40/0 .... 2 to 2½" ..... (OE) .... ❻ $23
□ III/40/1 .... 2½ to 2¾" ... (OE) .... ❶ $200-250
□ III/40/1 .... 2½ to 2¾" ... (OE) .... ❷ $150-200
□ III/40/1 .... 2½ to 2¾" ... (OE) .... ❸ $125-150

HUM 41
Singing Lesson (without base) (CN)
Factory book of models indicates this
piece is similar to HUM 34 (Singing Les-
son, Ashtray). Closed 31 October 1935.
No known examples.

□ 41 .... (CN) .... $5000 +

42/O   **42/I**

HUM 42
Good Shepherd
First modeled by master sculptor Reinhold Unger in 1935. Normally has a rust-colored gown. Factory sample of small size 42/0 has light blue gown but is doubtful that it was ever sold in blue color. Size 42/I is considered extremely rare and no longer produced in large size. Factory information states that (O) size designator will eventually be dropped from number. Current production still incised 42/0.

☐ 42/0 . . . . . . 6¼ to 6½" . . . (OE) . . . . ❶ $250-300
☐ 42/0 . . . . . . 6½ to 6½" . . . (OE) . . . . ❷ $150-200
☐ 42/0 . . . . . . 6¼ to 6½" . . . (OE) . . . . ❸ $100-125
☐ 42/0 . . . . . . 6¼ to 6½" . . . (OE) . . . . ❹ $75-85
☐ 42/0 . . . . . . 6¼" . . . . (OE) . . . . ❺ $66-75
☐ 42/0 . . . . . . 6¼" . . . . (OE) . . . . ❻ $66
☐ 42/I . . . . . . 7¼ to 7¾" . . . (CE) . . . . ❶ $3000-5000
☐ 42/I . . . . . . 7¼ to 7¾" . . . (CE) . . . . ❷ $2000-3000

HUM 43
March Winds
Many size variations with older pieces slightly larger. First modeled by master sculptor Reinhold Unger in 1935. Called "Urchin" in some old catalogues.

☐ 43	4¾ to 5½"	(OE)	❶	$200-250
☐ 43	4¾ to 5½"	(OE)	❷	$100-150
☐ 43	4¾ to 5½"	(OE)	❸	$75-100
☐ 43	4¾ to 5½"	(OE)	❹	$60-65
☐ 43	4¾ to 5½"	(OE)	❺	$55-60
☐ 43	4¾ to 5½"	(OE)	❻	$55

44 A   44 B

HUM 44 A
Culprits, Table Lamp
Originally modeled by master sculptor Arthur Moeller in 1935. Older models have a half-inch larger base, and hole for electrical switch on top of base. They usually have a 1935 copyright date incised.

HUM 44 B
Out of Danger, Table Lamp
Originally modeled by master sculptor Arthur Moeller in 1935. Older models have a half-inch larger base, and hole for electrical switch on top of base. They usually have a 1936 copyright date incised.

☐ 44A	8½ to 9½"	(OE)	❶	$350-500
☐ 44A	8½ to 9½"	(OE)	❷	$300-350
☐ 44A	8½ to 9½"	(OE)	❸	$250-300
☐ 44A	8½"	(OE)	❹	$225-250
☐ 44A	8½"	(OE)	❺	$205-225
☐ 44A	8½"	(OE)	❻	$205
☐ 44B	8½ to 9½"	(OE)	❶	$350-500
☐ 44B	8½ to 9½"	(OE)	❷	$300-350
☐ 44B	8½ to 9½"	(OE)	❸	$250-300
☐ 44B	8½"	(OE)	❹	$225-250
☐ 44B	8½"	(OE)	❺	$205-225
☐ 44B	8½"	(OE)	❻	$205

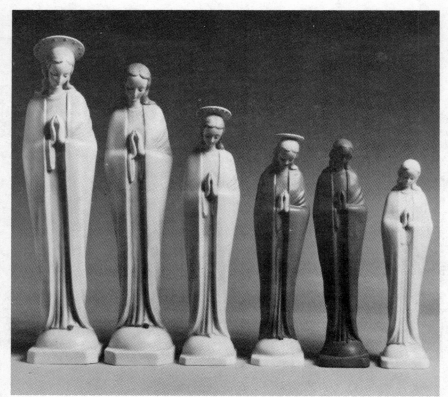

Many size and color variations

HUM 45
Madonna With Halo

HUM 46
Madonna Without Halo

These beautiful Madonnas were first modeled by master sculptor Reinhold Unger in 1935. Sometimes called "The Holy Virgin" in old catalogues. There are many size variations as well as color variations. Produced in white overglaze, pastel blue, pastel pink, heavy blue and ivory finish. Also has been found in reddish brown terra cotta finish signed "M.I. Hummel" but without incised number—height 11 inches. Some pieces have been mismarked 45 instead of 46, etc. Some pieces have been found with both 45 and 46 on the same piece. In the spring of 1982 the large sizes (45/III and 46/III) were listed by Goebel as a "temporary withdrawal," to be possibly reinstated at a future date. Sometimes an Arabic size designator is used on older models.

				Color	White
45/0	10½"	(OE)	❶	☐125-200	☐75-100
45/0	10½"	(OE)	❷	☐75-125	☐50-75
45/0	10½"	(OE)	❸	☐55-75	☐35-50
45/0	10½"	(OE)	❹	☐45-65	☐30-35
45/0	10½"	(OE)	❺	☐42-45	☐27-30
45/0	10½"	(OE)	❻	☐42	☐26.50
45/I	11½ to 13¼"	(OE)	❶	☐150-250	☐100-150

45/I ....11½ to 13¼" ...(OE) ...❷ ...☐ 100-150 ...☐ 75-100
45/I ....11½ to 13¼" ...(OE) ...❸ ...☐ 75-100 ....☐ 50-75
45/I ....11½ to 13¼" ...(OE) ...❹ ...☐ 55-75 .....☐ 35-50
45/I ....11½ to 13¼" ...(OE) ...❺ ...☐ 53-55 .....☐ 32-35
45/I ....11½ to 13¼" ...(OE) ...❻ ...☐ 52.50 .....☐ 31.50
45/III ...15½ to 16¾" ...(OE) ...❶ ...☐ 300-500 ...☐ 150-250
45/III ...15½ to 16¾" ...(OE) ...❷ ...☐ 200-300 ...☐ 100-150
45/III ...15½ to 16¾" ...(OE) ...❸ ...☐ 150-200 ...☐ 85-100
45/III ...15½ to 16¾" ...(OE) ...❹ ...☐ 110-150 ...☐ 75-85
45/III ...15½ to 16¾" ...(OE) ...❺ ...☐ 105-110 ...☐ 70-75
45/III ...15½ to 16¾" ...(OE) ...❻ ...☐ 105 ....☐ 70

....Color ....White .....
46/0 ...10¼" ....(OE)...❶ ...☐ $125-200 ...☐ $75-100
46/0 ...10¼" ....(OE)...❷ ...☐ $75-125 ...☐ $50-75
46/0 ...10¼" ....(OE)...❸ ...☐ $55-75 .....☐ $35-50
46/0 ...10¼" ....(OE)...❹ ...☐ $45-65 .....☐ $30-35
46/0 ...10¼" ....(OE)...❺ ...☐ $42-45 .....☐ $27-30
46/0 ...10¼" ....(OE)...❻ ...☐ $42 ....☐ $26-50
46/I ...11¼ to 13" .....(OE) ...❶ ...☐ $150-250 ...☐ $100-150
46/I ...11¼ to 13" .....(OE) ...❷ ...☐ $100-150 ...☐ $75-100
46/I ...11¼ to 13" .....(OE) ...❸ ...☐ $75-100 ....☐ $50-75
46/I ...11¼ to 13" .....(OE) ...❹ ...☐ $55-75 .....☐ $35-50
46/I ...11¼ to 13" .....(OE) ...❺ ...☐ $53-55 .....☐ $32-35
46/I ...11¼ to 13" .....(OE) ...❻ ...☐ $52.50 .....☐ $31.50
46/III ..15¼ to 16¼" ...(OE) ...❶ ...☐ $300-500 ...☐ $150-250
46/III ..15¼ to 16¼" ...(OE) ...❷ ...☐ $200-300 ...☐ $100-150
46/III ..15¼ to 16¼" ...(OE) ...❸ ...☐ $150-200 ...☐ $85-100
46/III ..15¼ to 16¼" ...(OE) ...❹ ...☐ $110-150 ...☐ $75-85
46/III ..15¼ to 16¼" ...(OE) ...❺ ...☐ $105-110 ...☐ $70-75
46/III ..15¼ to 16¼" ...(OE) ...❻ ...☐ $105 ......☐ $70

NOTE: HUM 1 through HUM 46 were all put on the market in 1935.

47/0 Crown

HUM 47
Goose Girl
First modeled by master sculptor Arthur Moeller in 1936. There are many size variations between the older and newer models. Sometimes called "Little Gooseherd" in old catalogues. Older models of size 47/0 have a blade of grass between the geese. This has been eliminated on newer models and on the small size 47/3/0. The large size 47/III was restyled with the new textured finish in the early 1970's. Sometimes incised 47/2 instead of 47/II.

☐ 47 3/0	4 to 4¼"	(OE)	❶	$200-300
☐ 47 3/0	4 to 4¼"	(OE)	❷	$125-180
☐ 47 3/0	4 to 4¼"	(OE)	❸	$90-120
☐ 47 3/0	4 to 4¼"	(OE)	❹	$75-80
☐ 47 3/0	4 to 4¼"	(OE)	❺	$70-75
☐ 47 3/0	4 to 4¼"	(OE)	❻	$66
☐ 47/0	4¾ to 5¼"	(OE)	❶	$350-425
☐ 47/0	4¾ to 5¼"	(OE)	❷	$175-350
☐ 47/0	4¾ to 5¼"	(OE)	❸	$130-170
☐ 47/0	4¾ to 5¼"	(OE)	❹	$100-115
☐ 47/0	4¾ to 5¼"	(OE)	❺	$90-100
☐ 47/0	4¾ to 5¼"	(OE)	❻	$90
☐ 47/II	7 to 7½"	(OE)	❶	$750-1000
☐ 47/II	7 to 7½"	(OE)	❷	$500-650
☐ 47/II	7 to 7½"	(OE)	❸	$300-375
☐ 47/II	7 to 7½"	(OE)	❹	$225-250
☐ 47/II	7 to 7½"	(OE)	❺	$200-225
☐ 47/II	7 to 7½"	(OE)	❻	$200

Current model

HUM 48
Madonna Plaque
This bas-relief plaque was first modeled by master sculptor Reinhold Unger in 1936. Old crown mark pieces are slightly smaller in size. Newer models have hole on back for hanging while older models have two small holes to use for hanging on wall with cord. Sometimes incised 48/2 instead of 48/II and 48/5 instead of 48/V. Also sold in white overglaze finish at one time in Belgium but are now considered extremely rare. Very early models have a flat back while all others have a recessed back.

☐ 48/0 . . . . . 3¼ x 4¼" . . . (OE) . . . . ❶ $250-300
☐ 48/0 . . . . . 3¼ x 4¼" . . . (OE) . . . . ❷ $100-150
☐ 48/0 . . . . . 3¼ x 4¼" . . . (OE) . . . . ❸ $75-100
☐ 48/0 . . . . . 3¼ x 4¼" . . . (OE) . . . . ❹ $60-70
☐ 48/0 . . . . . 3¼ x 4¼" . . . (OE) . . . . ❺ $53-60
☐ 48/0 . . . . . 3¼ x 4¼" . . . (OE) . . . . ❻ $52.50
☐ 48/II . . . . . 4¾ x 5¾" . . . (OE) . . . . ❶ $500-750
☐ 48/II . . . . . 4¾ x 5¾" . . . (OE) . . . . ❷ $350-500
☐ 48/II . . . . . 4¾ x 5¾" . . . (OE) . . . . ❸ $150-200
☐ 48/II . . . . . 4¾ x 5¾" . . . (OE) . . . . ❹ $105-125
☐ 48/II . . . . . 4¾ x 5¾" . . . (OE) . . . . ❺ $95-105
☐ 48/II . . . . . 4¾ x 5¾" . . . (OE) . . . . ❻ $94.50
☐ 48/V . . . . . 8¾ x 10¾" . . (CE) . . . . ❶ $1500-2000
☐ 48/V . . . . . 8¾ x 10¾" . . (CE) . . . . ❷ $1250-1500
☐ 48/V . . . . . 8¼ x 10¼" . . (CE) . . . . ❸ $1000-1250

White variation of 48/O

HUM 49   To Market

First modeled by master sculptor Arthur Moeller in 1936. Sometimes called "Brother and Sister" in old catalogues. Small size 49 3/0 never has bottle in basket. Some newly produced figurines in 6¼" size have appeared without a size designator. Only the number 49 is incised on the bottom along with the 5 trademark.

☐ 49 3/0 . . . . . 4" . . . . (OE) . . . . ❶ $225-300
☐ 49 3/0 . . . . . 4" . . . . (OE) . . . . ❷ $150-225
☐ 49 3/0 . . . . . 4" . . . . (OE) . . . . ❸ $100-150
☐ 49 3/0 . . . . . 4" . . . . (OE) . . . . ❹ $85-100
☐ 49 3/0 . . . . . 4" . . . . (OE) . . . . ❺ $80-85
☐ 49 3/0 . . . . . 4" . . . . (OE) . . . . ❻ $77.50
☐ 49/0 . . . . . . 5 to 5½" . . . . . (OE) . . . . ❶ $400-500
☐ 49/0 . . . . . . 5 to 5½" . . . . . (OE) . . . . ❷ $200-300
☐ 49/0 . . . . . . 5 to 5½" . . . . . (OE) . . . . ❸ $150-200
☐ 49/0 . . . . . . 5 to 5½" . . . . . (OE) . . . . ❹ $130-150
☐ 49/0 . . . . . . 5 to 5½" . . . . . (OE) . . . . ❺ $120-130
☐ 49/0 . . . . . . 5 to 5½" . . . . . (OE) . . . . ❻ $115.50
☐ 49/I . . . . . . 6¼ to 6½" . . . (OE) . . . . ❶ $1200-1500
☐ 49/I . . . . . . 6¼ to 6½" . . . (OE) . . . . ❷ $1000-1200
☐ 49/I . . . . . . 6¼ to 6½" . . . (OE) . . . . ❸ $350-500
☐ 49/I . . . . . . 6¼ to 6½" . . . (OE) . . . . ❹ $250-300
☐ 49/I . . . . . . 6¼ to 6½" . . . (OE) . . . . ❺ $240-250
☐ 49/I . . . . . . 6¼ to 6½" . . . (OE) . . . . ❻ $240
☐ 49 . . . . 6¼ to 6½" . . . (CE) . . . . ❶ $1200-1500
☐ 49 . . . . 6¼ to 6½" . . . (CE) . . . . ❺ $350-500

HUM 50
Volunteers
Originally modeled by master sculptor Reinhold Unger in 1936. Listed as "Playing Soldiers" in old catalogues. Sizes 50/0 and 50/I are difficult to find in older trademarks but were reinstated in 1979 with 5 trademark. The original drawing for this figurine was used by Ars Sacra Herbert Dubler on small note paper bearing a 1943 copyright date.

☐ 50 2/0 . . . . . 4¾ to 5" . . . . . (OE) . . . . ❷ $250-300
☐ 50 2/0 . . . . . 4¾ to 5" . . . . . (OE) . . . . ❸ $150-175
☐ 50 2/0 . . . . . 4¾ to 5" . . . . . (OE) . . . . ❹ $115-125
☐ 50 2/0 . . . . . 4¾ to 5" . . . . . (OE) . . . . ❺ $105-115
☐ 50 2/0 . . . . . 4¾ to 5" . . . . . (OE) . . . . ❻ $105
☐ 50/0 . . . . . . 5½ to 6" . . . . . (OE) . . . . ❶ $500-750
☐ 50/0 . . . . . . 5½ to 6" . . . . . (OE) . . . . ❷ $300-400
☐ 50/0 . . . . . . 5½ to 6" . . . . . (OE) . . . . ❸ $200-250
☐ 50/0 . . . . . . 5½ to 6" . . . . . (OE) . . . . ❹ $150-175
☐ 50/0 . . . . . . 5½ to 6" . . . . . (OE) . . . . ❺ $140-150
☐ 50/0 . . . . . . 5½ to 6" . . . . . (OE) . . . . ❻ $136.50
☐ 50/I . . . . . . 6½ to 7" . . . . . (OE) . . . . ❶ $750-1000
☐ 50/I . . . . . . 6½ to 7" . . . . . (OE) . . . . ❷ $500-750
☐ 50/I . . . . . . 6½ to 7" . . . . . (OE) . . . . ❸ $300-400
☐ 50/I . . . . . . 6½ to 7" . . . . . (OE) . . . . ❹ $250-300
☐ 50/I . . . . . . 6½ to 7" . . . . . (OE) . . . . ❺ $240-250
☐ 50/I . . . . . . 6½ to 7" . . . . . (OE) . . . . ❻ $240
☐ 50 . . . . 7" . . . . (CE) . . . . ❶ $1000-1500

HUM 51
Village Boy
First modeled by master sculptor Arthur Moeller in 1936. Has been slightly restyled several times through the years. Size 51/0 was restyled by Theo R. Menzenbach in 1960. Some newer models have a 1961 incised copyright date. Called "Country Boy" in old catalogues. Many size variations in the older pieces. One collector has small size 51 3/0 in crown trademark with yellow tie and blue jacket.

☐ 51 3/0 ..... 4" .... (OE).... ❶ $100-150
☐ 51 3/0 ..... 4" .... (OE).... ❷ $75-100
☐ 51 3/0 ..... 4" .... (OE).... ❸ $50-70
☐ 51 3/0 ..... 4" .... (OE).... ❹ $45-50
☐ 51 3/0 ..... 4" .... (OE).... ❺ $40-45
☐ 51 3/0 ..... 4" .... (OE).... ❻ $39
☐ 51 2/0 ..... 5" .... (OE).... ❷ $100-150
☐ 51 2/0 ..... 5" .... (OE).... ❸ $75-100
☐ 51 2/0 ..... 5" .... (OE).... ❹ $60-65
☐ 51 2/0 ..... 5" .... (OE).... ❺ $55-60
☐ 51 2/0 ..... 5" .... (OE).... ❻ $55
☐ 51/0 ...... 6 to 6¾" ..... (OE).... ❶ $300-400
☐ 51/0 ...... 6 to 6¾" ..... (OE).... ❷ $175-250
☐ 51/0 ...... 6 to 6¾" ..... (OE).... ❸ $125-150
☐ 51/0 ...... 6 to 6¾" ..... (OE).... ❹ $100-125
☐ 51/0 ...... 6 to 6¾" ..... (OE).... ❺ $90-100
☐ 51/0 ...... 6 to 6¾" ..... (OE).... ❻ $88
☐ 51/I ...... 7¼ to 8" ..... (OE).... ❶ $500-750
☐ 51/I ...... 7¼ to 8" ..... (OE).... ❷ $250-350
☐ 51/I ...... 7¼ to 8" ..... (OE).... ❸ $150-200
☐ 51/I ...... 7¼ to 8" ..... (OE).... ❹ $120-135
☐ 51/I ...... 7¼ to 8" ..... (OE).... ❺ $110-120
☐ 51/I ...... 7¼ to 8" ..... (OE).... ❻ $110

Old   52/I   New   Old   52/O   New

HUM 52   Going to Grandma's

Originally modeled in 1936 by master sculptor Reinhold Unger. Called "Little Mothers of the Family" in old catalogues. All large size and older small size figurines were produced with rectangular base. Small size was restyled in the early 1960's and changed to an oval base. The objects protruding from the cone represent candy and sweets rather than flowers. The cone appears empty on the large size models. In 1979 size 52/I was restyled with a new textured finish, an oval base and sweets in the cone. Both the old and new styles are found with 5 trademark.

☐ 52/0 ...... 4½ to 5" ..... (OE).... ❶ $400-500
☐ 52/0 ...... 4½ to 5" ..... (OE).... ❷ $250-300
☐ 52/0 ...... 4½ to 5" ..... (OE).... ❸ $150-200
☐ 52/0 ...... 4½ to 5" ..... (OE).... ❹ $110-125
☐ 52/0 ...... 4½ to 5" ..... (OE).... ❺ $100-110
☐ 52/0 ...... 4½ to 5" ..... (OE).... ❻ $100
☐ 52/I ...... 6 to 6¼" ..... (CE).... ❶ $1000-1250
☐ 52/I ...... 6 to 6¼" ..... (CE).... ❷ $600-750
☐ 52/I ...... 6 to 6¼" ..... (CE).... ❸ $400-500
☐ 52/I ...... 6 to 6¼" ..... (CE).... ❺ $240-500
☐ 52/I ...... 6 to 6¼" ..... (OE).... ❻ $240
☐ 52 .... 6¼" .... (CE).... ❶ $1250-1500
☐ 52 .... 6¼" .... (CE).... ❷ $750-1000

Old bowl style

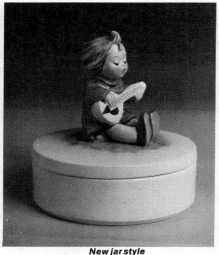

New jar style

HUM III/53
Joyful, Box
Bowl style box first produced in 1936. Jar style first produced and sold in 1964. Model number is found on underside of lid. "M.I. Hummel" signature is found on topside of lid directly behind figure.

HUM 53
Joyful
First modeled by master sculptor Reinhold Unger in 1936. Many size variations —older pieces usually much larger. Some early crown mark examples have orange dress and blue shoes—value: $500-750. Listed as "Singing Lesson" in some old catalogues. Current models have a brown-colored mandolin.

☐ 53	3½ to 4¼"	(OE)	❶	$250-300	
☐ 53	3½ to 4¼"	(OE)	❷	$125-150	
☐ 53	3½ to 4¼"	(OE)	❸	$70-80	
☐ 53	3½ to 4¼"	(OE)	❹	$50-60	
☐ 53	3½ to 4¼"	(OE)	❺	$45-50	
☐ 53	3½ to 4¼"	(OE)	❻	$44	
☐ III/53	6½"	(CE)	❶	$400-500	
☐ III/53	6½"	(CE)	❷	$350-400	
☐ III/53	6½"	(CE)	❸	$300-350	OLD STYLE
☐ III/53	5¾"	(OE)	❸	$110-135	NEW STYLE
☐ III/53	5¾"	(OE)	❹	$100-110	
☐ III/53	5¾"	(OE)	❺	$90-100	
☐ III/53	5¾"	(OE)	❻	$90	

HUM 54
Silent Night, Candleholder
This candleholder was first modeled by master sculptor Reinhold Unger in 1936. There are some color variations in the wings of angel. Early crown mark figurines are usually very light in color. Older pieces have smaller socket for candle. Almost identical to the model used for HUM 31 with the exception of the embossed earring and bare feet. Factory representatives state that a small quantity of HUM 54 were painted with a black child in the standing position—usually wearing shoes and a painted rather than an embossed earring.

☐ 54	3½ x 4¾"	(OE)	❶	$400-500	
☐ 54	3½ x 4¾"	(OE)	❷	$250-300	
☐ 54	3½ x 4¾"	(OE)	❸	$150-200	
☐ 54	3½ x 4¾"	(OE)	❹	$110-125	
☐ 54	3½ x 4¾"	(OE)	❺	$100-110	
☐ 54	3½ x 4¾"	(OE)	❻	$100	
☐ 54	3½ x 4¾"	(CE)	❷	$2000-3000	(with Black child)

HUM 55
Saint George
First modeled by master sculptor Reinhold Unger in 1936. Early crown mark models are sometimes found with bright orange-red saddle on horse. Old name: "Knight St. George" or "St. George and Dragon." Have not been able to trace location of Sister M.I. Hummel's original drawing for this figurine. Possibly painted on the wall of a church or religious building.

□ 55 .... 6¾" .... (OE).... ❶ $750-1000
□ 55 .... 6¾" .... (OE)....❷ $300-400
□ 55 .... 6¾" .... (OE)....❸ $200-275
□ 55 .... 6¾" .... (OE)....❹ $160-180
□ 55 .... 6¾" .... (OE)....❺ $144-160
□ 55 .... 6¾" .... (OE)....❻ $144

56 A   56 B

HUM 56 A
Culprits
Originally modeled in 1936 by master sculptor Arthur Moeller but has been restyled in later years. Restyled figurines have an extra branch by boy's feet. Variations in height and size of base. Old name "Apple Thief." Crown mark and early full bee trademarked pieces incised 56 only. Older models have the boy's eyes open while newer version eyes are looking down at dog.

HUM 56 B
Out of Danger
This companion figurine was first modeled by master sculptor Arthur Moeller in March of 1952, therefore will not be found with the crown trademark. Variation in height, and size of base. On older models the girl's eyes are open; on the newer version her eyes are looking down at dog. Full bee models have an extra flower on base.

□ 56 .... 6¼ to 6¾" ... (CE).... ❶ $350-500
□ 56/A...... 6¼ to 6¾" ... (OE)....❷ $200-275
□ 56/A...... 6¼ to 6¾" ... (OE)....❸ $125-150
□ 56/A...... 6¼ to 6¾" ... (OE)....❹ $115-125
□ 56/A...... 6¼ to 6¾" ... (OE)....❺ $105-115
□ 56/A...... 6¼ to 6¾" ... (OE)....❻ $105
□ 56/B...... 6¼ to 6¾" ... (OE)....❷ $200-275
□ 56/B...... 6¼ to 6¾" ... (OE)....❸ $125-150
□ 56/B...... 6¼ to 6¾" ... (OE)....❹ $115-125
□ 56/B...... 6¼ to 6¾" ... (OE)....❺ $105-115
□ 56/B...... 6¼ to 6¾" ... (OE)....❻ $105

HUM 57
Chick Girl

First modeled by master sculptor Reinhold Unger in 1936 and later remodeled by master sculptor Gerhard Skrobek in 1964. Small size has two chicks in basket while large size has three chicks. Old name: "Little Chicken Mother" or "The Little Chick Girl." There are three different styles of construction that have been used on bottom of base: quarter, doughnut and plain.

57/I   57/0

Old bowl style

New jar style

HUM III/57   Chick Girl, Box

Bowl style first produced in 1936. Jar style first produced and sold in 1964. Sometimes found with the incised number III 57/0 on the old bowl style pieces. Model number is found on underside of lid. "M.I. Hummel" signature is found on topside of lid directly behind figure.

☐ 57/0 . . . . . . 3½" . . . . (OE) . . . . ❶ $250-300
☐ 57/0 . . . . . . 3½" . . . . (OE) . . . . ❷ $150-175
☐ 57/0 . . . . . . 3½" . . . . (OE) . . . . ❸ $100-125
☐ 57/0 . . . . . . 3½" . . . . (OE) . . . . ❹ $75-95
☐ 57/0 . . . . . . 3½" . . . . (OE) . . . . ❺ $70-75
☐ 57/0 . . . . . . 3½" . . . . (OE) . . . . ❻ $66
☐ 57/I . . . . . . 4¼" . . . . (OE) . . . . ❶ $350-500
☐ 57/I . . . . . . 4¼" . . . . (OE) . . . . ❷ $250-300
☐ 57/I . . . . . . 4¼" . . . . (OE) . . . . ❸ $150-200
☐ 57/I . . . . . . 4¼" . . . . (OE) . . . . ❹ $125-150
☐ 57/I . . . . . . 4¼" . . . . (OE) . . . . ❺ $105-110

☐ 57/I	4¼"	(OE)	❻	$105	
☐ 57	4 to 4⅜"	(CE)	❶	$350-500	
☐ 57	4 to 4⅜"	(CE)	❷	$250-300	
☐ III/57	6 to 6¼"	(CE)	❶	$400-500	
☐ III/57	6 to 6¼"	(CE)	❷	$350-500	
☐ III/57	6 to 6¼"	(CE)	❸	$300-350	OLD STYLE
☐ III/57	5"	(OE)	❸	$110-135	NEW STYLE
☐ III/57	5"	(OE)	❹	$100-110	
☐ III/57	5"	(OE)	❺	$90-100	
☐ III/57	5"	(OE)	❻	$90	

58/I   58/O

HUM 58
Playmates
Originally modeled by master sculptor Reinhold Unger in 1936 and later restyled by master sculptor Gerhard Skrobek in 1964. Some size and color variations between old and new figurines. Both ears of rabbit pointing up on large size 58/I. Ears are separated on small size 58/0. Old name: "Just Friends." Three different styles of construction on bottom of base: quarter, doughnut and plain.

☐ 58/0	4"	(OE)	❶	$250-300
☐ 58/0	4"	(OE)	❷	$150-175
☐ 58/0	4"	(OE)	❸	$100-125
☐ 58/0	4"	(OE)	❹	$75-95
☐ 58/0	4"	(OE)	❺	$70-75
☐ 58/0	4"	(OE)	❻	$66
☐ 58/I	4¼"	(OE)	❶	$350-500
☐ 58/I	4¼"	(OE)	❷	$250-300
☐ 58/I	4¼"	(OE)	❸	$150-200
☐ 58/I	4¼"	(OE)	❹	$125-150
☐ 58/I	4¼"	(OE)	❺	$100-110
☐ 58/I	4¼"	(OE)	❻	$100
☐ 58	4 to 4½"	(CE)	❶	$350-600
☐ 58	4 to 4½"	(CE)	❷	$250-300

HUM III/58
Playmates, Box
Bowl style first produced in 1936. Jar style first produced and sold in 1964. Sometimes found with the incised number III 58/0 on the old bowl style pieces. Model number is found on underside of lid. "M.I. Hummel" signature is found on topside of lid directly behind figure.

Old bowl style

New jar style

☐ III/58	6¾"	(CE)	❶	$400-500	
☐ III/58	6¾"	(CE)	❷	$350-400	
☐ III/58	6¾"	(CE)	❸	$300-350	OLD STYLE
☐ III/58	5½"	(OE)	❸	$110-135	NEW STYLE
☐ III/58	5½"	(OE)	❹	$100-110	
☐ III/58	5½"	(OE)	❺	$90-100	
☐ III/58	5½"	(OE)	❻	$90	

Wooden poles   Plastic poles   Metal poles

HUM 59   Skier

First modeled by master sculptor Reinhold Unger in 1936. Older models were sold with wooden poles and fiber disks; newer models with plastic poles for a short period of time. The metal poles have been used since 1970. Many size variations; the full bee pieces usually the largest.

□ 59	5 to 6"	(OE)	❶	$350-400
□ 59	5 to 6"	(OE)	❷	$250-300
□ 59	5 to 6"	(OE)	❸	$125-150
□ 59	5 to 6"	(OE)	❹	$100-125
□ 59	5 to 6"	(OE)	❺	$90-100
□ 59	5 to 6"	(OE)	❻	$88

60/B   60/A

HUM 60 A
Farm Boy
HUM 60 B
Goose Girl, Bookends
First produced in September 1936. Trademarks usually stamped on wood base rather than on figurine. The number 60 A is found incised on bottom of feet of "Farm Boy" in crown and full bee trademarks. Have been unable to find a similar number on any "Goose Girls" that have been separated from wooden base. See HUM 148 and HUM 149 for additional information.

□ 60 A & B	4¾"	(OE)	❶	$750-1000
□ 60 A & B	4¾"	(OE)	❷	$400-600
□ 60 A & B	4¾"	(OE)	❸	$300-400
□ 60 A & B	4¾"	(OE)	❹	$250-300
□ 60 A & B	4¾"	(OE)	❺	$220-250
□ 60 A & B	4¾"	(OE)	❻	$220

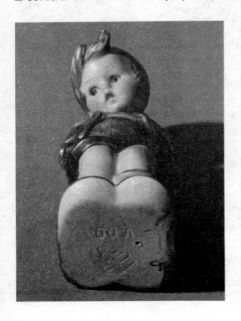

HUM 61 A
Playmates

HUM 61 B
Chick Girl, Bookends
First produced in November 1936. Trademarks stamped on wood base rather than on figurine.

☐ 61 A & B	.. 4"	....	(OE)	....❶....	$750-1000
☐ 61 A & B	.. 4"	....	(OE)	....❷....	$400-600
☐ 61 A & B	.. 4"	....	(OE)	....❸....	$300-400
☐ 61 A & B	.. 4"	....	(OE)	....❹....	$250-300
☐ 61 A & B	.. 4"	....	(OE)	....❺....	$220-250
☐ 61 A & B	.. 4"	....	(OE)	....❻....	$220

HUM 62
Happy Pastime, Ashtray
Slight difference in construction of ashtray on older models. Crown mark piece has "M.I. Hummel" signature on back of ashtray while newer models have signature on back of girl. First modeled by master sculptor Arthur Moeller in 1936.

☐ 62	.... 3½ x 6¼"	... (OE)	....❶....	$300-350
☐ 62	.... 3½ x 6¼"	... (OE)	....❷....	$150-225
☐ 62	.... 3½ x 6¼"	... (OE)	....❸....	$100-150
☐ 62	.... 3½ x 6¼"	... (OE)	....❹....	$90-100
☐ 62	.... 3½ x 6¼"	... (OE)	....❺....	$80-90
☐ 62	.... 3½ x 6¼"	... (OE)	....❻....	$80

HUM 63
Singing Lesson
First modeled by master sculptor Arthur Moeller in 1937. Some variations in size between old and new models. Sometimes a slight variation in tilt of boy's head and position of hand. Old name: "Duet" or "Critic." "Singing Lesson" is the motif used on the 1979 Annual Plate, HUM 272.

☐ 63	2¾ to 3"	(OE)	❶	$200-250
☐ 63	2¾ to 3"	(OE)	❷	$125-150
☐ 63	2¾ to 3"	(OE)	❸	$75-100
☐ 63	2¾ to 3"	(OE)	❹	$60-75
☐ 63	2¾ to 3"	(OE)	❺	$55-60
☐ 63	2¾ to 3"	(OE)	❻	$55

Old bowl style

New Jar style

HUM III/63   Singing Lesson, Box
Bowl style first produced in 1937. Jar style first produced and sold in 1964. Old name: "Duet" box. Model number is found on underside of lid. "M.I. Hummel" signature is found on topside of lid directly behind figure.

☐ III/63	5¾"	(CE)	❶	$400-500
☐ III/63	5¾"	(CE)	❷	$350-400
☐ III/63	5¾"	(CE)	❸	$300-350 (Old style)
☐ III/63	4¾"	(OE)	❸	$110-135 (New style)
☐ III/63	4¾"	(OE)	❹	$100-110
☐ III/63	4¾"	(OE)	❺	$90-100
☐ III/63	4¾"	(OE)	❻	$90

Old   *New*

HUM 64
Shepherd's Boy
First modeled by master sculptor Arthur Moeller in 1937. Restyled with the new textured finish in the late 1970's by master sculptor Gerhard Skrobek. Many size variations—note photo. Old name: "The Good Shepherd."

☐ 64	5½ to 6¼"	(OE)	❶	$350-400
☐ 64	5½ to 6¼"	(OE)	❷	$250-325
☐ 64	5½ to 6¼"	(OE)	❸	$150-175
☐ 64	5½ to 6¼"	(OE)	❹	$100-125
☐ 64	5½ to 6¼"	(OE)	❺	$90-100
☐ 64	5½ to 6¼"	(OE)	❻	$88

65   *65/I*   *65/O*

HUM 65
Farewell
First modeled by master sculptor Arthur Moeller in 1937. Restyled in 1964 by master sculptor Gerhard Skrobek. The small size (65/0) was modeled in 1955 by Gerhard Skrobek. 65/0 is extremely rare since only a few sample pieces were produced. Called "So Long" in some old catalogues. Many size variations. Currently produced in only one size with incised number 65 only.

☐ 65	4¾"	(OE)	❺	$110-120
☐ 65	4¾"	(OE)	❻	$110
☐ 65/0	4"	(CE)	❷	$3500-5000
☐ 65/I	4½ to 4⅞"	(CE)	❶	$350-500
☐ 65/I	4½ to 4⅞"	(CE)	❷	$250-375
☐ 65/I	4½ to 4⅞"	(CE)	❸	$150-175
☐ 65/I	4½ to 4⅞"	(CE)	❹	$120-150
☐ 65/I	4½ to 4⅞"	(CE)	❺	$110-120
☐ 65	4¾ to 5"	(CE)	❶	$350-500
☐ 65	4¾ to 5"	(CE)	❷	$250-375

HUM 66
Farm Boy
Many size variations. Old name: "Three Pals" or "Happy-Go-Lucky Fellow" in some catalogues. Originally modeled in 1937 by master sculptor Arthur Moeller.

☐ 66	5 to 5¾"	(OE)	❶	$300-400
☐ 66	5 to 5¾"	(OE)	❷	$200-250
☐ 66	5 to 5¾"	(OE)	❸	$150-175
☐ 66	5 to 5¾"	(OE)	❹	$100-125
☐ 66	5 to 5¾"	(OE)	❺	$90-100
☐ 66	5 to 5¾"	(OE)	❻	$88

Old   New

HUM 67
Doll Mother
First modeled by master sculptor Arthur Moeller in 1937 but has been restyled in recent years. Slight difference in hair ribbon on girl. Old name: "Little Doll Mother" or "Little Mother of Dolls" in some catalogues.

☐ 67	4¼ to 4¾"	(OE)	❶	$400-500
☐ 67	4¼ to 4¾"	(OE)	❷	$200-300
☐ 67	4¼ to 4¾"	(OE)	❸	$150-175
☐ 67	4¼ to 4¾"	(OE)	❹	$105-150
☐ 67	4¼ to 4¾"	(OE)	❺	$95-105
☐ 67	4¼ to 4¾"	(OE)	❻	$94.50

| 68 2/O | 68/O | 68 Crown | 68 Full Bee | 68 Double Crown |

HUM 68   Lost Sheep

Originally modeled by master sculptor Arthur Moeller in 1937 and later restyled by a combination of several modelers. Many size and color variations. Older models have dark brown trousers. Similar to HUM 64 "Shepherd's Boy" except for single lamb and different colors.

☐ 68 2/0 . . . . . 4¼ to 4½" . . . (OE) . . . . ❷ $125-150
☐ 68 2/0 . . . . . 4¼ to 4½" . . . (OE) . . . . ❸ $75-100
☐ 68 2/0 . . . . . 4¼ to 4½" . . . (OE) . . . . ❹ $60-70
☐ 68 2/0 . . . . . 4¼ to 4½" . . . (OE) . . . . ❺ $55-60
☐ 68 2/0 . . . . . 4¼ to 4½" . . . (OE) . . . . ❻ $55
☐ 68/0 . . . . . 5½" . . . . (OE) . . . . ❷ $200-225
☐ 68/0 . . . . . 5½" . . . . (OE) . . . . ❸ $100-150
☐ 68/0 . . . . . 5½" . . . . (OE) . . . . ❹ $85-100
☐ 68/0 . . . . . 5½" . . . . (OE) . . . . ❺ $80-85
☐ 68/0 . . . . . 5½" . . . . (OE) . . . . ❻ $77.50
☐ 68 . . . . 5½ to 6½" . . . (CE) . . . . ❶ $350-500
☐ 68 . . . . 5½ to 6½" . . . (CE) . . . . ❷ $250-350
☐ 68 . . . . 5½ to 6½" . . . (CE) . . . . ❸ $200-250

Early sample

HUM 69   Happy Pastime

First modeled by master sculptor Arthur Moeller in 1937. Very little difference between old and new models. Older models slightly larger. Called "Knitter" in old catalogues. The "M.I. Hummel" signature is very faint or difficult to see on some old models. "Happy Pastime" is the motif used on the 1978 Annual Plate, HUM 271.

- ☐ 69 .... 3½" .... (OE).... ❶ $300-350
- ☐ 69 .... 3½" .... (OE).... ❷ $150-200
- ☐ 69 .... 3½" .... (OE).... ❸ $100-125
- ☐ 69 .... 3½" .... (OE).... ❹ $75-85
- ☐ 69 .... 3½" .... (OE).... ❺ $70-75
- ☐ 69 .... 3½" .... (OE).... ❻ $66

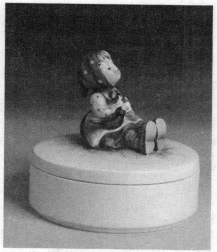

Old bowl style   *New jar style*

HUM III/69   Happy Pastime, Box

Bowl style first produced in 1937. Jar style first produced and sold in 1964. Model number is found on underside of lid. "M.I. Hummel" signature is found on topside of lid directly behind figure.

☐ III/69 . . . . . 6½" . . . . (CE). . . . ❶ $400-500
☐ III/69 . . . . . 6½" . . . . (CE). . . . ❷ $350-400
☐ III/69 . . . . . 6½" . . . . (CE). . . . ❸ . . . . $300-350 OLD STYLE
☐ III/69 . . . . . 5¼" . . . . (OE). . . . ❸ . . . . $110-135 NEW STYLE
☐ III/69 . . . . . 5¼" . . . . (OE). . . . ❹ $100-110
☐ III/69 . . . . . 5¼" . . . . (OE). . . . ❺ $90-100
☐ III/69 . . . . . 5¼" . . . . (OE). . . . ❻ $90

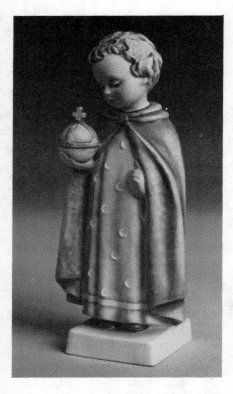

HUM 70
The Holy Child
Factory records indicate this was originally modeled in 1937 by a combination of modelers. Has been restyled in later years with newer models having the textured finish on gown and robe. Many size variations. Also listed as "Child Jesus" in some old catalogues.

☐ 70 . . . . 6¾ to 7½" . . . (OE) . . . . ❶ $250-300
☐ 70 . . . . 6¾ to 7½" . . . (OE) . . . . ❷ $200-250
☐ 70 . . . . 6¾ to 7½" . . . (OE) . . . . ❸ $90-125
☐ 70 . . . . 6¾ to 7½" . . . (OE) . . . . ❹ $70-80
☐ 70 . . . . 6¾ to 7½" . . . (OE) . . . . ❺ $63-70
☐ 70 . . . . 6¾ to 7½" . . . (OE) . . . . ❻ $63

New   Old   Full Bee

HUM 71   Stormy Weather

Originally modeled by master sculptor Reinhold Unger in 1937. Has been restyled several times through the years. Many size variations. Full bee models are usually the largest size. Old name: "Under One Roof." Slight difference between old and new models other than size. Several variations in structure of bottom of base design. This motif was used for the first Anniversary Plate, HUM 280 in 1975.

☐ 71 ...... 6 to 7" .... (OE).... ❶ $600-750
☐ 71 ...... 6 to 7" .... (OE).... ❷ $500-600
☐ 71 ...... 6 to 7" .... (OE).... ❸ $300-350
☐ 71 ...... 6 to 7" .... (OE).... ❹ $250-275
☐ 71 ...... 6 to 7" .... (OE).... ❺ $200-225
☐ 71 ...... 6 to 7" .... (OE).... ❻ $200

Old   *New*

HUM 72
Spring Cheer
First modeled in 1937 by master sculptor Reinhold Unger. Older models have yellow dress and no flowers in right hand. Restyled in 1965 by master sculptor Gerhard Skrobek who added flowers to right hand and changed color of dress to dark green. Older style can also be found with dark green dress. This variation would be considered rare and would bring a premium of usually anywhere from $250 to $750. Old name: "Spring Flowers." Crown mark pieces have a flower on reverse side. Later production pieces omitted this flower.

☐ 72 .... 5 to 5½" ..... (CE)....❶.... $250-300
☐ 72 .... 5 to 5½" ..... (CE)....❷.... $150-200
☐ 72 .... 5 to 5½" ..... (CE)....❸.... $75-100
☐ 72 .... 5 to 5½" ..... (OE)....❹.... $65-75
☐ 72 .... 5 to 5½" ..... (OE)....❺.... $55-65
☐ 72 .... 5 to 5½" ..... (OE)....❻.... $55

HUM 73
Little Helper
Very little variation between old and new pieces. Older figurines are usually slightly larger. Old name: "Diligent Betsy" or "The Little Sister." Originally modeled in 1937 by master sculptor Reinhold Unger.

☐ 73 .... 4¼ to 4½" ... (OE)....❶.... $200-250
☐ 73 .... 4¼ to 4½" ... (OE)....❷.... $100-150
☐ 73 .... 4¼ to 4½" ... (OE)....❸.... $75-100
☐ 73 .... 4¼ to 4½" ... (OE)....❹.... $65-75
☐ 73 .... 4¼ to 4½" ... (OE)....❺.... $55-65
☐ 73 .... 4¼ to 4½" ... (OE)....❻.... $55

Crown	Crown	Full	Stylized

HUM 74   Little Gardener

Originally modeled by master sculptor Reinhold Unger in 1937 but has undergone many changes through the years. Older models have an oval base. Restyled in the early 1960's and changed to a round base and smaller flower. Many color variations on girl's apron.

☐ 74	4 to 4½"	(OE)	❶	$200-250
☐ 74	4 to 4½"	(OE)	❷	$100-150
☐ 74	4 to 4½"	(OE)	❸	$75-100
☐ 74	4 to 4½"	(OE)	❹	$65-75
☐ 74	4 to 4½"	(OE)	❺	$55-65
☐ 74	4 to 4½"	(OE)	❻	$55

HUM 75
Holy Water Font, White Angel

First modeled by master sculptor Reinhold Unger in 1937. Newer models have hole for hanging font. Older models provide a hole only on back. Variation in construction of bowl. Also called "Angelic Prayer" in some catalogues.

☐ 75	3¼ to 4½"	(OE)	❶	$100-150
☐ 75	3¼ to 4½"	(OE)	❷	$50-75
☐ 75	3¼ to 4½"	(OE)	❸	$30-35
☐ 75	3¼ to 4½"	(OE)	❹	$20-25
☐ 75	3¼ to 4½"	(OE)	❺	$18-20
☐ 75	3¼ to 4½"	(OE)	❻	$17.50

HUM 76 A
Doll Mother

HUM 76 B
Prayer Before Battle, Bookends
No known examples other than this half of set which was located in Goebel factory. Originally modeled by master sculptor Arthur Moeller. Factory note indicates: "Not produced after 28 February 1938."

☐ 76 .... A & B" .... (CE) .... ❶ .... $5000 +

HUM 77
Holy Water Font, Cross With Doves
First modeled by master sculptor Reinhold Unger in 1937 but according to factory information was made as samples only and never in production. Listed as a closed edition on 21 October 1937. The only known example of this font, other than the factory archives specimen, was purchased at an estate sale in California in 1979. The original owner is now deceased and we are unable to confirm where she had first acquired the font.

☐ 77 .... 1¾ x 6¼" ... (CN) .... $5000 +

Old style   *New style*

HUM 78   Infant of Krumbad

This figurine has been produced in three different finishes. Produced in brownish bisque finish (U.S. Market); full color and white overglaze (various other countries), sometimes found in Belgium. Variations in older models. Restyled by Gerhard Skrobek in 1965. The two small holes on the back are designed to hold a wire halo. Full color and white overglaze pieces command varied premiums. First modeled by Erich Lautensack in 1937. (Lautensack died during the Second World War.)

B. C. W. . . . .

☐ ☐ ☐	78/0 . . . . 2¼"	(CE) . . ❷ . .	$150-200
☐ ☐ ☐	78/0 . . . . 2¼"	(CE) . . ❸ . .	$100-150
☐ ☐ ☐	78/I . . . . 2½"	(OE) . . ❶ . .	$150-200
☐ ☐ ☐	78/I . . . . 2½"	(OE) . . ❷ . .	$125-150
☐ ☐ ☐	78/I . . . . 2½"	(OE) . . ❸ . .	$30-35
☐ ☐ ☐	78/I . . . . 2½"	(OE) . . ❹ . .	$25-30
☐ ☐ ☐	78/I . . . . 2½"	(OE) . . ❺ . .	$21-25
☐ ☐ ☐	78/I . . . . 2½"	(OE) . . ❻ . .	$21
☐ ☐ ☐	78/II . . . . 3½"	(OE) . . ❶ . .	$200-250
☐ ☐ ☐	78/II . . . . 3½"	(OE) . . ❷ . .	$150-175
☐ ☐ ☐	78/II . . . . 3½"	(OE) . . ❸ . .	$35-40
☐ ☐ ☐	78/II . . . . 3½"	(OE) . . ❹ . .	$30-35
☐ ☐ ☐	78/II . . . . 3½"	(OE) . . ❺ . .	$27-30
☐ ☐ ☐	78/II . . . . 3½"	(OE) . . ❻ . .	$26.50
☐ ☐ ☐	78/III . . . 4½ to 5¼"	(OE) . . ❶ . .	$250-300
☐ ☐ ☐	78/III . . . 4½ to 5¼"	(OE) . . ❷ . .	$175-200
☐ ☐ ☐	78/III . . . 4½ to 5¼"	(OE) . . ❸ . .	$40-50
☐ ☐ ☐	78/III . . . 4½ to 5¼"	(OE) . . ❹ . .	$35-40
☐ ☐ ☐	78/III . . . 4½ to 5¼"	(OE) . . ❺ . .	$32-35
☐ ☐ ☐	78/III . . . 4½ to 5¼"	(OE) . . ❻ . .	$31.50
☐ ☐ ☐	78/V . . . . 7½ to 7¾"	(OE) . . ❶ . .	$400-500
☐ ☐ ☐	78/V . . . . 7½ to 7¾"	(OE) . . ❷ . .	$260-400
☐ ☐ ☐	78/V . . . . 7½ to 7¾"	(OE) . . ❸ . .	$100-125
☐ ☐ ☐	78/V . . . . 7½ to 7¾"	(OE) . . ❹ . .	$85-100
☐ ☐ ☐	78/V . . . . 7½ to 7¾"	(OE) . . ❺ . .	$75-85
☐ ☐ ☐	78/V . . . . 7½ to 7¾"	(OE) . . ❻ . .	$60
☐ ☐ ☐	78/VI . . . 10 to 11¼"	(OE) . . ❶ . .	$500-750
☐ ☐ ☐	78/VI . . . 10 to 11¼"	(OE) . . ❷ . .	$300-500

B. C. W. . . . .
☐ ☐ ☐ 78/VI . . .10 to 11¼" . . . . (OE) . . ❸ . .$150-200
☐ ☐ ☐ 78/VI . . .10 to 11¼" . . . . (OE) . . ❹ . .$150-200
☐ ☐ ☐ 78/VI . . .10 to 11¼" . . . . (OE) . . ❺ . .$150-175
☐ ☐ ☐ 78/VI . . .10 to 11¼" . . . . (OE) . . ❻ . .$120
☐ ☐ ☐ 78/VIII . .13¼ to 14¼" . . (OE) . . ❶ . .$750-1000
☐ ☐ ☐ 78/VIII . .13¼ to 14¼" . . (OE) . . ❷ . .$500-750
☐ ☐ ☐ 78/VIII . .13¼ to 14¼" . . (OE) . . ❸ . .$250-300
☐ ☐ ☐ 78/VIII . .13¼ to 14¼" . . (OE) . . ❹ . .$250-300
☐ ☐ ☐ 78/VIII . .13¼ to 14¼" . . (OE) . . ❺ . .$250-275
☐ ☐ ☐ 78/VIII . .13¼ to 14¼" . . (OE) . . ❻ . .$230

New   .   *Old*   *New*   *Old*

HUM 79   Globe Trotter

Originally modeled by master sculptor Arthur Moeller in 1937. Remodeled in 1955 at
which time the basket weave was changed from a double weave to a single weave.
Crown mark pieces usually have a tan-colored handle on umbrella while others are
black. Some variation of color on the inside of basket. Some old catalogues list name
as "Happy Traveler." Some older models have dark green hat. This motif is used on the
1973 Annual Plate, HUM 226.

☐ 79 . . . . 5 to 5¼" . . . . . (CE) . . . . ❶ $350-500
☐ 79 . . . . 5 to 5¼" . . . . . (CE) . . . . ❷ $200-350
☐ 79 . . . . 5 to 5¼" . . . . . (OE) . . . . ❸ $100-125
☐ 79 . . . . 5 to 5¼" . . . . . (OE) . . . . ❹ $80-90
☐ 79 . . . . 5 to 5¼" . . . . . (OE) . . . . ❺ $75-80
☐ 79 . . . . 5 to 5¼" . . . . . (OE) . . . . ❻ $72

HUM 80
Little Scholar
Original model made by master sculptor
Arthur Moeller in 1937. Some color variations. Old models have brown shoes. The
cone in boy's right arm is called Schultute
or Zuckertute, a paper cone containing
school supplies and other goodies, which
German parents traditionally give their
children on the first day of school.

☐ 80 .... 5¼ to 5¾" ... (OE).... ❶ $250-325
☐ 80 .... 5¼ to 5¾" ... (OE).... ❷ $150-225
☐ 80 .... 5¼ to 5¾" ... (OE).... ❸ $100-150
☐ 80 .... 5¼ to 5¾" ... (OE).... ❹ $80-100
☐ 80 .... 5¼ to 5¾" ... (OE).... ❺ $75-80
☐ 80 .... 5¼ to 5¾" ... (OE).... ❻ $72

81/0   *81 2/0*

HUM 81
School Girl

Old name: "Primer Girl." Original model made by master sculptor Arthur Moeller in 1937. Many size variations as well as color variations. Size 81 2/0 basket filled; all others, baskets empty. Old catalogue listing of 7¾" is in error. It is doubtful that the small size 81 2/0 was produced with crown trademark. This motif is used on the 1980 Annual Plate, HUM 273.

☐ 81 2/0	4¼ to 4¾"	(OE)	❶	$200-250
☐ 81 2/0	4¼ to 4¾"	(OE)	❷	$125-150
☐ 81 2/0	4¼ to 4¾"	(OE)	❸	$75-100
☐ 81 2/0	4¼ to 4¾"	(OE)	❹	$60-70
☐ 81 2/0	4¼ to 4¾"	(OE)	❺	$55-60
☐ 81 2/0	4¼ to 4¾"	(OE)	❻	$55
☐ 81/0	4¾ to 5¼"	(OE)	❶	$250-325
☐ 81/0	4¾ to 5¼"	(OE)	❷	$150-200
☐ 81/0	4¾ to 5¼"	(OE)	❸	$100-125
☐ 81/0	4¾ to 5¼"	(OE)	❹	$80-90
☐ 81/0	4¾ to 5¼"	(OE)	❺	$75-80
☐ 81/0	4¾ to 5¼"	(OE)	❻	$72
☐ 81	5⅛ to 5½"	(CE)	❶	$300-350
☐ 81	5⅛ to 5½"	(CE)	❷	$200-250

| 82/2 | 82/0 | 82/0 | 82 2/0 | 82 2/0 |

HUM 82   School Boy

First modeled by master sculptor Arthur Moeller in 1938. Many size variations. Old name: "Little Scholar," "School Days" or "Primer Boy." The larger size 82/II (82/2) has been considered rare but is once again back in current production. It is doubtful that the small size 82 2/0 was produced with crown trademark. See HUM 329.

☐ 82 2/0 . . . . . 4 to 4½" . . . . . (OE) . . . . ❶ $200-250
☐ 82 2/0 . . . . . 4 to 4½" . . . . . (OE) . . . . ❷ $125-150
☐ 82 2/0 . . . . . 4 to 4½" . . . . . (OE) . . . . ❸ $75-100
☐ 82 2/0 . . . . . 4 to 4½" . . . . . (OE) . . . . ❹ $60-70
☐ 82 2/0 . . . . . 4 to 4½" . . . . . (OE) . . . . ❺ $55-60
☐ 82 2/0 . . . . . 4 to 4½" . . . . . (OE) . . . . ❻ $55
☐ 82/0 . . . . . . 4¾ to 6" . . . . . (OE) . . . . ❶ $300-350
☐ 82/0 . . . . . . 4¾ to 6" . . . . . (OE) . . . . ❷ $150-200
☐ 82/0 . . . . . . 4¾ to 6" . . . . . (OE) . . . . ❸ $100-125
☐ 82/0 . . . . . . 4¾ to 6" . . . . . (OE) . . . . ❹ $80-90
☐ 82/0 . . . . . . 4¾ to 6" . . . . . (OE) . . . . ❺ $75-80
☐ 82/0 . . . . . . 4¾ to 6" . . . . . (OE) . . . . ❻ $72
☐ 82/II . . . . . . 7½" . . . . (OE) . . . . ❶ $750-1000
☐ 82/II . . . . . . 7½" . . . . (OE) . . . . ❷ $600-750
☐ 82/II . . . . . . 7½" . . . . (OE) . . . . ❸ $300-375
☐ 82/II . . . . . . 7½" . . . . (OE) . . . . ❺ $195-215
☐ 82/II . . . . . . 7½" . . . . (OE) . . . . ❻ $195

HUM 83
Angel Serenade
Old name: "Psalmist" in some early Goebel catalogues. First modeled by master sculptor Reinhold Unger in 1938. Very little change in design through the years. This figurine had not been produced in quantity since the early 1960's and was considered rare. It is now back on the market with the current trademark. The "Angel Serenade" name is also used for HUM 214/D (part of small Nativity set) and HUM 260/E (part of large Nativity set).

☐ 83	5½ to 5¾"	(OE)	❶	$400-500
☐ 83	5½ to 5¾"	(OE)	❷	$350-400
☐ 83	5½ to 5¾"	(OE)	❸	$250-350
☐ 83	5½ to 5¾"	(OE)	❹	$150-250
☐ 83	5½ to 5¾"	(OE)	❺	$84-95
☐ 83	5½ to 5¾"	(OE)	❻	$84

HUM 84
Worship
Originally modeled by master sculptor Reinhold Unger in 1938. Old name: "At The Wayside" or "Devotion" in some catalogues. The small size 84/0 was also sold in white overglaze at one time in Belgium and would now be considered extremely rare. Current models of the large size 84/V have "M.I. Hummel" signature on back of shrine while older models have signature on back of base. Sometimes incised 84/5 instead of 84/V.

☐ 84/0	5 to 5½"	(OE)	❶	$300-350
☐ 84/0	5 to 5½"	(OE)	❷	$150-200
☐ 84/0	5 to 5½"	(OE)	❸	$100-125
☐ 84/0	5"	(OE)	❹	$75-90
☐ 84/0	5"	(OE)	❺	$70-75
☐ 84/0	5"	(OE)	❻	$68.50
☐ 84/V	12½ to 13¼"	(OE)	❶	$2000-3000
☐ 84/V	12½ to 13¼"	(OE)	❷	$1500-2000
☐ 84/V	12½ to 13¼"	(OE)	❸	$800-1000
☐ 84/V	12½ to 13¼"	(OE)	❹	$700-800
☐ 84/V	12½ to 13¼"	(OE)	❺	$630-700
☐ 84/V	12½ to 13¼"	(OE)	❻	$630
☐ 84	5¼"	(CE)	❶	$350-500

Note fingers

HUM 85
Serenade
First modeled by master sculptor Arthur Moeller in 1938. Many size variations. Note variation of boy's fingers on flute—cannot be attributed to any one time period. Old model with 85/0 number has fingers up. Size 85/0 has recently been restyled with a new hair style and textured finish. Normal hat color is dark gray or black. Older models also found with light gray hat. Old large size figurine with crown trademark has 85 number. Also found with incised number 85.0. or 85. in crown trademark in the small size. Sometimes incised 85/2 instead of 85/II. One of several figurines that make up the Hummel orchestra. Old name: "The Flutist."

☐ 85/0	4¾ to 5¼"	(OE)	❶	$200-250
☐ 85/0	4¾ to 5¼"	(OE)	❷	$125-150

☐ 85/0	4¾ to 5¼"	(OE)	❸	$75-100
☐ 85/0	4¾ to 5¼"	(OE)	❹	$60-70
☐ 85/0	4¾ to 5¼"	(OE)	❺	$55-60
☐ 85/0	4¾ to 5¼"	(OE)	❻	$55
☐ 85	7 to 7½"	(CE)	❶	$750-1000
☐ 85	7 to 7½"	(CE)	❷	$400-750
☐ 85/II	7 to 7½"	(OE)	❶	$750-1000
☐ 85/II	7 to 7½"	(OE)	❷	$400-500
☐ 85/II	7 to 7½"	(OE)	❸	$250-300
☐ 85/II	7 to 7½"	(OE)	❹	$225-250
☐ 85/II	7 to 7½"	(OE)	❺	$195-215
☐ 85/II	7 to 7½"	(OE)	❻	$195

HUM 86
Happiness
Many size variations. Made with either square or rectangular base. Old name: "Wandersong" or "Traveller's Song" in early Goebel catalogue. First modeled by master sculptor Reinhold Unger in 1938.

☐ 86	4½ to 5"	(OE)	❶	$200-250
☐ 86	4½ to 5"	(OE)	❷	$125-150
☐ 86	4½ to 5"	(OE)	❸	$75-100
☐ 86	4½ to 5"	(OE)	❹	$60-70
☐ 86	4½ to 5"	(OE)	❺	$55-60
☐ 86	4½ to 5"	(OE)	❻	$55

HUM 87
For Father
First modeled in 1938 by master sculptor Arther Moeller. Some size and color variations between old and new models. Boy is carrying white radishes and beer stein. Some models have orange-colored vegetables that would appear to be carrots—usually found only with the early stylized trademark 3. The orange carrot variation normally sells in the $500 to $750 price range. Old name: "Father's Joy."

☐ 87	5½"	(OE)	❶	$300-375
☐ 87	5½"	(OE)	❷	$200-225
☐ 87	5½"	(OE)	❸	$125-150
☐ 87	5½"	(OE)	❹	$90-100
☐ 87	5½"	(OE)	❺	$85-90
☐ 87	5½"	(OE)	❻	$83

88/I   **88/2**

HUM 88
Heavenly Protection
Originally modeled by master sculptor Reinhold Unger in 1938. Some size and color variations between old and new models. Small size 88/I first put on the market in early 1960's. Some pieces have an incised 1961 copyright date on bottom.

☐ 88/I	6¼ to 6¾"	(OE)	❸	$250-300
☐ 88/I	6¼ to 6¾"	(OE)	❹	$175-200
☐ 88/I	6¼ to 6¾"	(OE)	❺	$155-175
☐ 88/I	6¼ to 6¾"	(OE)	❻	$155
☐ 88/II	8¾ to 9"	(OE)	❷	$500-750
☐ 88/II	8¾ to 9"	(OE)	❸	$350-500
☐ 88/II	8¾ to 9"	(OE)	❹	$255-290
☐ 88/II	8¾ to 9"	(OE)	❺	$231-255
☐ 88/II	8¾ to 9"	(OE)	❻	$231
☐ 88	9¼"	(CE)	❶	$1000-1250
☐ 88	9¼"	(CE)	❷	$750-1000
☐ 88	8¾ to 9¼"	(CE)	❸	$500-750

New   *Old*

HUM 89
Little Cellist

Modeled by master sculptor Arthur Moeller in 1938. Restyled in the early 1960's. Many size variations through the years. Older examples of size 89/I have eyes open and looking straight ahead. Newer pieces have eyes looking down. Older pieces have rectangular base while newer pieces have rectangular base with corners squared off. Name listed as "Musician" in some old catalogues.

☐ 89/I	5¼ to 6¼"	(OE)	❶	$350-400
☐ 89/I	5¼ to 6¼"	(OE)	❷	$250-325
☐ 89/I	5¼ to 6¼"	(OE)	❸	$125-150
☐ 89/I	5¼ to 6¼"	(OE)	❹	$95-110
☐ 89/I	5¼ to 6¼"	(OE)	❺	$90-95
☐ 89/I	5¼ to 6¼"	(OE)	❻	$88
☐ 89/II	7½ to 7¾"	(OE)	❶	$750-1000
☐ 89/II	7½ to 7¾"	(OE)	❷	$350-500
☐ 89/II	7½ to 7¾"	(OE)	❸	$250-300
☐ 89/II	7½ to 7¼"	(OE)	❹	$225-250
☐ 89/II	7½ to 7¾"	(OE)	❺	$195-215
☐ 89/II	7½ to 7¾"	(OE)	❻	$195

Factory sample

HUM 90
Eventide

HUM 90
Adoration (Without Shrine), Bookends
Records indicate that this set of book-
ends was made in 1938 by a team of art-
ists, which possibly included Reinhold
Unger. Factory sample only. Extremely
rare. Not produced after 28 February 1938.
Listed as a closed edition.

☐ 90 A&B ... . (CE) .... $5000 +

Old   *New*

HUM 91 A & B   Holy Water Font, Angels at Prayer
Angel facing left was apparently made first since early crown mark pieces are incised
91 only (not part of set). Angel facing right (91 B) was probably introduced slightly later.
Now listed as a pair—91 A & B. First modeled by master sculptor Reinhold Unger in
1938. Older models (left) do not have halos while more recent designs have halos and a
redesigned water bowl. Trademarks 1, 2 and 3 are without halos, 3, 4, 5 and 6 with
halos. Note: trademark 3 can be found either way.

☐ 91 .... 3¼ x 4½" ... (CE).... ❶ $200-250
☐ 91 A & B .. 3⅜ x 5" ...... (CE).... ❶ $200-300
☐ 91 A & B .. 3⅜ x 5" ...... (CE).... ❷ $150-200
☐ 91 A & B .. 3⅜ x 5" ...... (CE).... ❸ $125-150
☐ 91 A & B .. 3⅜ x 5" ...... (OE).... ❹ $40-50
☐ 91 A & B .. 3⅜ x 5" ...... (OE).... ❺ $35-40
☐ 91 A & B .. 3⅜ x 5" ...... (OE).... ❻ $35

Old   New

HUM 92   Merry Wanderer, Plaque

Many size variations. Crown mark pieces can be found in both sizes. Some have incised 1938 copyright date, others do not. Some pieces have "M.I. Hummel" signature on both front and back, while others have signature on back only. Some TM 2 plaques have copyright (© WG) on front lower right, signature on back. Originally modeled by master sculptor Arthur Moeller in 1938 but restyled several times in later years.

☐ 92	4½ x 5 to 5 x 5½"	(OE)	❶	$300-350
☐ 92	4½ x 5 to 5 x 5½"	(OE)	❷	$150-200
☐ 92	4½ x 5"	(OE)	❸	$100-125
☐ 92	4½ x 5"	(OE)	❹	$80-90
☐ 92	4½ x 5"	(OE)	❺	$70-80
☐ 92	4½ x 5"	(OE)	❻	$68.50

Rare old style   *New*

HUM 93   Little Fiddler, Plaque

Originally modeled by master sculptor Arthur Moeller in 1938. Many size variations. Two different backgrounds as noted in photograph. Older model (left) extremely rare. Some models have 1938 copyright date. Some pieces have "M.I. Hummel" signature on both front and back, while others have signature on back only, or front only. Also sold in white overglaze at one time. The background on the left is similar to HUM 107. Old style background $2,000-$3,000. .

☐ 93	4½ x 5 to 5 x 5½"	(OE)...	❶ ...	$300-350
☐ 93	4½ x 5 to 5 x 5½"	(OE)...	❷ ...	$150-200
☐ 93	4½ x 5"	(OE)...	❸ ...	$100-125
☐ 93	4½ x 5"	(OE)...	❹ ...	$80-90
☐ 93	4½ x 5"	(OE)...	❺ ...	$70-80
☐ 93	4½ x 5"	(OE)...	❻ ...	$68.50

HUM 94
Surprise

Records indicate this model was produced by a team of sculptors in 1938. Old name: "The Duet" or "Hansel and Gretel." Also found listed with name of: "What's Up?" Older pieces marked "94" or "94/I" have rectangular base. All newer models have oval base. Slight variation in suspender straps on older models. Numbering errors occur occasionally—as an example, we have size 94/I that is marked 94/II in trademark 3. This trademark, however, has been "slashed" indicating that it was probably sold to a factory employee.

☐ 94 3/0	4 to 4¼"	(OE)	❷	$150-175
☐ 94 3/0	4 to 4¼"	(OE)	❸	$100-125
☐ 94 3/0	4 to 4¼"	(OE)	❹	$75-90
☐ 94 3/0	4 to 4¼"	(OE)	❺	$70-75
☐ 94 3/0	4 to 4¼"	(OE)	❻	$66
☐ 94/I	5¼ to 5½"	(OE)	❶	$350-450
☐ 94/I	5¼ to 5½"	(OE)	❷	$200-275
☐ 94/I	5¼ to 5½"	(OE)	❸	$125-175
☐ 94/I	5¼ to 5½"	(OE)	❹	$100-115
☐ 94/I	5¼ to 5½"	(OE)	❺	$95-100
☐ 94/I	5¼ to 5½"	(OE)	❻	$94.50
☐ 94	5¾"	(CE)	❶	$400-500
☐ 94	5¾"	(CE)	❷	$250-300

HUM 95
Brother
Many size and color variations. Old name: "Our Hero" or "Hero of The Village." Same boy as used in HUM 94 "Surprise." Records indicate this figurine was first modeled in 1938 by a team of sculptors.

☐ 95 .... 5¼ to 5¾" ... (OE)....❶.... $200-300
☐ 95 .... 5¼ to 5¾" ... (OE)....❷.... $150-200
☐ 95 .... 5¼ to 5¾" ... (OE)....❸.... $100-125
☐ 95 .... 5¼ to 5¾" ... (OE)....❹.... $75-85
☐ 95 .... 5¼ to 5¾" ... (OE)....❺.... $70-75
☐ 95 .... 5¼ to 5¾" ... (OE)....❻.... $66

HUM 96
Little Shopper

Many size variations. Old name: "Errand Girl," "Gretel" or "Meg" in some older catalogues. Some catalogues and price lists indicate size as 5½". This is believed, by this author, to be in error. I have *never* seen it over 5 inches in twenty years of collecting. Records indicate this figurine was first modeled in 1938 by a team of sculptors possibly including master sculptor Reinhold Unger. Same girl as used in HUM 94 "Surprise."

☐ 96	4½ to 5"	(OE)	❶	$200-250
☐ 96	4½ to 5"	(OE)	❷	$125-150
☐ 96	4½ to 5"	(OE)	❸	$75-100
☐ 96	4½ to 5"	(OE)	❹	$60-75
☐ 96	4½ to 5"	(OE)	❺	$55-60
☐ 96	4½ to 5"	(OE)	❻	$55

HUM 97
Trumpet Boy

Originally modeled by master sculptor Arthur Moeller in 1938. Many size variations. Boy's coat is normally green. Old "U.S. Zone" specimen has blue coat shaded with green. Old name: "The Little Musician." There are a few rare pieces with the inscription "Design Patent No. 116,404" stamped on the bottom. This variation valued from $500-$750.

☐ 97	4½ to 4¾"	(OE)	❶	$200-250
☐ 97	4½ to 5¼"	(OE)	❷	$125-150
☐ 97	4½ to 5¼"	(OE)	❸	$75-100
☐ 97	4½ to 4¾"	(OE)	❹	$60-75
☐ 97	4½ to 4¾"	(OE)	❺	$55-60
☐ 97	4½ to 4¾"	(OE)	❻	$55

HUM 98
Sister

Originally modeled by master sculptor Arthur Moeller in 1938. Many size variations; otherwise very little change between old and new models. Old name: "The Shopper" or "The First Shopping" in some catalogues. Some pieces have an incised 1962 copyright date. A collector recently found this piece made with a purse instead of a basket. The purse, however, appears to be handmade rather than molded. Factory representatives believe that it *could* have been an experimental model, proposed by a sculptor but rejected even before a mold for the purse was produced.

☐ 98 2/0	4½ to 4¾"	(OE)	❸	$75-100
☐ 98 2/0	4½ to 4¾"	(OE)	❹	$60-75
☐ 98 2/0	4½ to 4¾"	(OE)	❺	$55-60
☐ 98 2/0	4½ to 4¾"	(OE)	❻	$55
☐ 98/0	5¼ to 5½"	(OE)	❸	$100-125
☐ 98/0	5¼ to 5½"	(OE)	❹	$75-95
☐ 98/0	5¼ to 5½"	(OE)	❺	$70-75
☐ 98/0	5¼ to 5½"	(OE)	❻	$66
☐ 98	5¾"	(CE)	❶	$250-300
☐ 98	5¾"	(CE)	❷	$175-200
☐ 98	5¾"	(CE)	❸	$150-175

HUM 99
Eventide

Records indicate this model was produced in 1938 by a combination of modelers. Almost identical with "Wayside Devotion" HUM 28 but without the shrine. Many size variations. Note photo of rare crown mark piece with lambs in different position. At one time this figurine was sold in Belgium in the white overglaze finish and would now be considered extremely rare.

☐ 99 ...... 4¼ x 5" ..... (OE).... ❶	$350-500
☐ 99 ...... 4¼ x 5" ..... (OE).... ❷	$250-350
☐ 99 ...... 4¼ x 5" ..... (OE).... ❸	$150-200
☐ 99 ...... 4¼ x 5" ..... (OE).... ❹	$135-150
☐ 99 ...... 4¼ x 5" ..... (OE).... ❺	$125-135
☐ 99 ...... 4¼ x 5" ..... (OE).... ❻	$125

HUM 100
Shrine, Table Lamp (CE)
This extremely rare lamp is similar to the figurine "Adoration" HUM 23. First modeled by Erich Lautensack in 1938 and produced in very limited quantities. Only a few examples known to exist. The example in our collection has a light beige-colored post, an incised crown trademark plus the stamped "U.S. Zone." Another example had a dark brown post, an incised crown trademark plus stamped "full bee." Also had 6/50 date.

☐ 100 ...... 7½" .... (CE).... ❶ .... $5000 +

Rare plain post

HUM 101 To Market, Table Lamp (CE)

Originally modeled by master sculptor Arthur Moeller in 1937. Listed as a closed edition on factory records 20 April 1937. Redesigned and limited quantity produced in early 1950's with "tree trunk" post. Some incised with number II/101, III/101 and others with 101 only. Lamp was adapted from figurine "To Market" HUM 49. Master sculptor Arthur Moeller redesigned this lamp in 1952 into the 9½ inch size HUM 223 which is still currently produced.

☐ 101 ..... 7½" .... (CE) .... ❶ .... $5000 +
☐ 101 ..... 7½" .... (CE) .... ❷ $500-750
☐ 101 ..... 7½" .... (CE) .... ❸ $250-500

Plain post   *Tree trunk post*

HUM 102
Volunteers, Table Lamp (CE)
Originally modeled by Erich Lautensack in 1937. Listed as a closed edition in factory records 20 April 1937. In 1979 a rare specimen was found in Seattle, Washington, and is now in the Robert L. Miller collection. This piece has a double crown (incised and stamped) trademark. Since 1979 several other specimens have been found and the Goebel factory now has one in their archives.

☐ 102 .... (CE).... ❶ .... $5000 +

HUM 103
Farewell, Table Lamp (CE)
Originally modeled by Erich Lautensack in 1937. Listed as a closed edition on factory records 20 April 1937. Several examples of this extremely rare lamp have recently been found and one is now in the Robert L. Miller collection. A second specimen was recently presented to the Goebel factory for their archives in Rodental, West Germany.

☐ 103 .... (CE).... ❶ .... $5000 +

HUM 104
Eventide, Table Lamp (CE)
Originally modeled by Reinhold Unger in 1938. Listed as a closed edition on factory records 3 March 1938. This lamp was originally called "Wayside Devotion" in our earlier books but is now correctly named "Eventide." The only know example of this extremely rare lamp base was recently purchased from its original owner in northern Indiana and is now in the Robert L. Miller collection. The lamp was located through the help of Ralph and Terry Kovel and their syndicated newspaper column on antiques. Notice the position of lambs in this photo and then compare with photo of "Eventide" HUM 99.

☐ 104 . . . . (CE) . . . . ❷ . . . . $5000 +

HUM 105 Adoration With Bird (CE)

Very limited production. Listed as a closed edition on factory records 24 May 1938. All known examples have double crown (incised and stamped) trademark. Notice difference in pigtail of little girl in this comparative photograph. Unable to locate information on original sculptor or date of original model; probably master sculptor Reinhold Unger who created model for "Adoration" HUM 23 which is similar in design. This figurine is considered extremely rare.

☐ 105 . . . . . . 4¾" . . . . (CE) . . . . ❶ . . . . $5000 +

HUM 106
Merry Wanderer,
Plaque with wood frame (CE)
Very limited production. Listed as a closed edition on factory records 1 August 1938. First modeled by master sculptor Arthur Moeller in 1938. Similar to the all-ceramic plaque of "Merry Wanderer" HUM 92 except for wood frame. Some variation in frames. Considered extremely rare.

HUM 107
Little Fiddler,
Plaque with wood frame (CE)
Very limited production. Listed as a closed edition on factory records 1 August 1938. First modeled by master sculptor Arthur Moeller in 1938. Similar to the all-ceramic plaque of "Little Fiddler" HUM 93 (rare old style background) except for the wood frame. Some variation in frames. Considered extremely rare. A specimen of this rare plaque was recently presented to the Goebel factory for their archives in Rodental, West Germany.

☐ 106 ...... 6 x 6" .... (CE) .... ❶ .... $5000 +

☐ 107 ...... 6 x 6" .... (CE) .... ❶ .... $5000 +

HUM 108
Angel With Two Children At Feet (CN)
Originally modeled by master sculptor Reinhold Unger in 1938. No known examples. Listed on factory records of 14 October 1938 as a wall decoration. Pictured here is Goebel item HS 01 listed in 1950 Goebel catalogue. Factory representatives state that this is possibly a Hummel design—probably rejected by Siessen Convent and then later marketed as a Goebel item. The "MM" painted on gown indicates this is a "muster" (the German word for sample). When and if found with the "M.I. Hummel" signature and incised 108 would have a value of $5,000 + .

☐ 108 . . . . (CN) . . . .

HUM 109
Happy Traveller

First modeled by master sculptor Arthur Moeller in 1938 and has been produced in all trademark periods. The large size only was permanently retired by Goebel in the spring of 1982. Early pieces were usually incised 109/2 instead of 109/II. Small size only is still in current production. Sometimes the small size is found without the size designator in trademarks 3, 4 and 5. Listed as "Wanderer" in old catalogues. Small size was restyled in 1980 with the new textured finish.

☐ 109/0	4¾ to 5"	(OE)	❷	$125-150
☐ 109/0	4¾ to 5"	(OE)	❸	$75-100
☐ 109	4¾ to 5"	(OE)	❸	$75-100
☐ 109/0	4¾ to 5"	(OE)	❹	$60-75
☐ 109	4¾ to 5"	(OE)	❹	$60-75
☐ 109/0	4¾ to 5"	(OE)	❺	$55-60
☐ 109	4¾ to 5"	(OE)	❺	$55-60
☐ 109/0	4¾ to 5"	(OE)	❻	$55
☐ 109/II	7½"	(OE)	❷	$500-600
☐ 109/II	7½"	(OE)	❸	$300-350
☐ 109/II	7½"	(OE)	❹	$225-300
☐ 109/II	7½"	(OE)	❺	$195-225
☐ 109/II	7½"	(OE)	❻	$195
☐ 109	7¾"	(CE)	❶	$750-1000

HUM 110   Let's Sing

Originally modeled by master sculptor Reinhold Unger in 1938. There are many size variations. Some have an incised 1938 copyright date. Some incised model numbers are difficult to read because of the extremely small bases.

☐ 110/0 . . . . . 3 to 3¼" . . . . . (OE) . . . . ❶ $125-200
☐ 110/0 . . . . . 3 to 3¼" . . . . . (OE) . . . . ❷ $100-125
☐ 110/0 . . . . . 3 to 3¼" . . . . . (OE) . . . . ❸ $60-90
☐ 110/0 . . . . . 3 to 3¼" . . . . . (OE) . . . . ❹ $55-60
☐ 110/0 . . . . . 3 to 3¼" . . . . . (OE) . . . . ❺ $50-55
☐ 110/0 . . . . . 3 to 3¼" . . . . . (OE) . . . . ❻ $50
☐ 110/I . . . . . 3½ to 4" . . . . . (OE) . . . . ❷ $200-250
☐ 110/I . . . . . 3½ to 4" . . . . . (OE) . . . . ❸ $100-125
☐ 110/I . . . . . 3½ to 4" . . . . . (OE) . . . . ❹ $80-100
☐ 110/I . . . . . 3½ to 4" . . . . . (OE) . . . . ❺ $75-80
☐ 110/I . . . . . 3½ to 4" . . . . . (OE) . . . . ❻ $72
☐ 110 . . . . . . 4" . . . . (CE) . . . . ❶ $300-350
☐ 110 . . . . . . 4" . . . . (CE) . . . . ❷ $200-250

Old bowl style

New jar style

HUM III/110   Let's Sing, Box

Bowl style first produced in 1938. Jar style first produced and sold in 1964. Model number is found on underside of lid. The "M.I. Hummel" signature is found on topside of lid directly behind figure.

☐ III/110 . . . . 6¼" . . . . (CE) . . . . ❶ $400-500
☐ III/110 . . . . 6¼" . . . . (CE) . . . . ❷ $350-400
☐ III/110 . . . . 6¼" . . . . (CE) . . . . ❸ . . . . $300-350 OLD STYLE
☐ III/110 . . . . 5¼" . . . . (OE) . . . . ❸ . . . . $110-135 NEW STYLE
☐ III/110 . . . . 5¼" . . . . (OE) . . . . ❹ $100-110
☐ III/110 . . . . 5¼" . . . . (OE) . . . . ❺ $90-100
☐ III/110 . . . . 5¼" . . . . (OE) . . . . ❻ $90

HUM 111
Wayside Harmony
First modeled in 1938 by master sculptor Reinhold Unger. There are many size variations. Normally has green-colored socks, but some crown and full bee trademark pieces have yellow socks in the small (111 3/0) size. Old name: "Just Sittin-Boy." Some models have a 1938 incised copyright date.

☐ 111 3/0 .... 3¾ to 4" ..... (OE) .... ❶ $225-275
☐ 111 3/0 .... 3¾ to 4" ..... (OE) .... ❷ $125-175
☐ 111 3/0 .... 3¾ to 4" ..... (OE) .... ❸ $100-125
☐ 111 3/0 .... 3¾ to 4" ..... (OE) .... ❹ $70-80
☐ 111 3/0 .... 3¾ to 4" ..... (OE) .... ❺ $65-70
☐ 111 3/0 .... 3¾ to 4" ..... (OE) .... ❻ $63
☐ 111/I ..... 5 to 5½" ..... (OE) .... ❶ $350-425
☐ 111/I ..... 5 to 5½" ..... (OE) .... ❷ $200-275
☐ 111/I ..... 5 to 5½" ..... (OE) .... ❸ $125-175
☐ 111/I ..... 5 to 5½" ..... (OE) .... ❹ $105-125
☐ 111/I ..... 5 to 5½" ..... (OE) .... ❺ $95-105
☐ 111/I ..... 5 to 5½" ..... (OE) .... ❻ $94.50
☐ 111 ...... 5½" .... (CE) .... ❶ $400-500

II/111   **224/I**

HUM II/111
Wayside Harmony, Table Lamp (CE)
This number was used briefly in the early 1950's. Later changed to 224/I. The only difference is that the boy is slightly larger. Some models have been found with number III/111/I.

☐ II/111 ..... 7½" .... (CE).... ❶ $500-750
☐ II/111 ..... 7½" .... (CE).... ❷ $400-500
☐ II/111 ..... 7½" .... (CE).... ❸ $350-500

HUM 112
Just Resting
First modeled in 1938 by master sculptor Reinhold Unger. Many size variations. Old name: "Just Sittin-Girl." Some models have a 1938 incised copyright date. There is an unusual example of size 112/I without a basket in front of the girl (not shown).

☐ 112 3/0 .... 3¾ to 4" ..... (OE).... ❶ $225-275
☐ 112 3/0 .... 3¾ to 4" ..... (OE).... ❷ $125-175
☐ 112 3/0 .... 3¾ to 4" ..... (OE).... ❸ $100-125
☐ 112 3/0 .... 3¾ to 4" ..... (OE).... ❹ $70-80
☐ 112 3/0 .... 3¾ to 4" ..... (OE).... ❺ $65-70
☐ 112 3/0 .... 3¾ to 4" ..... (OE).... ❻ $63.00
☐ 112/I ..... 4¾ to 5½" ... (OE).... ❶ $350-425
☐ 112/I ..... 4¾ to 5½" ... (OE).... ❷ $200-275
☐ 112/I ..... 4¾ to 5½" ... (OE).... ❸ $125-175

```
□ 112/I ..... 4¾ to 5½" ... (OE)....❹.... $105-125
□ 112/I ..... 4¾ to 5½" ... (OE)....❺.... $95-105
□ 112/I ..... 4¾ to 5½" ... (OE)....❻.... $94.50
□ 112 ...... 5½" ........ (CE)....❶.... $400-500
```

II/112 **225/I**

HUM II/112
Just Resting, Table Lamp
This number was used briefly in the early 1950's. Later changed to 225/I. The only difference is that the girl is slightly larger. Some models have a 1938 incised copyright date. Some models have been found with numbers III/112/I and 2/112/I. Extremely rare.

```
□ II/112..... 7½" ........ (CE)....❶.... $500-750
□ II/112..... 7½" ........ (CE)....❷.... $400-500
□ II/112..... 7½" ........ (CE)....❸.... $350-500
```

HUM 113
Heavenly Song, Candleholder (CE)
Originally modeled by master sculptor Arthur Moeller in 1938 but was produced in very limited quantities. Sometimes mistaken for HUM 54 "Silent Night," which is similar. Was scheduled for production again in 1978 and listed in some catalogues and price lists. Because of its similarity to HUM 54 "Silent Night" the factory decided it should not be produced again so in 1980 it was listed as a closed edition. At least one piece is known to exist with the 5 trademark. All specimens would now be considered extremely rare.

```
□ 113 ...... 3½ x 4¾" ... (CE)....❶.... $3000-5000
□ 113 ...... 3½ x 4¾" ... (CE)....❷.... $2000-3000
□ 113 ...... 3½ x 4¾" ... (CE)....❸.... $2000-2500
□ 113 ...... 3½ x 4¾" ... (CE)....❺.... $2000-2500
```

Old   **New**

HUM 114 Let's Sing, Ashtray

First modeled in 1938 by master sculptor Reinhold Unger with the ashtray on the left (boy's right). Restyled in 1959 by master sculptor Theo R. Menzenbach with the ashtray on the right (boy's left). Old style would be considered rare. Both styles can be found with full bee trademark.

☐ 114 ...... 3½ x 6¼" ... (CE).... ❶ $850-1000
☐ 114 ...... 3½ x 6¼" ... (CE).... ❷ $500-850
☐ 114 ...... 3½ x 6¼" ... (OE).... ❸ $100-125
☐ 114 ...... 3½ x 6¼" ... (OE).... ❹ $75-90
☐ 114 ...... 3½ x 6¼" ... (OE).... ❺ $65-70
☐ 114 ...... 3½ x 6¼" ... (OE).... ❻ $65

115   116   117

HUM 115
Advent Candlestick, Girl With Nosegay
HUM 116
Advent Candlestick, Girl With Fir Tree
HUM 117
Advent Candlestick, Boy With Horse
These three figurines were first modeled by master sculptor Reinhold Unger in 1939. They are similar to HUM 239 A, B & C (without candleholders). Very early models were incised with "Mel" instead of "M.I. Hummel." Reportedly sold only in Germany. Note: "Mel" is the last three letters of Hum*mel*. Some "Mel" pieces have been found with the early stylized trademark indicating that both "Hummel" and "Mel" pieces were being produced and marketed at the same time. Mel 1, Mel 2, and Mel 3 usually sell for $100 to $150 each depending on the condition.

☐ 115	3½"	(OE)	❶	$100-150
☐ 115	3½"	(OE)	❷	$50-75
☐ 115	3½"	(OE)	❸	$35-50
☐ 115	3½"	(OE)	❹	$30-35
☐ 115	3½"	(OE)	❺	$27-30
☐ 115	3½"	(OE)	❻	$26.50
☐ 116	3½"	(OE)	❶	$100-150
☐ 116	3½"	(OE)	❷	$50-75
☐ 116	3½"	(OE)	❸	$35-50
☐ 116	3½"	(OE)	❹	$30-35
☐ 116	3½"	(OE)	❺	$27-30
☐ 116	3½"	(OE)	❻	$26.50
☐ 117	3½"	(OE)	❶	$100-150
☐ 117	3½"	(OE)	❷	$50-75
☐ 117	3½"	(OE)	❸	$35-50
☐ 117	3½"	(OE)	❹	$30-35
☐ 117	3½"	(OE)	❺	$27-30
☐ 117	3½"	(OE)	❻	$26.50

New   **Old**

HUM 118
Little Thrifty, Bank
This figurine is actually a bank. Made with a metal lock & key on bottom. Originally modeled by master sculptor Arthur Moeller in 1939. Restyled by Rudolf Wittman in 1963. Older models have a slightly different base design as noted in photograph. The object into which "Little Thrifty" is putting her coin is a medieval form of a poor box, something which can still be found in old European churches.

☐ 118 ...... 5 to 5½" ..... (CE).... ❶ $400-500
☐ 118 ...... 5 to 5½" ..... (CE).... ❷ $250-300
☐ 118 ...... 5 to 5½" ..... (CE).... ❸ $125-150
☐ 118 ...... 5 to 5½" ..... (OE).... ❺ $66-75
☐ 118 ...... 5 to 5½" ..... (OE).... ❻ $66

Current   **Stylized**   **Full Bee**

HUM 119
Postman
Many size variations although officially made in one size only. First modeled by master sculptor Arthur Moeller in 1939. Later restyled by the current master sculptor Gerhard Skrobek in 1970 giving it the new textured finish.

☐ 119 ...... 5 to 5½" ..... (OE).... ❶ $300-375
☐ 119 ...... 5 to 5½" ..... (OE).... ❷ $200-250
☐ 119 ...... 5 to 5½" ..... (OE).... ❸ $125-150
☐ 119 ...... 5 to 5½" ..... (OE).... ❹ $95-125
☐ 119 ...... 5 to 5½" ..... (OE).... ❺ $85-95
☐ 119 ...... 5 to 5½" ..... (OE).... ❻ $83

HUM 120
Joyful and Let's Sing (on wooden base), Bookends (CE)

No known examples. Listed as a closed edition on factory records 16 June 1939. Records indicate this was made in 1939 by a combination of sculptors. Probably similar in design to HUM 122.

☐ 120 .... (CE).... ❶ .... $5000 +

HUM 121
Wayside Harmony and Just Resting (on a wooden base), Bookends (CE)

No known examples. Listed as a closed edition on factory records 16 June 1939. Records indicate this was made in 1939 by a combination of sculptors. Probably similar in design to HUM 122.

☐ 121 .... (CE).... ❶ .... $5000 +

Factory prototype

HUM 122
Puppy Love and Serenade With Dog (on wooden base), Bookends (CE)

Factory sample only. Listed as a closed edition on factory records 16 June 1939. Records indicate this was made in 1939 by a combination of sculptors.

☐ 122 .... (CE).... ❶ .... $5000 +

HUM 123
Max and Moritz
First modeled by master sculptor Arthur
Moeller in 1939. Restyled in the early
1970's with the new textured finish. Old
name: "Good Friends" in some catalogues.

☐ 123	5 to 5½"	(OE)	❶	$300-375
☐ 123	5 to 5½"	(OE)	❷	$200-250
☐ 123	5 to 5½"	(OE)	❸	$100-150
☐ 123	5 to 5½"	(OE)	❹	$85-100
☐ 123	5 to 5½"	(OE)	❺	$80-85
☐ 123	5 to 5½"	(OE)	❻	$77.50

Current   *Full Bee*   *Crown*

HUM 124
Hello
Many size variations. Earliest models
produced had gray coat, gray trousers
and pink vest. Changed to brown coat,
green trousers and pink vest in early
1950's. Changed to dark brown coat, light
brown trousers and blue-white vest in
mid-1960's. Originally modeled by master
sculptor Arthur Moeller in 1939. Has been
restyled several times through the years.
Old name: "The Boss" or "Der Chef." The
large size 124/I had been difficult to find
but was put back on the market in 1978,
then in the spring of 1982 was listed as a
"temporary withdrawal" by Goebel, to be
reinstated at a later date. The small size
only is still in current production.

☐ 124/0	5¾ to 6¼"	(OE)	❷	$200-250
☐ 124/0	5¾ to 6¼"	(OE)	❸	$125-150
☐ 124/0	5¾ to 6¼"	(OE)	❹	$85-100
☐ 124/0	5¾ to 6¼"	(OE)	❺	$80-85

☐ 124/0	5¾ to 6¼"	(OE)	❻	$77.50
☐ 124/I	6¾ to 7"	(OE)	❶	$750-1000
☐ 124/I	6¾ to 7"	(OE)	❷	$350-500
☐ 124/I	6¾ to 7"	(OE)	❸	$250-350
☐ 124/I	6¾ to 7"	(OE)	❹	$110-125
☐ 124/I	6¾ to 7"	(OE)	❺	$110
☐ 124	6½"	(CE)	❶	$750-1000
☐ 124	6½"	(CE)	❷	$350-500

New   **Old**

HUM 125   Vacation Time, Plaque

First modeled in 1939 by master sculptor Arthur Moeller. Restyled in 1960 by master
sculptor Theo R. Menzenbach. The newer model has five fence posts while the older
one has six. Old name: "Happy Holidays" or "On Holiday." Newer models produced
without string for hanging, only a hole on back for hanging.

☐ 125	4⅜ x 5¼"	(CE)	❶	$350-500
☐ 125	4⅜ x 5¼"	(CE)	❷	$250-350
☐ 125	4 x 4¾"	(OE)	❸	$150-200
☐ 125	4 x 4¾"	(OE)	❹	$125-150
☐ 125	4 x 4¾"	(OE)	❺	$100-110
☐ 125	4 x 4¾"	(OE)	❻	$100

HUM 126
Retreat to Safety, Plaque
First modeled by master sculptor Arthur Moeller in 1939. Older plaques are slightly larger. Slight color variations on older models. This same motif is also produced as a figurine by the same name although the colors are different. See "Retreat to Safety" HUM 201.

☐ 126	4¾ x 4¾ to 5 x 5"	(OE) ... ❶ ...	$350-500
☐ 126	4¾ x 4¾ to 5 x 5"	(OE) ... ❷ ...	$200-275
☐ 126	4¾ x 4¾"	(OE) ... ❸ ...	$150-200
☐ 126	4¾ x 4¾"	(OE) ... ❹ ...	$125-150
☐ 126	4¾ x 4¾"	(OE) ... ❺ ...	$100-110
☐ 126	4¾ x 4¾"	(OE) ... ❻ ...	$100

HUM 127
Doctor
Originally modeled by master sculptor Arthur Moeller in 1939. Has been restyled with the new textured finish. Many variations in size through the years with older examples slightly larger. Old name: "The Doll Doctor."

☐ 127	4¾ to 5¼"	(OE)	❶	$250-300
☐ 127	4¾ to 5¼"	(OE)	❷	$125-175
☐ 127	4¾ to 5¼"	(OE)	❸	$100-125
☐ 127	4¾ to 5¼"	(OE)	❹	$70-95
☐ 127	4¾ to 5¼"	(OE)	❺	$65-70
☐ 127	4¾ to 5¼"	(OE)	❻	$63

HUM 128
Baker

This figurine was first modeled in 1939 by master sculptor Arthur Moeller. Has been restyled several times during the years— most recently in the mid-1970's with the new textured finish. Slight color variations can be noticed. The little baker is holding a "Gugelhupf" round pound cake, a popular Bavarian treat.

☐ 128	4¾ to 5"	(OE)	❶	$300-325
☐ 128	4¾ to 5"	(OE)	❷	$130-195
☐ 128	4¾ to 5"	(OE)	❸	$90-100
☐ 128	4¾ to 5"	(OE)	❹	$80-90
☐ 128	4¾ to 5"	(OE)	❺	$75-80
☐ 128	4¾ to 5"	(OE)	❻	$72

HUM 129
Band Leader
First modeled by master sculptor Arthur Moeller in 1939. Many size and color variations. Old name: "Leader." One of several figurines that make up the Hummel orchestra.

☐ 129	5 to 5⅞"	(OE)	❶	$350-400
☐ 129	5 to 5⅞"	(OE)	❷	$200-250
☐ 129	5 to 5⅞"	(OE)	❸	$125-150
☐ 129	5 to 5⅞"	(OE)	❹	$100-125
☐ 129	5 to 5⅞"	(OE)	❺	$90-100
☐ 129	5 to 5⅞"	(OE)	❻	$88

Old base variation

HUM 130
Duet
Many size variations—from 5 to 5½". Originally modeled in 1939 by master sculptor Arthur Moeller. Early crown mark pieces have incised notes as well as painted notes on sheet music. Some early crown mark examples have a small "lip" on top edge of base. This variation should be valued from $500 to $750. Old name: "The Songsters." One of several figurines that make up the Hummel orchestra. "Duet" is similar to a combination of "Street Singer" HUM 131 and "Soloist" HUM 135.

☐ 130	......	5 to 5½"	..... (OE)....	❶	$350-450
☐ 130	......	5 to 5½"	..... (OE)....	❷	$250-300
☐ 130	......	5 to 5½"	..... (OE)....	❸	$150-175
☐ 130	......	5 to 5½"	..... (OE)....	❹	$115-135
☐ 130	......	5 to 5½"	..... (OE)....	❺	$105-115
☐ 130	......	5 to 5½"	..... (OE)....	❻	$105

HUM 131
Street Singer
Many size variations as well as some slight color variations of this popular figurine. Originally modeled by master sculptor Arthur Moeller in 1939. Old name: "Soloist." One of several figurines that make up the Hummel orchestra.

131	......	5 to 5½"	..... (OE)....	❶	$250-300
131	......	5 to 5½"	..... (OE)....	❷	$125-175
131	......	5 to 5½"	..... (OE)....	❸	$90-120
131	......	5 to 5½"	..... (OE)....	❹	$75-85
☐ 131	......	5 to 5½"	..... (OE)....	❺	$70-75
☐ 131	......	5 to 5½"	..... (OE)....	❻	$66

New model   **Old model**

HUM 132   Star Gazer

A very few older models have blue shirt. Most models in all trademark periods have purple shirts. Also some color variations on telescope. No cross-strap on boy's lederhosen on older models. "M.I. Hummel" signature is straight on early models; curved on later models. First modeled by master sculptor Arthur Moeller in 1939. Restyled by current master sculptor Gerhard Skrobek in 1980 with the new textured finish and slightly rounded corners on the base.

☐ 132 ...... 4¾" .... (OE).... ❶ $300-350
☐ 132 ...... 4¾" .... (OE).... ❷ $175-225
☐ 132 ...... 4¾" .... (OE).... ❸ $125-150
☐ 132 ...... 4¾" .... (OE).... ❹ $100-125
☐ 132 ...... 4¾" .... (OE).... ❺ $90-100
☐ 132 ...... 4¾ to 5" ..... (OE).... ❻ $88

HUM 133
Mother's Helper
This is the only figurine (in current production) produced with a cat. A similar figurine with a cat is named "Helping Mother" HUM 325 which is classified as a (PFE) possible future edition, and may be released at a later date. Older figurines are slightly larger in size. Originally modeled in 1939 by master sculptor Arthur Moeller.

☐ 133 ...... 4¾ to 5" ..... (OE) .... ❶ $300-400
☐ 133 ...... 4¾ to 5" ..... (OE) .... ❷ $200-250
☐ 133 ...... 4¾ to 5" ..... (OE) .... ❸ $125-150
☐ 133 ...... 4¾ to 5" ..... (OE) .... ❹ $100-125
☐ 133 ...... 4¾ to 5" ..... (OE) .... ❺ $90-100
☐ 133 ...... 4¾ to 5" ..... (OE) .... ❻ $88

HUM 134   Quartet, Plaque

First modeled by master sculptor Arthur Moeller in 1939. Older models have "M.I. Hummel" signature on back while newer models have signature incised on front. Older models provided with two holes for cord to hang on wall while newer models have a centered hole on back for hanging.

☐ 134 ...... 5½ x 6¼" ... (OE)....❶.... $500-700
☐ 134 ...... 5½ x 6¼" ... (OE)....❷.... $250-425
☐ 134 ...... 5½ x 6¼" ... (OE)....❸.... $185-225
☐ 134 ...... 5½ x 6¼" ... (OE)....❹.... $165-185
☐ 134 ...... 5½ x 6¼" ... (OE)....❺.... $150-165
☐ 134 ...... 5½ x 6¼" ... (OE)....❻.... $147

HUM 135
Soloist
Many size variations between old and new figurines. Originally modeled in 1940 by master sculptor Arthur Moeller. Old name: "High Tenor." Similar to singer in figurine "Duet" HUM 130. One of several figurines that can be used to make up the Hummel orchestra.

☐ 135 ...... 4½ to 5" ..... (OE).... ❶ $200-250
☐ 135 ...... 4½ to 5" ..... (OE).... ❷ $125-150
☐ 135 ...... 4½ to 5" ..... (OE).... ❸ $75-100
☐ 135 ...... 4½ to 5" ..... (OE).... ❹ $60-75
☐ 135 ...... 4½ to 5" ..... (OE).... ❺ $55-60
☐ 135 ...... 4½ to 5" ..... (OE).... ❻ $55

HUM 136
Friends

Originally modeled by master sculptor Reinhold Unger in 1940. Spots on deer will vary slightly—sometimes three rows rather than two rows. Old name: "Good Friends" or "Friendship." The small size 136/I usually has an incised 1947 copyright date. Sold at one time in reddish-brown terra cotta finish in size 136 (10½") with incised crown trademark. Very limited production in this finish; would be considered extremely rare. Value: $5,000 +. Also old crown trademark example (large size) found in white overglaze finish, but probably not sold that way.

□ 136/I	5 to 5⅜"	(OE)	❶	$300-500
□ 136/I	5 to 5⅜"	(OE)	❷	$250-300
□ 136/I	5 to 5⅜"	(OE)	❸	$125-150
□ 136/I	5 to 5⅜"	(OE)	❹	$100-125
□ 136/I	5 to 5⅜"	(OE)	❺	$90-100
□ 136/I	5 to 5⅜"	(OE)	❻	$88
□ 136/V	10¾ to 11"	(OE)	❶	$1500-2000
□ 136/V	10¾ to 11"	(OE)	❷	$1000-1500
□ 136/V	10¾ to 11"	(OE)	❸	$600-750
□ 136/V	10¾ to 11"	(OE)	❹	$550-600
□ 136/V	10¾ to 11"	(OE)	❺	$525-550
□ 136/V	10¾ to 11"	(OE)	❻	$525
□ 136	10½"	(CE)	❶	$2000-2500
□ 136	10½"	(CE)	❷	$1500-2000

HUM 137
Child in Bed, Wall Plaque
HUM 137 A (Child looking left) (CE)
HUM 137 B (Child looking right) (CE)
Apparently this was intended to be a set of two rings, one looking right and one looking left. Child looking right HUM 137 B has been on the market for years and can be found in all trademark periods. Child looking left HUM 137 A has never been found and factory is not sure that it was ever produced—there are no known examples. The original model was made by master sculptor Arthur Moeller in 1940. Current production number is 137 only, incised on the back along with the "M.I. Hummel" signature. Also called "Baby Ring with Ladybug" or "Ladybug Plaque" in old catalogues.

☐ 137A	3 x 3"	(CE)		
☐ 137B	3 x 3"	(CE)	❶	$300-500
☐ 137B	3 x 3"	(CE)	❷	$150-200
☐ 137B	3 x 3"	(CE)	❸	$75-100
☐ 137B	3 x 3"	(CE)	❹	$35-50
☐ 137B	3 x 3"	(CE)	❺	$32-35
☐ 137	3 x 3"	(OE)	❺	$32-35
☐ 137	3 x 3"	(OE)	❻	$31.50

HUM 138 (CN)
Tiny Baby In Crib, Wall Plaque
According to factory information this small plaque was never produced for sale. The original model was made by master sculptor Arthur Moeller in 1940. Now listed on factory records as a Closed Number (CN) meaning that this design was produced as a sample model, but then for various reasons never authorized for release. Apparently, a very few examples left the factory and have been found in Germany. This plaque would be considered extremely rare.

☐ 138	2¼ x 3"	(CN)	❷	$2000-3000

Crown *Stylized* *Full Bee*

HUM 139   Flitting Butterfly, Wall Plaque

First modeled by master sculptor Arthur Moeller in 1940, this plaque is also known as "Butterfly Plaque." Early crown mark pieces have no dots on girl's dress. The "M.I. Hummel" signature has been on the back during all time periods. Redesigned in the 1960's with no air space behind girl's head. Some design and color variations through the years of production.

☐ 139	2½ x 2½"	(OE)	❶	$300-350
☐ 139	2½ x 2½"	(OE)	❷	$200-250
☐ 139	2½ x 2½"	(OE)	❸	$100-150
☐ 139	2½ x 2½"	(OE)	❺	$32-35
☐ 139	2½ x 2½"	(OE)	❻	$31.50

HUM 140
The Mail Is Here, Plaque

Originally modeled by master sculptor Arthur Moeller in 1940, this plaque can be found in all trademark periods. At one time it was sold in Belgium in the white overglaze finish and would now be considered extremely rare. Old name: "Post Carriage." Also known to collectors as "Mail Coach" plaque. In 1952 this same motif was made into a figurine by the same name (HUM 226) by master sculptor Arthur Moeller.

☐ 140	4¼ x 6¾"	(OE)	❶	$400-500
☐ 140	4¼ x 6¾"	(OE)	❷	$300-350
☐ 140	4¼ x 6¾"	(OE)	❸	$175-225
☐ 140	4¼ x 6¾"	(OE)	❹	$150-175
☐ 140	4¼ x 6¾"	(OE)	❺	$130-140
☐ 140	4¼ x 6¾"	(OE)	❻	$126

141/V   Old   141/I   New   Old   141 3/O   New

HUM 141   Apple Tree Girl

First modeled by master sculptor Arthur Moeller in 1940 and has been restyled many times during the years that it has been produced. There are many size variations and early models have a tapered brown base. The smaller models have always been made without the bird in the tree. Size 141/V was first produced in the early 1970's and is found in 4, 5 and 6 trademarks only. Size 141/X was first produced in 1975. Old name: "Spring" or "Springtime." This same motif is used on the 1976 Annual Plate, HUM 269; Table Lamp, HUM 229; and Bookends, HUM 252 A.

- ☐ 141 3/0 . . . . 4 to 4¼" . . . . . (OE) . . . . ❶ $200-250
- ☐ 141 3/0 . . . . 4 to 4¼" . . . . . (OE) . . . . ❷ $125-150
- ☐ 141 3/0 . . . . 4 to 4¼" . . . . . (OE) . . . . ❸ $75-95
- ☐ 141 3/0 . . . . 4 to 4¼" . . . . . (OE) . . . . ❹ $60-75
- ☐ 141 3/0 . . . . 4 to 4¼" . . . . . (OE) . . . . ❺ $55-60
- ☐ 141 3/0 . . . . 4 to 4¼" . . . . . (OE) . . . . ❻ $55
- ☐ 141 . . . . . . 6 to 6¾" . . . . (CE) . . . . ❶ $350-500
- ☐ 141/I . . . . 6 to 6¾" . . . . . (OE) . . . . ❶ $350-500
- ☐ 141/I . . . . 6 to 6¾" . . . . . (OE) . . . . ❷ $200-275
- ☐ 141/I . . . . 6 to 6¾" . . . . . (OE) . . . . ❸ $150-175
- ☐ 141/I . . . . 6 to 6¾" . . . . . (OE) . . . . ❹ $115-135
- ☐ 141/I . . . . 6 to 6¾" . . . . . (OE) . . . . ❺ $105-115
- ☐ 141/I . . . . 6 to 6¾" . . . . . (OE) . . . . ❻ $105
- ☐ 141/V . . . . . 10¼" . . . . (OE) . . . . ❹ $550-650
- ☐ 141/V . . . . . 10¼" . . . . (OE) . . . . ❺ $525-550
- ☐ 141/V . . . . . 10¼" . . . . (OE) . . . . ❻ $525
- ☐ 141/X . . . . . 32" . . . . (OE) . . . . ❺ $8000-13,100
- ☐ 141/X . . . . . 32" . . . . (OE) . . . . ❻ . . . . $13,100 (List price)

141/V   Old   142/I   New   Old   142 3/O   New

HUM 142   Apple Tree Boy

This companion figurine to "Apple Tree Girl" was also modeled by master sculptor Arthur Moeller in 1940, and has been restyled many times during the years. There are many size variations and early models have a tapered brown base. The small size 142 3/O with trademark 2 usually has a red feather in the boy's hat. Size 142/V was first produced in the early 1970's and is found in 4, 5 and 6 trademarks only. Size 142/X was first produced in the mid-1960's with number 142/10 incised and the stylized mark is incised rather than stamped. Old name: "Autumn" or "Fall." Smaller models have always been made without the bird in the tree. This same motif is used on the 1977 Annual Plate, HUM 270; Table Lamp, HUM 230; and Bookends, HUM 252 B.

☐ 142 3/0 . . . . 4 to 4¼" . . . . . (OE) . . . ❶ $200-250
☐ 142 3/0 . . . . 4 to 4¼" . . . . . (OE) . . . ❷ $125-150
☐ 142 3/0 . . . . 4 to 4¼" . . . . . (OE) . . . ❸ $75-95
☐ 142 3/0 . . . . 4 to 4¼" . . . . . (OE) . . . ❹ $60-75
☐ 142 3/0 . . . . 4 to 4¼" . . . . . (OE) . . . ❺ $55-60
☐ 142 3/0 . . . . 4 to 4¼" . . . . . (OE) . . . ❻ $55
☐ 142 . . . . . . 6 to 6⅞" . . . . . (CE) . . . ❶ $350-500
☐ 142/I . . . . . 6 to 6⅞" . . . . . (OE) . . . ❶ $350-500
☐ 142/I . . . . . 6 to 6⅞" . . . . . (OE) . . . ❷ $200-275
☐ 142/I . . . . . 6 to 6⅞" . . . . . (OE) . . . ❸ $150-175
☐ 142/I . . . . . 6 to 6⅞" . . . . . (OE) . . . ❹ $115-135
☐ 142/I . . . . . 6 to 6⅞" . . . . . (OE) . . . ❺ $105-115
☐ 142/I . . . . . 6 to 6⅞" . . . . . (OE) . . . ❻ $105
☐ 142/V . . . . 10¼" . . . . (OE) . . . ❹ $550-650
☐ 142/V . . . . 10¼" . . . . (OE) . . . ❺ $525-550
☐ 142/V . . . . 10¼" . . . . (OE) . . . ❻ $525
☐ 142/X . . . . 30" . . . . (OE) . . . ❸ $10,000-13,100
☐ 142/X . . . . 30" . . . . (OE) . . . ❹ $9000-13,100
☐ 142/X . . . . 30" . . . . (OE) . . . ❺ $8000-13,100
☐ 142/X . . . . 30" . . . . (OE) . . . ❻ . . . . $13,100 (LIST PRICE)

HUM 143
Boots
First modeled by master sculptor Arthur Moeller in 1940. There are many size variations—from 5 to 5½" on the small; from 6 to 6¾" on the large. Old name: "Shoemaker." Both sizes were restyled with the new textured finish by current master modeler Gerhard Skrobek in the late 1970's.

☐ 143/O .... 5 to 5½" ..... (OE).... ❶ $250-325
☐ 143/O .... 5 to 5½" ..... (OE).... ❷ $175-200
☐ 143/O .... 5 to 5½" ..... (OE).... ❸ $90-100
☐ 143/O .... 5 to 5½" ..... (OE).... ❹ $80-90
☐ 143/O .... 5 to 5½" ..... (OE).... ❺ $75-80
☐ 143/O .... 5 to 5½" ..... (OE).... ❻ $72
☐ 143/I ..... 6½ to 6¾" ... (OE).... ❶ $350-500
☐ 143/I ..... 6½ to 6¾" ... (OE).... ❷ $200-300
☐ 143/I ..... 6½ to 6¾" ... (OE).... ❸ $150-200
☐ 143/I ..... 6½ to 6¾" ... (OE).... ❹ $125-150
☐ 143/I ..... 6½ to 6¾" ... (OE).... ❺ $110-125
☐ 143/I ..... 6½ to 6¾" ... (OE).... ❻ $110
☐ 143 ...... 6¾" .... (CE).... ❶ $500-750
☐ 143 ...... 6¾" .... (CE).... ❷ $300-500

HUM 144
Angelic Song
Originally modeled in 1941 by master sculptor Reinhold Unger. Little variation between old and new models. Old name: "Angels" or "Holy Communion."

☐ 144 ...... 4" .... (OE).... ❶ $200-300
☐ 144 ...... 4" .... (OE).... ❷ $125-175
☐ 144 ...... 4" .... (OE).... ❸ $85-100
☐ 144 ...... 4" .... (OE).... ❹ $70-85
☐ 144 ...... 4" .... (OE).... ❺ $65-70
☐ 144 ...... 4" .... (OE).... ❻ $63

HUM 145
Little Guardian
This figurine was first modeled by master sculptor Reinhold Unger in 1941. The only noticeable difference would be in size, with the older pieces slightly larger.

☐ 145	......	3¾ to 4"	.....	(OE)	....❶....	$200-300
☐ 145	......	3¾ to 4"	.....	(OE)	....❷....	$125-175
☐ 145	......	3¾ to 4"	.....	(OE)	....❸....	$85-100
☐ 145	......	3¾ to 4"	.....	(OE)	....❹....	$70-85
☐ 145	......	3¾ to 4"	.....	(OE)	....❺....	$65-70
☐ 145	......	3¾ to 4"	.....	(OE)	....❻....	$63

Old   *New*

HUM 146
Holy Water Font, Angel Duet
First modeled by master sculptor Reinhold Unger in 1941. This font has been restyled several times through the years with noticeable variations in the shape of angels' wings, construction of the back, holes for hanging and holes between angels' heads and wings. Newer examples are completely solid and have the new textured finish.

☐ 146	......	3½ x 4¾"	...	(OE)	....❶....	$100-150
☐ 146	......	3½ x 4¾"	...	(OE)	....❷....	$50-75
☐ 146	......	3½ x 4¾"	...	(OE)	....❸....	$30-35
☐ 146	......	3½ x 4¾"	...	(OE)	....❹....	$25-30
☐ 146	......	3½ x 4¾"	...	(OE)	....❺....	$23-25
☐ 146	......	3½ x 4¾"	...	(OE)	....❻....	$23

Old   *New*

HUM 147
Holy Water Font, Angel Shrine
Originally modeled in 1941 by master sculptor Reinhold Unger and has been produced in all trademark periods. Older models are usually larger. Some variation in construction of back of font and water bowl. Old name: "Angel Devotion."

☐ 147	3 x 5 to 3⅛ x 5¼"	......	(OE)	...❶ ...	$200-250
☐ 147	3 x 5 to 3⅛ x 5¼"	......	(OE)	...❷ ...	$75-100
☐ 147	3 x 5"	....	(OE)	...❸ ...	$30-35
☐ 147	3 x 5"	....	(OE)	...❹ ...	$25-30
☐ 147	3 x 5"	....	(OE)	...❺ ...	$23-25
☐ 147	3 x 5"	....	(OE)	...❻ ...	$23

HUM 148 (CN)
Factory records indicate this was the same as the boy from HUM 60/A (Farm Boy, Bookend). Modeled in 1941 by a combination of the modelers. Listed as a Closed Number on 28 February 1941. No known examples or photographs.

☐ 148.... .... (CN).......

HUM 149 (CN)
Factory records indicate this was the same as the girl from HUM 60/B (Goose Girl, Bookend). Modeled in 1941 by a combination of modelers. Listed as a Closed Number on 28 February 1941. No known examples or photographs. A Closed Number (CN): an indentification number in W. Goebel's numerical identification system, used to identify a design or sample model intended for possible production but then for various reasons never authorized for release.

☐ 149.... .... (CN).......

HUM 150
Happy Days
"Happy Days" was the very first "M.I. Hummel" figurine my wife, Ruth, acquired to start her collection. It reminded her of our daughter and son. We no longer have this first piece, as one of the children broke it; has since been replaced by an intact piece! "Happy Days" was first modeled in 1942 by a combination of modelers. All large size and older pieces have an extra flower on the base. The large size in the crown trademark usually does not have a size designator; incised 150 only. Sizes 150/O and 150/I had been in very limited production, but are once again back on the market.

☐ 150 2/0.... 4¼" .... (OE).... ❷.... $125-175
☐ 150 2/0.... 4¼" .... (OE).... ❸.... $100-125
☐ 150 2/0.... 4¼" .... (OE).... ❹.... $95-100
☐ 150 2/0.... 4¼" .... (OE).... ❺.... $83-95
☐ 150 2/0.... 4¼" .... (OE).... ❻.... $83

□ 150/0 ..... 5 to 5¼" ..... (OE) .... ❷ $300-350
□ 150/0 ..... 5 to 5¼" ..... (OE) .... ❸ $150-200
□ 150/0 ..... 5 to 5¼" ..... (OE) .... ❹ $140-150
□ 150/0 ..... 5 to 5¼" ..... (OE) .... ❺ $125-140
□ 150/0 ..... 5 to 5¼" ..... (OE) .... ❻ $125
□ 150/I ..... 6¼ to 6½" ... (OE) .... ❶ $900-1150
□ 150/I ..... 6¼ to 6½" ... (OE) .... ❷ $500-700
□ 150/I ..... 6¼ to 6½" ... (OE) .... ❸ $350-500
□ 150/I ..... 6¼ to 6½" ... (OE) .... ❹ $240-250
□ 150/I ..... 6¼ to 6½" ... (OE) .... ❻ $240
□ 150 ...... 6¼" .... (CE) .... ❶ $1000-1250
□ 150 ...... 6¼" .... (CE) .... ❷ $500-750

HUM 151
Madonna Holding Child
Known as the "Madonna with the Blue Cloak." Modeled by master sculptor Reinhold Unger in 1942. Was produced in five color variations: white overglaze (OE), pastel blue cloak (OE), dark blue cloak (CE), brown cloak (CE), ivory finish (CE). All of the closed editions are considered extremely rare. This figurine had not been produced for many years but has recently been put into current production in white overglaze and pastel blue. Can now be found in 5 and 6 trademarks.

□ 151 ...... 12½" Blue ... (OE) .... ❶ $2000-3000
□ 151 ...... 12½" Blue ... (OE) .... ❷ $2000-2500
□ 151 ...... 12½" Blue ... (OE) .... ❺ $475-525
□ 151 ...... 12½" Blue ... (OE) .... ❻ $472.50
□ 151 ...... 12½" White .. (OE) .... ❶ $1500-2500
□ 151 ...... 12½" White .. (OE) .... ❷ $1000-2000
□ 151 ...... 12½" White .. (OE) .... ❺ $175-200
□ 151 ...... 12½" White .. (OE) .... ❻ $175
□ 151 ...... 12½" Brown . (CE) .... ❶ .... $5000 +
□ 151 ...... 12½" Ivory ... (CE) .... ❶ .... $5000 +
□ 151 ...... 12½" Dk. Blue (CE) .... ❶ .... $5000 +

152A TM④   **152B TM④**

HUM 152 A
Umbrella Boy

Originally modeled by master sculptor Arthur Moeller in 1942. The crown mark piece in our collection is incised 152 only and is considered rare with that trademark. The large size was restyled in 1972 with a thin umbrella and new textured finish. Older models have the umbrella handle fastened on boy's right shoe while in newer models the handle is fastened to his left shoe. The small size was first produced in 1954 and can be found in all trademarks except the crown. Some small size examples have a *stamped* 1951 copyright date while others have an *incised* 1957 date. Old name: "In Safety" or "Boy Under Umbrella."

HUM 152 B
Umbrella Girl

Originally modeled by master sculptor Arthur Moeller in 1949. We have never been able to locate "Umbrella Girl" with the crown trademark for our collection. It would be considered extremely rare, if it actually does exist. The large size was restyled in 1972 with a thin umbrella and new textured finish. The small size was first produced in 1954 and can be found in all trademarks except the crown. Some small size examples have an incised 1951 copyright date while others have an incised 1957 date. Old name: "In Safety" or "Girl Under Umbrella."

☐ 152/0A .... 4¾" .... (OE) .... ❷ $500-750
☐ 152/0A .... 4¾" .... (OE) .... ❸ $325-375
☐ 152/0A .... 4¾" .... (OE) .... ❹ $290-325
☐ 152/0A .... 4¾" .... (OE) .... ❺ $265-290
☐ 152/0A .... 4¾" .... (OE) .... ❻ $265
☐ 152 ...... 8" .... (OE) .... ❶ $1500-2000
☐ 152 A ..... 8" .... (OE) .... ❷ $1000-1500
☐ 152 A ..... 8" .... (OE) .... ❸ $850-1000
☐ 152 A ..... 8" .... (OE) .... ❹ $800-850
☐ 152/II A ... 8" .... (OE) .... ❺ $750-800
☐ 152/II A ... 8" .... (OE) .... ❻ $750
☐ 152/0B .... 4¾" .... (OE) .... ❷ $500-750
☐ 152/0B .... 4¾" .... (OE) .... ❸ $325-375
☐ 152/0B .... 4¾" .... (OE) .... ❹ $290-325
☐ 152/0B .... 4¾" .... (OE) .... ❺ $265-290
☐ 152/0B .... 4¾" .... (OE) .... ❻ $265

□ 152 B . . . . . 8" . . . . (OE) . . . . ❶ $1500-2000
□ 152 B . . . . . 8" . . . . (OE) . . . . ❷ $1000-1500
□ 152 B . . . . . 8" . . . . (OE) . . . . ❸ $850-1000
□ 152 B . . . . . 8" . . . . (OE) . . . . ❹ $800-850
□ 152/II B . . . 8" . . . . (OE) . . . . ❺ $750-800
□ 152/II B . . . 8" . . . . (OE) . . . . ❻ $750

153/O   153/I   153/O Boy with hat (CE)

HUM 153 Auf Wiedersehen

Originally modeled by master sculptor Arthur Moeller in 1943. First produced in the large size only with plain 153 incised number. The small size was introduced in the early 1950's with the boy wearing a hat and waving his hand—always with full bee trademark and "O" size designator directly under the number "153"—considered rare. This style was made in the small size only. Both sizes have been restyled in recent years. Both styles of the small size can be found in full bee trademark. Also called "Good Bye" in old catalogues.

□ 153/0 . . . . . 5½ to 6" . . . . . (OE) . . . . ❷ $200-275
□ 153/0 . . . . . 5½ to 6" . . . . . (OE) . . . . ❸ $150-175
□ 153/0 . . . . . 5½ to 6" . . . . . (OE) . . . . ❹ $105-130
□ 153/0 . . . . . 5½ to 6" . . . . . (OE) . . . . ❺ $95-105
□ 153/0 . . . . . 5½ to 6" . . . . . (OE) . . . . ❻ $94.50
□ 153/0 . . . . . 5¼" . . . . (CE) . . . . ❷ . . . . $1500-2500 (With hat)
□ 153 . . . . . 6¾ to 7" . . . . . (CE) . . . . ❶ $750-1000
□ 153 . . . . . 6¾ to 7" . . . . . (CE) . . . . ❷ $450-550
□ 153/I . . . . . 6¾ to 7" . . . . . (OE) . . . . ❶ $500-850
□ 153/I . . . . . 6¾ to 7" . . . . . (OE) . . . . ❷ $400-500
□ 153/I . . . . . 6¾ to 7" . . . . . (OE) . . . . ❸ $350-400
□ 153/I . . . . . 6¾ to 7" . . . . . (OE) . . . . ❹ $300-350
□ 153/I . . . . . 6¾ to 7" . . . . . (OE) . . . . ❺ $125-140
□ 153/I . . . . . 6¾ to 7" . . . . . (OE) . . . . ❻ $125

| 154/O | 154/O | 154/I | 154 (CE) |

HUM 154   Waiter

Originally modeled by master sculptor Arthur Moeller in 1943. Was first produced in the 6½" size and incised number 154 only, with gray coat and gray striped trousers. In the early 1950's the colors were changed to blue coat and tan striped trousers, and "Waiter" was produced in two sizes: 154/O and 154/I. Has been produced with various names on bottle. "Rhein-wine" or "Rhein Wine" are the most common. "Whisky," "Hiher Mchie" and other illegible names have been used. Old name: "Chef of Service" in some old catalogues. Both sizes have recently been restyled with the new textured finish.

☐ 154/0 . . . . . 6 to 6¼" . . . . . (OE) . . . . ❶ $300-400
☐ 154/0 . . . . . 6 to 6¼" . . . . . (OE) . . . . ❷ $150-250
☐ 154/0 . . . . . 6 to 6¼" . . . . . (OE) . . . . ❸ $125-150
☐ 154/0 . . . . . 6 to 6¼" . . . . . (OE) . . . . ❹ $100-125
☐ 154/0 . . . . . 6 to 6¼" . . . . . (OE) . . . . ❺ $90-100
☐ 154/0 . . . . . 6 to 6¼" . . . . . (OE) . . . . ❻ $88
☐ 154/I . . . . . 6½ to 7" . . . . . (OE) . . . . ❶ $500-750
☐ 154/I . . . . . 6½ to 7" . . . . . (OE) . . . . ❷ $250-350
☐ 154/I . . . . . 6½ to 7" . . . . . (OE) . . . . ❸ $150-200
☐ 154/I . . . . . 6½ to 7" . . . . . (OE) . . . . ❹ $125-150
☐ 154/I . . . . . 6½ to 7" . . . . . (OE) . . . . ❺ $110-125
☐ 154/I . . . . . 6½ to 7" . . . . . (OE) . . . . ❻ $110
☐ 154 . . . . . . 6½" . . . . (CE) . . . . ❶ $750-1000
☐ 154 . . . . . . 6½" . . . . (CE) . . . . ❷ $350-500

HUM 155 (CN)
Factory records indicate: Madonna with cloak, sitting with child on her lap, Reinhold Unger in 1943. Listed as Closed Number on 18 May 1943. No known examples or photographs.

☐ 155 . . . . (CN) . . . .

HUM 156 (CN)
Factory records indicate: Wall picture with sitting woman and child, Arthur Moeller in 1943. Listed as Closed Number on 18 May 1943. No known examples or photographs.

☐ 156 . . . . (CN) . . . .

HUM 157 (CN)
Factory records indicate: Boy standing with flower basket. Sample model sculpted by Arthur Moeller in 1943. Considered for production but was never made. This factory sample does not have "M.I. Hummel" signature. Listed as Closed Number on 17 September 1943.

☐ 157 . . . . (CN) . . . .

HUM 158 (CN)
Factory records indicate: Girl standing with dog in her arms. Sample model sculpted by Arthur Moeller in 1943. Considered for production but was never made. This factory sample does not have "M.I. Hummel" signature. Listed as Closed Number on 17 September 1943.

☐ 158 .... (CN) ....

HUM 159 (CN)
Factory records indicate: Girl standing with flowers in her arms. Sample model sculpted by Arthur Moeller in 1943. Considered for production but was never made. This factory sample does not have "M.I. Hummel" signature. Listed as Closed Number on 17 September 1943.

☐ 159 .... (CN) ....

HUM 160 (CN)
Factory records indicate: Girl standing in tiered dress and bouquet of flowers. Sample model sculpted by Reinhold Unger in 1943. Considered for production but was never made. This factory sample does not have "M.I. Hummel" signature. Listed as Closed Number on 17 September 1943.

☐ 160 .... (CN) ....

HUM 161 (CN)
Factory records indicate: Girl standing with hands in her pockets. Sample model sculpted by Reinhold Unger in 1943. Considered for production but was never made. This factory sample does not have "M.I. Hummel" signature. Listed as Closed Number on 17 September 1943.

☐ 161 .... (CN) ....

HUM 162 (CN)
Factory records indicate: Girl standing with pocket-book (handbag). Sample model sculpted by Reinhold Unger in 1943. Listed as Closed Number on 11 October 1943. No known examples or photographs.

☐ 162 .... (CN) ....

Old   *New*

HUM 163
Whitsuntide
Originally modeled by master sculptor Arthur Moeller in 1946. Can be found in all trademarks except TM 4. Older models are larger than newer models. Old name: "Christmas." Sometimes referred to as "Happy New Year." Angel on base holds red or yellow candle on older models. Unusual variation has small hole in angel's cupped hands where candle should be. Had been considered rare at one time, but was put back into current production in 1978 and can be found with TM 5 and TM 6.

☐ 163 ...... 6½ to 7" ..... (OE).... ❶ $1000-1200
☐ 163 ...... 6½ to 7" ..... (OE).... ❷ $750-1000
☐ 163 ...... 6½ to 7" ..... (OE).... ❸ $500-750
☐ 163 ...... 6½ to 7" ..... (OE).... ❺ $125-150
☐ 163 ...... 6½ to 7" ..... (OE).... ❻ $125

Old   *New*

HUM 164
Holy Water Font, Worship
First modeled by master sculptor Reinhold Unger in 1946. There are variations in construction of this font in that older models do not have a rim on back side of bowl while newer models do. Also color variations on lip of water bowl—older ones were handpainted; newer ones are shaded with airbrush.

☐ 164 ...... 3¼ x 5" ..... (OE).... ❶ $200-250
☐ 164 ...... 3¼ x 5" ..... (OE).... ❷ $100-150
☐ 164 ...... 3¼ x 5" ..... (OE).... ❸ $40-50
☐ 164 ...... 3¼ x 5" ..... (OE).... ❹ $30-40
☐ 164 ...... 3¼ x 5" ..... (OE).... ❺ $27-30
☐ 164 ...... 3¼ x 5" ..... (OE).... ❻ $26.50

Stylized trademark

HUM 165
Swaying Lullaby, Wall Plaque
Originally modeled by master sculptor Arthur Moeller in 1946. Not pictured in older catalogues; most collectors were not aware of the existence of this plaque until the early 1970's. Our first purchase came through an American soldier who had been stationed in Panama. Put back into current production in 1978 and now available in TM 5 and TM 6. Older models have the "M.I. Hummel" signature on the back while newer models have signature on front lower right corner. Old name: "Child in a Hammock." Inscription reads: "Dreaming of better times." Considered rare in crown, full bee, and stylized trademarks. Restyled in 1979. Current production models are slightly thicker in depth, with signature on back.

☐ 165	...... 4½ x 5¼"	... (OE)	.... ❶	.... $750-1000
☐ 165	...... 4½ x 5¼"	... (OE)	.... ❷	.... $500-750
☐ 165	...... 4½ x 5¼"	... (OE)	.... ❸	.... $350-500
☐ 165	...... 4½ x 5¼"	... (OE)	.... ❺	.... $80-90
☐ 165	...... 4½ x 5¼"	... (OE)	.... ❻	.... $80

HUM 166
Boy With Bird, Ashtray
This ashtray was modeled by master sculptor Arthur Moeller in 1946. Only slight variations in color and construction through the years; no major differences between old and new models.

☐ 166	...... 3¼ x 6"	..... (OE)	.... ❶	.... $250-350
☐ 166	...... 3¼ x 6"	..... (OE)	.... ❷	.... $200-250
☐ 166	...... 3¼ x 6"	..... (OE)	.... ❸	.... $100-125
☐ 166	...... 3¼ x 6"	..... (OE)	.... ❹	.... $90-100
☐ 166	...... 3¼ x 6"	..... (OE)	.... ❺	.... $80-90
☐ 166	...... 3¼ x 6"	..... (OE)	.... ❻	.... $80

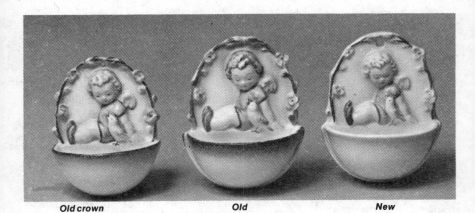

Old crown   Old   New

HUM 167 Holy Water Font, Angel Sitting

Also referred to as: "Angel-Bird" or "Angel with Bird" font. Newer models have a hole at top of font for hanging. Older models have hole on back of font for hanging. We recently found old crown (TM 1) font that has both hole at top and on back, is smaller in size and has no rim on back edge of bowl. Variations in color on lip of water bowl—older ones were handpainted; newer ones are shaded with airbrush. First modeled by Reinhold Unger in 1945.

☐ 167	...... 3¼ x 4⅛"	.... (OE)	.... ❶	....	$200-250
☐ 167	...... 3¼ x 4⅛"	.... (OE)	.... ❷	....	$100-150
☐ 167	...... 3¼ x 4⅛"	.... (OE)	.... ❸	....	$40-50
☐ 167	...... 3¼ x 4⅛"	.... (OE)	.... ❹	....	$30-35
☐ 167	...... 3¼ x 4⅛"	.... (OE)	.... ❺	....	$23-25
☐ 167	...... 3¼ x 4⅛"	.... (OE)	.... ❻	....	$23

Stylized trademark

HUM 168
Standing Boy, Wall Plaque

Originally modeled by master sculptor Arthur Moeller in 1948. Not pictured in older catalogues; most collectors were not aware of the existence of this plaque until the early 1970's. Very limited early production, probably sold mostly in European market. Put back into current production in 1978 and now available in TM 5 and TM 6. Older models have only "Hummel" on front, lower left, along with "© WG" in lower right corner. Newer models have "M.I. Hummel" signature incised on back. This same motif was made into a figurine in 1979 by current master sculptor Gerhard Skrobek; see HUM 399 "Valentine Joy."

□ 168 ...... 4⅛ x 5½ " .... (OE)....❶.... $750-1000
□ 168 ...... 4⅛ x 5½ " .... (OE)....❷.... $500-750
□ 168 ...... 4⅛ x 5½ " .... (OE)....❸.... $350-500
□ 168 ...... 4⅛ x 5½ " .... (OE)....❺.... $80-90
□ 168 ...... 4⅛ x 5½ " .... (OE)....❻.... $80

Old   **New**

HUM 169   Bird Duet
Originally modeled in 1945 by master sculptor Arthur Moeller; later restyled in 1967 by current master sculptor Gerhard Skrobek. Many variations between old and new figurines. Variations are noted in angel's wings, gown and position of baton. Color variation in birds, angel's hair and gown, as well as music stand.

□ 169 ...... 3¾ to 4" ..... (OE)....❶.... $200-300
□ 169 ...... 3¾ to 4" ..... (OE)....❷.... $125-175
□ 169 ...... 3¾ to 4" ..... (OE)....❸.... $100-125
□ 169 ...... 3¾ to 4" ..... (OE)....❹.... $75-90
□ 169 ...... 3¾ to 4" ..... (OE)....❺.... $70-75
□ 169 ...... 3¾ to 4" ..... (OE)....❻.... $66

170/I

HUM 170
School Boys

First modeled by master sculptor Reinhold Unger in 1943 and later remodeled by present master sculptor Gerhard Skrobek in 1961. Originally produced in one size with incised number 170 only. Small size first produced in the early 1960's and has an incised 1961 copyright date. Old name: "Difficult Problems." Some color variations on older models. Large size was again restyled in the early 1970's with the new textured finish and 1972 copyright date. In the sping of 1982 the large size (170/III) was permanently retired by Goebel and will not be produced again. The small size 170/I is still in current production.

☐ 170/I	7¼ to 7½"	(OE)	❸	$600-750
☐ 170/I	7¼ to 7½"	(OE)	❹	$550-600
☐ 170/I	7¼ to 7½"	(OE)	❺	$525-550
☐ 170/I	7¼ to 7½"	(OE)	❻	$525
☐ 170	10 to 10¼"	(CE)	❶	$2000-2500
☐ 170	10 to 10¼"	(CE)	❷	$1500-2000
☐ 170/III	10 to 10¼"	(CE)	❸	$1400-1500
☐ 170/III	10 to 10¼"	(CE)	❹	$1350-1400
☐ 170/III	10 to 10¼"	(CE)	❺	$1310-1350
☐ 170/III	10 to 10¼"	(CE)	❻	$1310

HUM 171
Little Sweeper

This figurine was first modeled by master sculptor Reinhold Unger in 1944. Very little change between older and newer models. Old name: "Mother's Helper." Restyled in 1981 by present master sculptor Gerhard Skrobek. The current production now has the new textured finish and is slightly larger.

☐ 171	4¼"	(OE)	❶	$200-250
☐ 171	4¼"	(OE)	❷	$100-150
☐ 171	4¼"	(OE)	❸	$75-100
☐ 171	4¼"	(OE)	❹	$60-75
☐ 171	4¼"	(OE)	❺	$55-60
☐ 171	4¼ to 4½"	(OE)	❻	$55

Crown   Full Bee   Stylized

HUM 172 Festival Harmony (Mandolin)

Originally modeled in 1947 by master sculptor Reinhold Unger in the large size only with incised number 172. Old crown mark and some full bee examples have the bird resting on flowers in front of angel (rare). Restyled in the early 1950's with bird resting on mandolin and one flower at hem of angel's gown. Restyled again in the late 1960's with the new textured finish and flowers placed at angel's feet. There are variations in color of gown and color of birds. The small size (172/O) was modeled by master sculptor Theo R. Menzenbach in 1961 and can be found in one style only.

☐ 172/0	8"	(OE)	❸	$150-200	
☐ 172/0	8"	(OE)	❹	$130-150	
☐ 172/0	8"	(OE)	❺	$115-130	
☐ 172/0	8"	(OE)	❻	$115	
☐ 172/II	10¼ to 10¾"	(OE)	❷	$750-1000	
☐ 172/II	10¼ to 10¾"	(OE)	❸	$350-400	
☐ 172/II	10¼ to 10¾"	(OE)	❹	$250-300	
☐ 172/II	10¼ to 10¾"	(OE)	❺	$220-250	
☐ 172/II	10¼ to 10¾"	(OE)	❻	$220	
☐ 172	10¾"	(CE)	❶	$2000-2500	(Bird in front)
☐ 172	10¾"	(CE)	❷	$1500-2000	(Bird in front)

Crown   ***Full Bee***   *Stylized*

HUM 173   Festival Harmony (Flute)

Originally modeled in 1947 by master sculptor Reinhold Unger in the large size only with incised number 173. Old crown mark and some full bee examples have a much larger bird and flower in front of angel (rare). Restyled in the early 1950's with smaller bird and one flower at hem of angel's gown. Restyled again in the late 1960's with the new textured finish and flowers placed at angel's feet. There are variations in color of gown and color of birds. The small size (173/O) was modeled by master sculptor Theo R. Menzenbach in 1961 and can be found in one style only.

☐ 173/0	8"	(OE)	❸	$150-200
☐ 173/0	8"	(OE)	❹	$130-150
☐ 173/0	8"	(OE)	❺	$115-130
☐ 173/0	8"	(OE)	❻	$115
☐ 173/II	10¼ to 11"	(OE)	❷	$750-1000
☐ 173/II	10¼ to 11"	(OE)	❸	$350-400
☐ 173/II	10¼ to 11"	(OE)	❹	$250-300
☐ 173/II	10¼ to 11"	(OE)	❺	$220-225
☐ 173/II	10¼ to 11"	(OE)	❻	$220
☐ 173	11"	(CE)	❶	$2000-2500 (Flowers up front of dress)
☐ 173	11"	(CE)	❷	$1500-2000 (Flowers up front of dress)

Current　　　　　　　　　*Full Bee*

HUM 174　She Loves Me, She Loves Me Not!

Originally modeled by master sculptor Arthur Moeller in 1945. Has been restyled several times. Early crown mark pieces have smaller feather in boy's hat, no flower on left fence post and eyes are open. The 2, 3 and 4 trademark period pieces have a flower on left fence post and eyes open. Current production pieces have no flower on left fence post (same as crown mark piece) but with eyes looking down.

☐ 174 ...... 4¼" .... (OE)....❶.... $300-375
☐ 174 ...... 4¼" .... (OE)....❷.... $200-250
☐ 174 ...... 4¼" .... (OE)....❸.... $100-150
☐ 174 ...... 4¼" .... (OE)....❹.... $80-100
☐ 174 ...... 4¼" .... (OE)....❺.... $75-80
☐ 174 ...... 4¼" .... (OE)....❻.... $72

Newer model

HUM 175
Mother's Darling
Older models have pink and green-colored kerchiefs (bags) while newer models have blue ones. Older models do not have polka dots on head scarf. Old name: "Happy Harriet." First modeled by master sculptor Arthur Moeller in 1945, and has been restyled several times since then.

☐ 175	5½"	(OE)	❶	$300-400
☐ 175	5½"	(OE)	❷	$200-250
☐ 175	5½"	(OE)	❸	$150-175
☐ 175	5½"	(OE)	❹	$100-125
☐ 175	5½"	(OE)	❺	$90-100
☐ 175	5½"	(OE)	❻	$88

176/I New   *176/I Old*

HUM 176 Happy Birthday

When first modeled in 1945 by master sculptor Arthur Moeller this figurine was produced in one size only with the incised number 176. A smaller size was issued in the
mid-1950's with the incised number 176/O and an oval base. At the same time, the large
size was changed to 176/I. The large size figurine has always had a round base until it
was completely restyled in 1979 and now has an oval base, also.

☐ 176/0 . . . . . 5 to 5¼ " . . . . . (OE) . . . . ❷ $250-300
☐ 176/0 . . . . . 5 to 5¼ " . . . . . (OE) . . . . ❸ $150-175
☐ 176/0 . . . . . 5 to 5¼ " . . . . . (OE) . . . . ❹ $105-120
☐ 176/0 . . . . . 5 to 5¼ " . . . . . (OE) . . . . ❺ $95-105
☐ 176/0 . . . . . 5 to 5¼ " . . . . . (OE) . . . . ❻ $94.50
☐ 176/I . . . . . 5¾ to 6 " . . . . . (OE) . . . . ❶ $500-650
☐ 176/I . . . . . 5¾ to 6 " . . . . . (OE) . . . . ❷ $350-500
☐ 176/I . . . . . 5¾ to 6 " . . . . . (OE) . . . . ❸ $300-350
☐ 176/I . . . . . 5¾ to 6 " . . . . . (OE) . . . . ❹ $250-300
☐ 176/I . . . . . 5¾ to 6 " . . . . . (OE) . . . . ❺ $140-155
☐ 176/I . . . . . 5¾ to 6 " . . . . . (OE) . . . . ❻ $136.50
☐ 176 . . . . . . 5½ " . . . . (CE) . . . . ❶ $650-750
☐ 176 . . . . . . 5½ " . . . . (CE) . . . . ❷ $350-500

177/I

HUM 177
School Girls

First modeled by master sculptor Reinhold Unger in 1946 and later remodeled by master sculptor Theo R. Menzenbach in 1961. Originally produced in one size with incised number 177 only. Small size first produced in the early 1960's and has an incised 1961 copyright date. Old name: "Master Piece." Some slight color variations on older models, particularly the shoes. Large size again restyled in the early 1970's with the new textured finish and a 1972 incised copyright date. In the spring of 1982 the large size (177/III) was permanently retired by Goebel and will not be produced again. The small size (170/I) is still in current production. See HUM 225 "Stitch in Time" and HUM 256 "Knitting Lesson" for interesting comparison.

☐ 177/I	7½"	(OE)	❸	$600-750
☐ 177/I	7½"	(OE)	❹	$550-600
☐ 177/I	7½"	(OE)	❺	$525-550
☐ 177/I	7½"	(OE)	❻	$525
☐ 177	9½"	(CE)	❶	$2000-2500
☐ 177	9½"	(CE)	❷	$1500-2000
☐ 177/III	9½"	(CE)	❸	$1400-1500
☐ 177/III	9½"	(CE)	❹	$1350-1400
☐ 177/III	9½"	(CE)	❺	$1310-1350
☐ 177/III	9½"	(CE)	❻	$1310

Newer model

HUM 178
Photographer

Originally modeled by master sculptor Reinhold Unger in 1948 and has been restyled several times through the years. There are many size variations with the older models being larger. Some color variations on dog and camera. Newer models have a 1948 copyright date.

As prices change and new issues are made, revised editions of this book will be published. If you would like to be notified when the next edition becomes available, please fill in your name and street address on the card below, affix 13¢ postage and mail it to us.

AFFIX
13¢
STAMP

PORTFOLIO PRESS CORP.
170 FIFTH AVENUE
NEW YORK, NY 10010

As prices change and new issues are made, revised editions of this book will be published. If you would like to be notified when the next edition becomes available, please fill in your name and street address on the card below, affix 13¢ postage and mail it to us.

☐ Please notify me when the next edition of **The No. 1 Price Guide to M.I. Hummel**, by Robert L. Miller, becomes available.

(Please print)

Name _____

Address _____

City _____ State _____ Zip _____

☐ 178	......	4¾ to 5¼"	... (OE)	....❶....	$300-500
☐ 178	......	4¾ to 5¼"	... (OE)	....❷....	$200-300
☐ 178	......	4¾ to 5¼"	... (OE)	....❸....	$150-200
☐ 178	......	4¾ to 5¼"	... (OE)	....❹....	$115-125
☐ 178	......	4¾ to 5¼"	... (OE)	....❺....	$105-115
☐ 178	......	4¾ to 5¼"	... (OE)	....❻....	$105

Older model

HUM 179
Coquettes
Modeled originally by master sculptor Arthur Moeller in 1946 and has been restyled in recent years. Older examples are usually slightly larger in size. Minor color variations can be found in older models.

☐ 179	......	5 to 5½"	.... (OE)	....❶....	$300-500
☐ 179	......	5 to 5¼"	.... (OE)	....❷....	$200-300
☐ 179	......	5 to 5¼"	.... (OE)	....❸....	$150-200
☐ 179	......	5 to 5¼"	.... (OE)	....❹....	$115-125
☐ 179	......	5 to 5¼"	.... (OE)	....❺....	$105-115
☐ 179	......	5 to 5¼"	.... (OE)	....❻....	$105

New style   *Old style*

HUM 180   Tuneful Good Night, Wall Plaque
Modeled by master sculptor Arthur Moeller in 1946. Recently restyled in 1981 by master sculptor Rudolf Wittman, a twenty-five-year veteran of the Goebel factory. In the restyled version, the position of the girl's head and hairstyle have been changed, as well as the position of the horn which is no longer attached to the heart-shaped back. Old name: "Happy Bugler" plaque. Had been considered rare and was difficult to find, but is again in current production with 5 and 6 trademarks.

☐ 180	5 x 4¾"	(OE)	❶	$500-750
☐ 180	5 x 4¾"	(OE)	❷	$350-500
☐ 180	5 x 4¾"	(OE)	❸	$250-350
☐ 180	5 x 4¾"	(OE)	❹	$150-250
☐ 180	5 x 4¾"	(OE)	❺	$100-125
☐ 180	5 x 4¾"	(OE)	❻	$94.50

HUM 181
Old Man Reading Newspaper (CN)
This unusual piece was made as a sample only in 1948 by master sculptor Arthur Moeller and was not approved by the Siessen Convent for production. It was not considered typical of Sister M.I. Hummel's work, although it is an exact reproduction of one of her early sketches. This early sample *does* have the familiar "M.I. Hummel" signature and is part of the Robert L. Miller collection. Listed as a Closed Number on 18 February 1948 and will not be produced again. Often referred to as one of the "Mamas" and the "Papas." Also produced as lamp base; see HUM 202.

☐ 181	6¾"	(CN)	$5000 +

New style   Old style

HUM 182   Good Friends
Originally modeled by master sculptor Arthur Moeller in 1946 and later restyled by
master sculptor Gerhard Skrobek in 1976. The current model is slightly larger and has
the new textured finish. Called "Friends" in old catalogues.

☐ 182 ...... 4 to 4¼" ..... (OE).... ❶ $300-450
☐ 182 ...... 4 to 4¼" ..... (OE).... ❷ $200-250
☐ 182 ...... 4 to 4¼" ..... (OE).... ❸ $100-150
☐ 182 ...... 4 to 4¼" ..... (OE).... ❹ $90-100
☐ 182 ...... 4 to 4¼" ..... (OE).... ❺ $85-90
☐ 182 ...... 4 to 4¼" ..... (OE).... ❻ $83

Older model

HUM 183
Forest Shrine

First modeled in 1946 by master sculptor Reinhold Unger and can be found with all trademarks except trademark 4. Had been considered rare by was put back into production in 1977 and can be found with 5 and 6 trademarks. Older models have a shiny finish on the deer while newer models have a dull finish. Old name: "Doe at Shrine." This figurine has recently been restyled with a more lifelike finish on the deer.

☐ 183	9"	(OE)	❶	$1000-1500
☐ 183	9"	(OE)	❷	$750-1000
☐ 183	9"	(OE)	❸	$300-500
☐ 183	9"	(OE)	❺	$273-300
☐ 183	9"	(OE)	❻	$273

New style   Old style

HUM 184
Latest News

First modeled by master sculptor Arthur Moeller in 1946. Older models were made with square base and boy's eyes open. Restyled in the mid-1960's and changed to round base and boy's eyes looking down at paper. At one time the newspaper was produced without any name so that visitors to the factory could have the name of their choice put on. An endless variety of names can be found. Most common names are: "Das Allerneueste," "Munchener Presse" and "Latest News." Some collectors specialize in collecting the different names on the newspaper and will pay from $500 to $1,000 for some names. Some catalogues list as 184/O.S. which means: Ohne Schrift (without lettering).

☐ 184	5 to 5¼"	(OE)	❶	$350-500
☐ 184	5 to 5¼"	(OE)	❷	$300-350
☐ 184	5 to 5¼"	(OE)	❸	$150-225
☐ 184	5 to 5¼"	(OE)	❹	$125-150
☐ 184	5 to 5¼"	(OE)	❺	$120-125
☐ 184	5 to 5¼"	(OE)	❻	$115.50

New   **Old**

HUM 185
Accordion Boy

First modeled by master sculptor Reinhold Unger in 1947, this figurine has never had a major restyling although there are many size variations due mainly to "mold growth." In the early years, the molds were made of plaster of paris and had a tendency to "wash out" or erode with use, thereby producing figurines each being slightly larger than the last. Since 1954, the use of acrylic resin for modeling has led to greater uniformity in the figurines themselves. There are some slight color variations on the accordion. Old name: "On the Alpine Pasture." One of several figurines that make up the Hummel orchestra.

☐ 185	5 to 6"	(OE)	❶	$250-350
☐ 185	5 to 6"	(OE)	❷	$150-200
☐ 185	5 to 6"	(OE)	❸	$100-125
☐ 185	5"	(OE)	❹	$80-100
☐ 185	5"	(OE)	❺	$75-80
☐ 185	5"	(OE)	❻	$72

New   **Old**

HUM 186
Sweet Music

Originally modeled in 1947 by master sculptor Reinhold Unger. Many size variations. Was restyled slightly in the mid-1960's. Some old crown mark pieces have white slippers with blue-green stripes instead of the normal brownish color. This variation will usually sell for $500 to $1,000. Old name: "Playing To The Dance." One of several figurines that make up the Hummel orchestra.

☐ 186	5 to 5½"	(OE)	❶	$350-750
☐ 186	5 to 5½"	(OE)	❷	$200-250
☐ 186	5 to 5½"	(OE)	❸	$100-150
☐ 186	5"	(OE)	❹	$90-100
☐ 186	5"	(OE)	❺	$85-90
☐ 186	5"	(OE)	❻	$83

HUM 187
M.I. Hummel Plaques (in English)
There seems to have been an endless variety of plaques throughout the years, some for dealers and some for collectors. Originally modeled by master sculptor Reinhold Unger in 1947 and later restyled by Gerhard Skrobek in 1962. Two incised copyright dates have been used, 1947 and 1976. Current display plaques for collectors are incised 187 A. At one time in recent years, dealers' names were printed

on the plaques for Australian dealers
only. Pictured here is only a small portion
of the many variations issued.

☐ 187	5½ x 4"	(CE)	❶	$1000-1500
☐ 187	5½ x 4"	(CE)	❷	$500-750
☐ 187	5½ x 4"	(CE)	❸	$200-500
☐ 187	5½ x 4"	(CE)	❹	$200-350
☐ 187A	5½ x 4"	(CE)	❺	$42-50
☐ 187A	5½ x 4"	(OE)	❻	$42

HUM 187 (SPECIAL)
W.G.P. "Service" Plaque
This service plaque was first introduced in the late 1950's and has become a Goebel tradition. Each employee of W. Goebel Porzellanfabrik, regardless of his position or the department she/he is working in receives such a special plaque on the occasion of his/her 25th, 40th or 50th anniversary with Goebel.

HUM 188
Celestial Musician
Originally modeled by master sculptor Reinhold Unger in 1948, this figurine has never had a major restyling. Older models are slightly larger, have a bluish-green gown and an open quartered base. Newer models are slightly smaller, have a green gown and a closed flat base, and some have 1948 incised copyright date. According to factory information, this figurine was also sold in white overglaze finish at one time, but would now be considered extremely rare in that finish. A new smaller size was first released in 1983. Designed by master sculptor Gerhard Skrobek in 1982, this new size measures 5½" and is incised 188/O on the bottom. Original issue price was $80 in 1983. The older large size will eventually be renumbered 188/I.

☐ 188	7"	(OE)	❶	$500-750
☐ 188	7"	(OE)	❷	$250-350
☐ 188	7"	(OE)	❸	$150-200
☐ 188	7"	(OE)	❹	$130-150
☐ 188	7"	(OE)	❺	$120-130
☐ 188	7"	(OE)	❻	$115.50
☐ 188/0	5½"	(OE)	❻	$80

Incised "M.I. Hummel"

HUM 189
Old Woman Knitting (CN)

This unusual piece was made as a sample only in 1948 by master sculptor Arthur Moeller and was not approved by the Siessen Convent for production. It was not considered typical of Sister M.I. Hummel's work, although it is an exact replica of one of her early sketches. This early sample *does* have the familiar "M.I. Hummel" signature and is part of the Robert L. Miller collection. Listed as a Closed Number on 18 February 1948 and will not be produced again. Often referred to as one of the "Mamas" and the "Papas."

□ 189 . . . . . . 6¾" . . . . (CN) . . . . $5000 +

Incised "M.I. Hummel"

HUM 190
Old Woman Walking To Market (CN)

This unusual piece was made as a sample only in 1948 by master sculptor Arthur Moeller and was not approved by the Siessen Convent for production. It was not considered typical of Sister M.I. Hummel's work, although it is an exact replica of one of her early sketches. This early sample *does* have the familiar "M.I. Hummel" signature and is part of the Robert L. Miller collection. Listed as a Closed Number on 18 February 1948 and will not be produced again. Often referred to as one of the "Mamas" and the "Papas."

□ 190 . . . . . . 6¾" . . . . (CN) . . . . $5000 +

Incised "M.I. Hummel"

HUM 191
Old Man Walking To Market (CN)

This unusual piece was made as a sample only in 1948 by master sculptor Arthur Moeller and was not approved by the Siessen Convent for production. It was not considered typical of Sister M.I. Hummel's work, although it is an exact replica of one of her early sketches. This early sample *does* have the familiar "M.I. Hummel" signature and is part of the Robert L. Miller collection. Listed as a Closed Number on 18 February 1948 and will not be produced again. Often referred to as one of the "Mamas" and the "Papas."

☐ 191 . . . . . . 6¾" . . . . (CN) . . . . $5000 +

New style   *Old style*

HUM 192
Candlelight, Candleholder

Originally modeled by master sculptor Reinhold Unger in 1948 with a long red ceramic candle. Later restyled by master sculptor Theo R. Menzenbach in 1958 with a short candleholder ending in angel's hands. Both models have a receptical for holding a wax candle. Older models are slightly larger. Old name: "Carrier of Light." The incised copyright date on both models is 1948.

□ 192	6¾ x 7"	(OE)	❶	$600-750
□ 192	6¾ x 7"	(OE)	❷	$500-600
□ 192	6¾ x 7"	(OE)	❸	$300-375
□ 192	6¾ x 7"	(OE)	❹	$80-100
□ 192	6¾ x 7"	(OE)	❺	$70-80
□ 192	6¾ x 7"	(OE)	❻	$70

HUM 193 Angel Duet, Candleholder

First modeled by master sculptor Reinhold Unger in 1948 and later restyled by master sculptor Theo R. Menzenbach in 1958. Notice the position of angel's arm in rear view—this was changed by Menzenbach because he thought it would be easier for artists to paint—looks better and is a more natural position. Menzenbach began working at the Goebel factory in October 1948, at the age of 18. He left the factory in October 1961 to start his own business as a commercial artist. He is still living and resides in Germany, near Coburg. According to factory information, this figurine was also sold in white overglaze finish at one time—extremely rare. Also produced without holder for candle —see HUM 261.

□ 193	5"	(OE)	❶	$350-500
□ 193	5"	(OE)	❷	$200-250
□ 193	5"	(OE)	❸	$125-150
□ 193	5"	(OE)	❹	$100-125
□ 193	5"	(OE)	❺	$85-95
□ 193	5"	(OE)	❻	$84

HUM 194
Watchful Angel
Originally modeled by master sculptor Reinhold Unger in 1948 and later restyled by master sculptor Gerhard Skrobek in 1959. Older models are usually larger. Most models have an incised 1948 copyright date. Old name: "Angelic Care" or "Guardian Angel."

☐ 194	6¼ to 6¾"	(OE)	❶	$500-650
☐ 194	6¼ to 6¾"	(OE)	❷	$250-350
☐ 194	6¼ to 6¾"	(OE)	❸	$200-250
☐ 194	6¼"	(OE)	❹	$150-175
☐ 194	6¼"	(OE)	❺	$140-150
☐ 194	6¼"	(OE)	❻	$136.50

195/I

HUM 195
Barnyard Hero
First modeled by master sculptor Reinhold Unger in 1948. Originally made in one size only with the incised number 195. A smaller size was produced in the mid-1950's with the incised number 195 2/O. Both sizes have been restyled in recent years. Many size variations as well as variation in position of boy's hands in small size only: old model has one hand on each side of fence; new model, one hand on top of the other one. Most models have an incised 1948 copyright date.

☐ 195 2/0	3¾ to 4"	(OE)	❷	$150-195
☐ 195 2/0	3¾ to 4"	(OE)	❸	$100-125
☐ 195 2/0	3¾ to 4"	(OE)	❹	$80-100
☐ 195 2/0	3¾ to 4"	(OE)	❺	$75-80
☐ 195 2/0	3¾ to 4"	(OE)	❻	$72
☐ 195/I	5½"	(OE)	❷	$300-350
☐ 195/I	5½"	(OE)	❸	$150-200
☐ 195/I	5½"	(OE)	❹	$135-150
☐ 195/I	5½"	(OE)	❺	$125-135
☐ 195/I	5½"	(OE)	❻	$125
☐ 195	5¾ to 6"	(CE)	❶	$500-650
☐ 195	5¾ to 6"	(CE)	❷	$350-500

196/O

HUM 196
Telling Her Secret
When first modeled in 1948 by master sculptor Reinhold Unger this figurine was produced in one size only with the incised number 196. A smaller size was issued in the mid-1950's with the incised number 196/O. Some older models have "O" size designator directly under the 196 rather than 196/O. Slightly restyled in recent years. Most models have an incised 1948 copyright date. Old name: "The Secret." The girl on the right is the same as HUM 258 "Which Hand?"

☐ 196/0	5 to 5½"	(OE)	❷	$300-350
☐ 196/0	5 to 5½"	(OE)	❸	$150-200
☐ 196/0	5 to 5½"	(OE)	❹	$135-150
☐ 196/0	5 to 5½"	(OE)	❺	$125-135
☐ 196/0	5 to 5½"	(OE)	❻	$125
☐ 196/I	6½ to 6¾"	(OE)	❷	$500-750
☐ 196/I	6½ to 6¾"	(OE)	❸	$350-450
☐ 196/I	6½ to 6¾"	(OE)	❹	$250-300
☐ 196/I	6½ to 6¾"	(OE)	❺	$240-250
☐ 196/I	6½ to 6¾"	(OE)	❻	$240
☐ 196	6¾"	(CE)	❶	$750-1000
☐ 196	6¾"	(CE)	❷	$500-750

197/I

HUM 197
Be Patient
When first modeled in 1948 by master sculptor Reinhold Unger this figurine was produced in one size only with the incised number 197. A smaller size was issued in the mid-1950's with the incised number 197 2/O. At the same time, the large size was changed to 197/I. Both sizes have been restyled with the new textured finish and usually have an incised 1948 copyright date. Old name: "Mother of Ducks."

☐ 197 2/0.... 4¼ to 4½".. . (OE).... ❷ $150-200
☐ 197 2/0.... 4¼ to 4½".. . (OE).... ❸ $100-125
☐ 197 2/0.... 4¼ to 4½".. . (OE).... ❹ $85-100
☐ 197 2/0.... 4¼ to 4½".. . (OE).... ❺ $80-95
☐ 197 2/0.... 4¼ to 4½".. . (OE).... ❻ $77.50
☐ 197/I ..... 6 to 6¼"..... (OE).... ❷ $200-300
☐ 197/I ..... 6 to 6¼"..... (OE).... ❸ $150-200
☐ 197/I ..... 6 to 6¼"..... (OE).... ❹ $110-125
☐ 197/I ..... 6 to 6¼"..... (OE).... ❺ $105-110
☐ 197/I ..... 6 to 6¼"..... (OE).... ❻ $105
☐ 197 ...... 6¼" .... (CE).... ❶ $400-500
☐ 197 ...... 6¼" .... (CE).... ❷ $300-400

198/I

HUM 198
Home From Market
When first modeled in 1948 by master sculptor Arthur Moeller this figurine was produced in one size only with the incised number 198. A smaller size was issued in the mid-1950's with the incised number 198 2/O. At the same time, the large size was changed to 198/I. Many size variations with older models slightly larger than new. Both sizes have been restyled and now have an incised 1948 copyright date.

☐ 198 2/0	4½ to 4¾"	(OE)	❷	$125-150
☐ 198 2/0	4½ to 4¾"	(OE)	❸	$75-100
☐ 198 2/0	4½ to 4¾"	(OE)	❹	$60-75
☐ 198 2/0	4½ to 4¾"	(OE)	❺	$55-60
☐ 198 2/0	4½ to 4¾"	(OE)	❻	$55
☐ 198/I	5½"	(OE)	❷	$200-250
☐ 198/I	5½"	(OE)	❸	$125-150
☐ 198/I	5½"	(OE)	❹	$100-125
☐ 198/I	5½"	(OE)	❺	$90-95
☐ 198/I	5½"	(OE)	❻	$88
☐ 198	5¾ to 6"	(CE)	❶	$350-400
☐ 198	5¾ to 6"	(CE)	❷	$250-325

Old style **New style**

HUM 199 Feeding Time

When first modeled in 1948 by master sculptor Arthur Moeller this figurine was produced in one size only with the incised number 199. A smaller size was issued in the
mid-1950's with the incised number 199/O. At the same time, the large size was changed
to 199/I. Both sizes were restyled in the mid-1960's by master sculptor Gerhard Skrobek. The girl is blonde on older figurines—changed to dark hair and new facial fea-
tures on newer ones. Note position of girl's hand under bowl in new style figurines. All
small size and the new large size figurines have an incised 1948 copyright date.

☐ 199/0 . . . . . 4¼ to 4½" . . . (OE) . . . . ❷ $250-300
☐ 199/0 . . . . . 4¼ to 4½" . . . (OE) . . . . ❸ $150-200
☐ 199/0 . . . . . 4¼ to 4½" . . . (OE) . . . . ❹ $100-125
☐ 199/0 . . . . . 4¼ to 4½" . . . (OE) . . . . ❺ $90-100
☐ 199/0 . . . . . 4¼ to 4½" . . . (OE) . . . . ❻ $88
☐ 199/I . . . . . 5½ to 5¾" . . . (OE) . . . . ❷ $300-350
☐ 199/I . . . . . 5½ to 5¾" . . . (OE) . . . . ❸ $200-250
☐ 199/I . . . . . 5½ to 5¾" . . . (OE) . . . . ❹ $125-150
☐ 199/I . . . . . 5½ to 5¾" . . . (OE) . . . . ❺ $95-105
☐ 199/I . . . . . 5½ to 5¾" . . . (OE) . . . . ❻ $94.50
☐ 199 . . . . . . 5¾" . . . . (CE) . . . . ❶ $400-450
☐ 199 . . . . . . 5¾" . . . . (CE) . . . . ❷ $300-400

200/I (New style

HUM 200
Little Goat Herder
When first modeled in 1948 by master sculptor Arthur Moeller this figurine was made in one size only with the incised number 200. A smaller size was issued in the mid-1950's with the incised number 200/O. At the same time, the large size was changed to 200/I. Both sizes have been restyled with only minor changes. Older models have a blade of grass between hind legs of the small goat. Newer models do not. Newer models have an incised 1948 copyright date. Older pieces slightly larger. Old name: "Goat Boy."

☐ 200/0	4½ to 4¾"	(OE)	❷	$200-250
☐ 200/0	4½ to 4¾"	(OE)	❸	$100-150
☐ 200/0	4½ to 4¾"	(OE)	❹	$95-100
☐ 200/0	4½ to 4¾"	(OE)	❺	$85-95
☐ 200/0	4½ to 4¾"	(OE)	❻	$83
☐ 200/I	5 to 5½"	(OE)	❷	$225-275
☐ 200/I	5 to 5½"	(OE)	❸	$125-175
☐ 200/I	5 to 5½"	(OE)	❹	$105-125
☐ 200/I	5 to 5½"	(OE)	❺	$95-105
☐ 200/I	5 to 5½"	(OE)	❻	$94.50
☐ 200	5½ to 5¾"	(CE)	❶	$400-450
☐ 200	5½ to 5¾"	(CE)	❷	$250-350

HUM 201
Retreat To Safety
When first modeled in 1948 by master sculptor Reinhold Unger this figurine was produced in one size only with the incised number 201. A smaller size was issued in the mid-1950's with the incised number 201 2/O. At the same time, the large size was changed to 201/I. Both sizes have been restyled in recent years. Many size variations as well as variation in position of boy's hands in small size only: old model has one hand on each side of fence; new model, one hand on top of the other one. Most models have an incised 1948 copyright date. Old name: "Afraid."

☐ 201 2/0	3¾ to 4"	(OE)	❷	$150-195
☐ 201 2/0	3¾ to 4"	(OE)	❸	$100-125
☐ 201 2/0	3¾ to 4"	(OE)	❹	$80-100
☐ 201 2/0	3¾ to 4"	(OE)	❺	$75-80
☐ 201 2/0	3¾ to 4"	(OE)	❻	$72
☐ 201/I	5½ to 5¾"	(OE)	❷	$300-350
☐ 201/I	5½ to 5¾"	(OE)	❸	$150-200
☐ 201/I	5½ to 5¾"	(OE)	❹	$135-150
☐ 201/I	5½ to 5¾"	(OE)	❺	$125-135
☐ 201/I	5½ to 5¾"	(OE)	❻	$125
☐ 201	5¾ to 6"	(CE)	❶	$500-600
☐ 201	5¾ to 6"	(CE)	❷	$350-400

Factory sample

HUM 202
Old Man Reading Newspaper, Table Lamp (CN)
This unusual piece was made as a sample only in 1948 by master sculptor Arthur Moeller and was not approved by the Siessen Convent for production. It was not considered typical of Sister M.I. Hummel's work, although it is an exact replica of one of her early sketches. Same figure as HUM 181 except on lamp base. Listed as a Closed Number on 18 August 1948. This sample model is from Goebel factory archives.

☐ 202	8¼"	(CN)		$5000 +

| 203/I | 203 2/O (New style) | 203 2/O (Old style) |

HUM 203   Signs of Spring

When first modeled in 1948 by master sculptor Arthur Moeller this figurine was produced in one size only with the incised number 203. A smaller size was issued in the
mid-1950's with the incised number 203 2/O. At the same time, the large size was
changed to 203/I. Many size variations. At one time, small size only, was made with the
girl wearing both shoes. Full bee trademark pieces found both with or without shoe.
Newer models have an incised 1948 copyright date. Old name: "Scandal." "Two shoe"
variety considered rare, usually sells for $350 to $500.

☐ 203 2/0	4"	(CE)	❷	$350-500 (WITH TWO SHOES)
☐ 203 2/0	4"	(OE)	❷	$150-195
☐ 203 2/0	4"	(OE)	❸	$100-125
☐ 203 2/0	4"	(OE)	❹	$80-100
☐ 203 2/0	4"	(OE)	❺	$75-80
☐ 203 2/0	4"	(OE)	❻	$72
☐ 203/I	5 to 5½"	(OE)	❷	$225-275
☐ 203/I	5 to 5½"	(OE)	❸	$125-175
☐ 203/I	5 to 5½"	(OE)	❹	$105-125
☐ 203/I	5 to 5½"	(OE)	❺	$95-105
☐ 203/I	5 to 5½"	(OE)	❻	$94.50
☐ 203	5¼"	(CE)	❶	$350-500
☐ 203	5¼"	(CE)	❷	$250-300

Rear view

HUM 204
Weary Wanderer
Many size variations. Most models have 1949 as the incised copyright date. Old name: "Tired Little Traveler." Has been restyled with the new textured finish. The word "Lauterbach" on the back of fig-urine is the name of a village used in an old German song. The first model was made by master sculptor Reinhold Unger in 1949.

☐ 204 ...... 5½ to 6" ..... (OE).... ❶ $350-500
☐ 204 ......: 5½ to 6" ..... (OE).... ❷ $250-300
☐ 204 ...... 5½ to 6" ..... (OE).... ❸ $150-200
☐ 204 ...... 5½ to 6" ..... (OE).... ❹ $100-125
☐ 204 ...... 5½ to 6" ..... (OE).... ❺ $90-100
☐ 204 ...... 5½ to 6" ..... (OE).... ❻ $88

HUM 205
M.I. Hummel Dealer's Plaque
(in German) (CE)

This German dealer's plaque was first modeled by master sculptor Reinhold Unger in 1949. There are three color variations of lettering: all black lettering, black and red combination as pictured, and all black except the capital letters O, H and F in red lettering. Usually has an incised crown mark in addition to other trademark. The all-black variety usually has "Made in U.S. Zone, Germany" stamped on bottom. Listed in factory records as a Closed Edition on 18 June 1949 although it is found with the stylized trademark (in addition to the crown), indicating they were painted at a later date.

☐ 205 . . . . . . 5½ x 4¼" . . . (CE) . . . . ❶ $900-1000
☐ 205 . . . . . . 5½ x 4¼" . . . (CE) . . . . ❷ $750-900
☐ 205 . . . . . . 5½ x 4¼" . . . (CE) . . . . ❸ $500-750

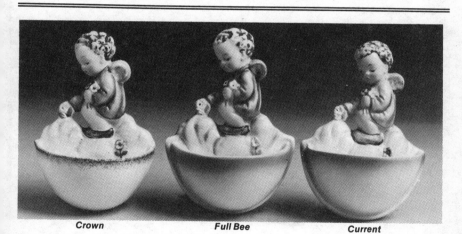

| Crown | Full Bee | Current |

HUM 206   Holy Water Font, Angel Cloud

This holy water font was originally modeled by master sculptor Reinhold Unger in 1949 but has been restyled several times. At least three different variations. Early models do not have rim on back side of bowl. Also color variations on lip of water bowl. Has been considered rare in the older trademarks but was put back into current production in 1978 and can now be found with 5 and 6 trademarks at more reasonable prices. Newer models have an incised 1949 copyright date.

☐ 206 . . . . . . 3¼ x 4¾" . . . (OE) . . . . ❶ $350-500
☐ 206 . . . . . . 3¼ x 4¾" . . . (OE) . . . . ❷ $250-350
☐ 206 . . . . . . 3¼ x 4¾" . . . (OE) . . . . ❸ $200-250
☐ 206 . . . . . . 3¼ x 4¾" . . . (OE) . . . . ❹ $50-75
☐ 206 . . . . . . 3¼ x 4¾" . . . (OE) . . . . ❺ $23-25
☐ 206 . . . . . . 3¼ x 4¾" . . . (OE) . . . . ❻ $23

New style   **Old style**

HUM 207
Holy Water Font, Heavenly Angel
This holy water font was originally modeled by master sculptor Reinhold Unger in 1949 and is the highest numbered piece with the crown trademark. Older models have a hole on the back for hanging while the newer models have a visible hole on the front. Early models do not have rim on back side of bowl. Newer models have an incised 1949 copyright date. The "Heavenly Angel" motif was used on the First Annual Plate HUM 264 in 1971.

☐ 207	3 x 5"	(OE)	❶	$200-250
☐ 207	3 x 5"	(OE)	❷	$75-100
☐ 207	3 x 5"	(OE)	❸	$30-35
☐ 207	3 x 5"	(OE)	❹	$25-30
☐ 207	3 x 5"	(OE)	❺	$23-25
☐ 207	3 x 5"	(OE)	❻	$23

Newer model

HUM 208
M.I. Hummel Dealer's Plaque
(in French) (CE)
Originally modeled in 1949 by master sculptor Reinhold Unger. Two known variations. Made with dotted "i" and without quotation marks on Hummel. Newer model has quotation marks: "HUMMEL" + "Reg. trade mark."

HUM 209
M.I. Hummel Dealer's Plaque
(in Swedish) (CE)
This extremely rare plaque was first modeled in 1949 by master sculptor Reinhold Unger and was apparently issued in extremely limited quantities. Some have sold for over $5,000.

☐ 208	5½ x 4"	(CE)	❷	$2000-2500
☐ 209	5½ x 4"	(CE)	❷	$2000-3000

HUM 210
M.I. Hummel Dealer's Plaque
(Schmid Bros.) (CE)
Normal dealer's plaque in English with "SCHMID BROS. INC. BOSTON" embossed on side of satchel of "Merry Wanderer." This extremely rare plaque was first modeled in 1950 by master sculptor Reinhold Unger. Also made with dotted "i" and without quotation marks. Very few are known to exist. Schmid Bros. was one of the early importers of "M.I. Hummel" figurines in 1935.

] 210 ...... 5½ x 4" ..... (CE).... ❷ .... $5000 +

Unpainted sample

UM 211   M.I. Hummel Dealer's Plaque (in English) (CE)
his is probably the most rare of all "M.I. Hummel" dealer's plaques. The only known ainted example was located in 1975 by Major Larry Spohn and his wife Anne while ey were living in Germany, and is now in the Robert L. Miller collection. All the lettering on this plaque is in lower case and the word "Oeslau" is used as the location of W. oebel Porzellanfabrik. Modeled in 1950 by master sculptor Reinhold Unger. The exct purpose or reason for designing this plaque still remains a mystery today.

| 211 ...... 5½ x 4" ..... (CE)....❷ .... $5000 +

HUM 212
Orchestra (CN)

Most notes from the Goebel factory state: "No information available" on this number. However, one old list indicates "Orchestra A-F" and the date "13 May 51." This is possibly a number assigned to a Hummel orchestra as a set, such as Hummel Nativity Set HUM 214. Another note states: "Modeled by Arthur Moeller in 1951."

☐ 212 .... (CN) ....

HUM 213
M.I. Hummel Dealer's Plaque
(in Spanish) (CE)

This Spanish dealer's plaque was first modeled in 1951 by master sculptor Reinhold Unger and apparently only a very limited number were produced. Considered extremely rare.

☐ 213 ...... 5¾ x 4¼" ... (CE).... ❷ $2000-3000

Nativity set in color

Discontinued white nativity set

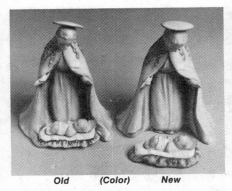

Old   (Color)   New   Old   (White)   New

Rare white pieces

Incised signature (HUM 214E)   Painted signature

New   *Old*

HUM 214   Nativity Set with Wooden Stable

This set was modeled by master sculptor Reinhold Unger in 1951. First produced and sold in 1952. Normally sold as a set but is also available in individual pieces. At one time this set was produced and sold in white overglaze finish but is no longer sold this way. The white overglaze finish is considered rare and usually brings a premium. Early production of HUM 214 A (Virgin Mary and Infant Jesus) was made in one piece. Because of production problems, it was later produced as two separate pieces, both with the same number (214 A) incised on the bottom of each piece. The one-piece unit was sold in white overglaze finish as well as full color finish and both are considered rare today. Two different styles of lambs (HUM 214/0) have been used with the Nativity sets —note variations in photo. Some Nativity set pieces have an incised 1951 copyright date. HUM 214/C, 214/D, 214/E and 214/H are not always included in sets and are considered "optional" pieces. The wooden stable is usually sold separately. The sixteenth piece, "Flying Angel" HUM 366, was added to the set in 1963. Goebel also produces three different camels to match this set which do not have the "M.I. Hummel" signature since they were not designed by Sister Hummel.

214 A Virgin Mary and Infant Jesus (one piece—CE)
214/A Virgin Mary
214/A Infant Jesus
214/B Joseph
214/C Angel standing, "Good Night"
214/D Angel kneeling, "Angel Serenade"
214/E We Congratulate
214/F Shepherd standing with sheep
214/G Shepherd kneeling
214/H Shepherd Boy, kneeling with flute "Little Tooter"
214/J Donkey
214/K Ox (cow)
214/L Moorish king, standing
214/M King, kneeling on one knee
214/N King, kneeling, with cash-box
214/O Lamb
366 Flying Angel

				COLOR	WHITE
☐ 214	SET 14 PIECES		❷	$2000-2500	☐ $2500-3000
☐ 214	SET 15 PIECES		❷	$1100-1250	☐ $1600-1750
☐ 214	SET 15 PIECES		❸	$1000-1100	☐ $1500-1600
☐ 214	SET 16 PIECES		❹	$950-1000	☐ $1400-1500
☐ 214	SET 16 PIECES		❺	$900-950	— —
☐ 214	SET 16 PIECES		❻	$888	—
☐ 214	SET 10 PIECES		❷	$1700-2150	☐ $2000-2500
☐ 214	SET 11 PIECES		❷	$850-900	☐ $1100-1250
☐ 214	SET 11 PIECES		❸	$800-850	☐ $1000-1100
☐ 214	SET 12 PIECES		❹	$750-800	☐ $900-1000
☐ 214	SET 12 PIECES		❺	$700-750	— —
☐ 214	SET 12 PIECES		❻	$695	—

				COLOR	WHITE
☐ 214A	1 PIECE 6½"	(CE)	❷	1500-2000	☐ 1750-2250
☐ 214A	6¼ to 6½"	(OE)	❷	120-150	☐ 150-200
☐ 214A	6¼ to 6½"	(OE)	❸	105-120	☐ 125-150
☐ 214A	6¼ to 6½"	(OE)	❹	90-105	☐ 100-125
☐ 214A	6¼ to 6½"	(OE)	❺	83-90	☐ 50-55
☐ 214A	6¼ to 6½"	(OE)	❻	82.50	☐ 50
☐ 214A	1½ x 3½"	(OE)	❷	40-50	☐ 60-75
☐ 214A	1½ x 3½"	(OE)	❸	35-40	☐ 50-60
☐ 214A	1½ x 3½"	(OE)	❹	30-35	☐ 40-50
☐ 214A	1½ x 3½"	(OE)	❺	28-30	☐ 20-22
☐ 214A	1½ x 3½"	(OE)	❻	27.50	☐ 20
☐ 214B	7½"	(OE)	❷	120-150	☐ 150-200
☐ 214B	7½"	(OE)	❸	105-120	☐ 125-150
☐ 214B	7½"	(OE)	❹	90-105	☐ 100-125
☐ 214B	7½"	(OE)	❺	83-90	☐ 56-60
☐ 214B	7½"	(OE)	❻	83	☐ 55.50
☐ 214C	3½"	(OE)	❷	60-70	☐ 200-250
☐ 214C	3½"	(OE)	❸	50-60	☐ 150-200
☐ 214C	3½"	(OE)	❹	43-50	☐ 100-150
☐ 214C	3½"	(OE)	❺	39-43	— —
☐ 214C	3½"	(OE)	❻	39	—
☐ 214D	3"	(OE)	❷	$45-60	☐ $125-150
☐ 214D	3"	(OE)	❸	$40-45	☐ $100-125
☐ 214D	3"	(OE)	❹	$35-40	☐ $75-100
☐ 214D	3"	(OE)	❺	$33-35	— —
☐ 214D	3"	(OE)	❻	$33	—
☐ 214E	3¾"	(OE)	❷	$90-120	☐ $200-250
☐ 214E	3¾"	(OE)	❸	$85-90	☐ $150-200
☐ 214E	3¾"	(OE)	❹	$75-85	☐ $100-150
☐ 214E	3¾"	(OE)	❺	$66-75	— —
☐ 214E	3¾"	(OE)	❻	$66	—
☐ 214F	7"	(OE)	❷	$110-160	☐ $150-200
☐ 214F	7"	(OE)	❸	$100-110	☐ $125-150
☐ 214F	7"	(OE)	❹	$95-100	☐ $100-125
☐ 214F	7"	(OE)	❺	$88-95	— —
☐ 214F	7"	(OE)	❻	$88	—
☐ 214G	5"	(OE)	❷	$80-100	☐ $125-150

				COLOR	WHITE
☐ 214G	5"	(OE)	❸	$75-80	☐ $100-125
☐ 214G	5"	(OE)	❹	$65-75	☐ $75-100
☐ 214G	5"	(OE)	❺	$60-65	— —
☐ 214G	5"	(OE)	❻	$60	—
☐ 214H	3¾ to 4"	(OE)	❷	$65-90	☐ $125-150
☐ 214H	3¾ to 4"	(OE)	❸	$60-65	☐ $100-125
☐ 214H	3¾ to 4"	(OE)	❹	$55-60	☐ $75-100
☐ 214H	3¾ to 4"	(OE)	❺	$50-55	— —
☐ 214H	3¾ to 4"	(OE)	❻	$50	—
☐ 214J	5"	(OE)	❷	$45-55	☐ $85-100
☐ 214J	5"	(OE)	❸	$40-45	☐ $75-85
☐ 214J	5"	(OE)	❹	$35-40	☐ $60-75
☐ 214J	5"	(OE)	❺	$31-35	— —
☐ 214J	5"	(OE)	❻	$30.50	—
☐ 214K	3½ x 6¼"	(OE)	❷	$45-55	☐ $85-100
☐ 214K	3½ x 6¼"	(OE)	❸	$40-45	☐ $75-85
☐ 214K	3½ x 6¼"	(OE)	❹	$35-40	☐ $60-75
☐ 214K	3½ x 6¼"	(OE)	❺	$31-35	— —
☐ 214K	3½ x 6¼"	(OE)	❻	$30.50	—
☐ 214L	8 to 8¼"	(OE)	❷	$100-150	☐ $150-200
☐ 214L	8 to 8¼"	(OE)	❸	$95-100	☐ $125-150
☐ 214L	8 to 8¼"	(OE)	❹	$90-95	☐ $100-125
☐ 214L	8 to 8¼"	(OE)	❺	$85-90	— —
☐ 214L	8 to 8¼"	(OE)	❻	$83	—
☐ 214M	5½"	(OE)	❷	$100-150	☐ $150-200
☐ 214M	5½"	(OE)	❸	$95-100	☐ $125-150
☐ 214M	5½"	(OE)	❹	$90-95	☐ $100-125
☐ 214M	5½"	(OE)	❺	$85-90	— —
☐ 214M	5½"	(OE)	❻	$83	—
☐ 214N	5½"	(OE)	❷	$100-150	☐ $150-200
☐ 214N	5½"	(OE)	❸	$95-100	☐ $125-150
☐ 214N	5½"	(OE)	❹	$85-95	☐ $100-125
☐ 214N	5½"	(OE)	❺	$77-85	— —
☐ 214N	5½"	(OE)	❻	$77	—
☐ 214O	1¾ x 2½"	(OE)	❷	$15-25	☐ $40-50
☐ 214O	1¾ x 2½"	(OE)	❸	$12-15	☐ $25-40
☐ 214O	1¾ x 2½"	(OE)	❹	$10-12	☐ $20-25
☐ 214O	1¾ x 2½"	(OE)	❺	$9-10	— —
☐ 214O	1¾ x 2½"	(OE)	❻	$9	—
☐ 366	3½"	(OE)	❹	$60-75	☐ $25-30
☐ 366	3½"	(OE)	❺	$55-60	☐ $20-25
☐ 366	3½"	(OE)	❻	$55	☐ $20

☐ Wooden stable................Current retail $55

HUM 215 (CN)

Factory records indicate: A child Jesus standing with lamb in arms. Listed as a Closed Number on 16 August 1951. No known examples.

HUM 216 (CN)

Factory records indicate: Joyful, ashtray without rest for cigarette. Listed as a Closed Number on 10 September 1951. No known examples.

☐ 215 .... (CN) ....
☐ 216 .... (CN) ....

HUM 217
Boy With Toothache

First modeled by master sculptor Arthur Moeller in 1951. Older figurines are slightly larger. Older models have "©WG" after the "M.I. Hummel" signature. Old name: "At the Dentist" or "Toothache." Newer models have an incised 1951 copyright date. Some slight variations in color are found, but would not affect value.

☐ 217 ...... 5¼ to 5½" ... (OE) .... ❷ $125-185
☐ 217 ...... 5¼ to 5½" ... (OE) .... ❸ $100-125
☐ 217 ...... 5¼ to 5½" ... (OE) .... ❹ $85-100
☐ 217 ...... 5¼ to 5½" ... (OE) .... ❺ $80-85
☐ 217 ...... 5¼ to 5½" ... (OE) .... ❻ $77.50

New style (OE)	*Old style (CE)*

HUM 218 Birthday Serenade

First modeled by master sculptor Reinhold Unger in 1952. Early models bearing an incised 1952 copyright date have boy playing horn, girl playing accordion. Remodeled in 1964 by master sculptor Gerhard Skrobek. Newer models bearing an incised 1965 copyright date have boy playing accordion, girl playing horn. This change was made at the request of the convent. The large size (HUM 218/0) had been considered rare but is again back in production with current trademark with boy playing accordion and girl playing horn with an incised 1952 copyright date. This was an error as it should have been 1965. Note that a tie has been added to the boy when he plays the accordion. Both styles can be found with TM 4.

☐ 218 2/0 .... 4¼ to 4½" ... (OE) .... ❹ $85-100
☐ 218 2/0 .... 4¼ to 4½" ... (OE) .... ❺ $80-85
☐ 218 2/0 .... 4¼ to 4½" ... (OE) .... ❻ $77.50
☐ 218 2/0 .... 4¼ to 4½" ... (CE) .... ❷ $450-500
☐ 218 2/0 .... 4¼ to 4½" ... (CE) .... ❸ $400-450
☐ 218 2/0 .... 4¼ to 4½" ... (CE) .... ❹ $300-400
☐ 218/0 ..... 5¼" .... (OE) .... ❺ $125-140
☐ 218/0 ..... 5¼" .... (OE) .... ❻ $125
☐ 218/0 ..... 5¼" .... (CE) .... ❷ $600-750
☐ 218/0 ..... 5¼" .... (CE) .... ❸ $550-650
☐ 218/0 ..... 5¼" .... (CE) .... ❹ $500-600
☐ 218 ...... 5¼" .... (CE) .... ❷ $750-800

"Little Velma"

HUM 219
Little Velma (CE)
This figurine was designed in 1952 by master sculptor Reinhold Unger. According to factory records this figurine was produced in very limited numbers (possibly less than 50 pieces) because of its similarity to other models. The name "Little Velma" was affectionately assigned to this piece in honor of the lady who first brought it to the attention of, and sold it to, this author. Most of these figurines must have been shipped to Canada as most known examples can be traced to that country.

☐ 219 2/0.... 4" .... (CN) ... ❷ ... $3000-5000

220 2/O (with base)

HUM 220
We Congratulate (with base)
First modeled by master sculptor Arthur Moeller in 1952. Early production pieces have the incised number 220 2/0. Later production dropped the 2/0 size designator and added the 1952 incised copyright date. This figurine is the same as HUM 214/E and HUM 260/F in the Nativity Sets, except with base and no flowers in girl's hair. Also note lederhosen straps added to boy.

☐ 220 ...... 3¾ to 4" ..... (OE).... ❷ $150-195
☐ 220 ...... 3¾ to 4" ..... (OE).... ❸ $100-125
☐ 220 ...... 3¾ to 4" ..... (OE).... ❹ $80-95
☐ 220 ...... 3¾ to 4" ..... (OE).... ❺ $75-80
☐ 220 ...... 3¾ to 4" ..... (OE).... ❻ $72
☐ 220 2/0.... 4" .... (CE).... ❷ $250-325

(Factory sample)

HUM 221
Happy Pastime, Candy Jar (CN)
This candy jar was made as a sample only and was never produced for sale. First modeled by master sculptor Arthur Moeller in 1952. To my knowledge, there are no examples in private collections.

☐ 221 .... (CN) .... $5000 +

Two variations

HUM 222
Madonna Plaque (with metal frame) (CE)
Originally modeled by master sculptor Reinhold Unger in 1952. There are basically two different styles of metal frames —both pictured here. Found without frame with full bee trademark but unconfirmed if actually sold that way. Similar in design to HUM 48 "Madonna Plaque." Usually found with gray felt backing, which would have to be removed to see the incised number.

☐ 222 ...... 4 x 5" .... (CE).... ❷ $750-1250
☐ 222 ...... 4 x 5" .... (CE).... ❸ $750-1000

223   **101**

HUM 223
To Market, Table Lamp

This lamp was originally modeled by master sculptor Arthur Moeller in 1937 as HUM 101 and later restyled by him in 1952. It is similar to the original model with the exception of the size and a flower added to branch of tree trunk. Measures 5¼″ across the base. Called "Surprise" in old 1955 catalogue.

☐ 223	9½″	(OE)	❷	$350-500
☐ 223	9½″	(OE)	❸	$260-275
☐ 223	9½″	(OE)	❹	$250-260
☐ 223	9½″	(OE)	❺	$240-250
☐ 223	9½″	(OE)	❻	$240

224/II   **224/I**

HUM 224
Wayside Harmony, Table Lamp

This lamp was modeled by master sculptor Reinhold Unger in 1952 and is actually a restyling of HUM II/111 "Wayside Harmony" lamp made in 1938. Large size same as small with the exception of a flower on branch of tree trunk. Small size measures 4¼″ across base. Large size measures 6¼″ across base. Early examples of the large (9½″) size usually found without size designator, incised 224 only and usually have a switch on the base.

☐ 224/I	7½″	(OE)	❷	$300-325
☐ 224/I	7½″	(OE)	❸	$200-225

☐ 224/I	7½"	(OE)	❹	$190-200
☐ 224/I	7½"	(OE)	❺	$180-190
☐ 224/I	7½"	(OE)	❻	$180
☐ 224/II	9½"	(OE)	❷	$350-500
☐ 224/II	9½"	(OE)	❸	$275-350
☐ 224/II	9½"	(OE)	❹	$245-275
☐ 224/II	9½"	(OE)	❺	$220-245
☐ 224/II	9½"	(OE)	❻	$220
☐ 224	9½"	(CE)	❷	$350-500

225/II   **225/I**

HUM 225
Just Resting, Table Lamp
This lamp was modeled by master sculptor Reinhold Unger in 1952 and is actually a restyling of HUM II/112 "Just Resting" lamp made in 1938. Large size same as small with the exception of a flower on branch of tree trunk. Small size measures 4¼" across base. Large size measures 6¼" across base. Early examples of the large (9½") size usually found without size designator, incised 225 only and usually have a switch on the base.

☐ 225/I	7½"	(OE)	❷	$300-325
☐ 225/I	7½"	(OE)	❸	$200-225
☐ 225/I	7½"	(OE)	❹	$190-200
☐ 225/I	7½"	(OE)	❺	$180-190
☐ 225/I	7½"	(OE)	❻	$180
☐ 225/II	9½"	(OE)	❷	$350-500
☐ 225/II	9½"	(OE)	❸	$275-350
☐ 225/II	9½"	(OE)	❹	$245-275
☐ 225/II	9½"	(OE)	❺	$220-245
☐ 225/II	9½"	(OE)	❻	$220
☐ 225	9½"	(CE)	❷	$350-500

HUM 226   The Mail Is Here
Originally modeled by master sculptor Arthur Moeller in 1952. Older pieces are slightly
larger in size. Also called "Mail Coach." Usually has an incised 1952 copyright date.
Some older examples have a very faint "M.I. Hummel" signature while others have the
signature painted on because of this light impression.

☐ 226 . . . . . . 4¼ x 6 to
           4½ x 6¼" . . . (OE). . . . ❷ $500-750
☐ 226 . . . . . . 4¼ x 6" . . . . . (OE). . . . ❸ $350-500
☐ 226 . . . . . . 4¼ x 6" . . . . . (OE). . . . ❹ $300-350
☐ 226 . . . . . . 4¼ x 6" . . . . . (OE). . . . ❺ $265-300
☐ 226 . . . . . . 4¼ x 6" . . . . . (OE). . . . ❻ $265

227   228

HUM 227
She Loves Me, She Loves Me Not
Table Lamp
This lamp was first modeled in 1953 by
master sculptor Arthur Moeller and has
been restyled several times. On the older
lamps the figure much larger and the
boy's eyes are open. On the newer
models the eyes are looking down. Same
motif as HUM 174 of the same name.
Measures 4″ across the base. Refer to
HUM 251 for matching bookends.

HUM 228
Good Friends, Table Lamp
This lamp was first modeled in 1953 by
master sculptor Arthur Moeller and has
been restyled several times. On the older
lamps the figure is much larger and the
tree trunk post has a smoother finish.
Same motif as HUM 182 of the same
name. Measures 4¼″ across the base.
Refer to HUM 251 for matching bookends.

☐ 227	7½″	(OE)	❷	$350-500
☐ 227	7½″	(OE)	❸	$200-250
☐ 227	7½″	(OE)	❹	$185-200
☐ 227	7½″	(OE)	❺	$170-185
☐ 227	7½″	(OE)	❻	$168
☐ 228	7½″	(OE)	❷	$350-500
☐ 228	7½″	(OE)	❸	$200-250
☐ 228	7½″	(OE)	❹	$185-200
☐ 228	7½″	(OE)	❺	$170-185
☐ 228	7½″	(OE)	❻	$168

229   230

HUM 229
Apple Tree Girl, Table Lamp
This lamp was first modeled in 1953 by master sculptor Arthur Moeller and has been restyled several times. On the older lamps the figure is much larger but the post still measures only 7½ inches. Measures 4¼″ across base. Old name: "Spring" or "Springtime." Refer to HUM 252 for matching bookends.

HUM 230
Apple Tree Boy, Table Lamp
This lamp was first modeled in 1953 by master sculptor Arthur Moeller and has been restyled several times. On the older lamps the figure is much larger but the post still measures only 7½ inches. Measures 4¼″ across base. Old name: "Autumn" or "Fall" table lamp. Refer to HUM 252 for matching bookends.

☐ 229	7½″	(OE)	❷	$500-750
☐ 229	7½″	(OE)	❸	$200-250
☐ 229	7½″	(OE)	❹	$185-200
☐ 229	7½″	(OE)	❺	$170-185
☐ 229	7½″	(OE)	❻	$168
☐ 230	7½″	(OE)	❷	$500-750
☐ 230	7½″	(OE)	❸	$200-250
☐ 230	7½″	(OE)	❹	$185-200
☐ 230	7½″	(OE)	❺	$170-185
☐ 230	7½″	(OE)	❻	$168

231　　New　　234　　　　231　　Old　　234

HUM 231
Birthday Serenade, Table Lamp
This lamp was first modeled by master sculptor Reinhold Unger and was restyled in 1976 by master sculptor Rudolf Wittman. The early model measures 6" across the base and has a hole for electrical switch on top of the base. Had been considered rare but is again in current production with 5 and 6 trademarks. Early models have an incised 1954 copyright date. The musical instruments have been reversed on the current production models. Refer to HUM 218 "Birthday Serenade" figurine for more details.

HUM 234
Birthday Serenade, Table Lamp
This smaller size lamp was also modeled in 1954 by master sculptor Reinhold Unger and the first sample was painted in October 1954 by artist Georg Mechtold (initials "GM"). Similar to HUM 231 with the exception of having no flower on branch of tree trunk. Older models have an incised 1954 copyright date. Restyled in 1976 by master sculptor Rudolf Wittmann with the musical instruments in the reverse position. Had been considered rare but is again in current production. Trademark 4 examples can be found in either style.

☐ 231	9¾"	(OE)	❺	$240-265
☐ 231	9¾"	(OE)	❻	$240
☐ 231	9¾"	(CE)	❷	$2000-3000
☐ 234	7¾"	(OE)	❺	$210-230
☐ 234	7¾"	(OE)	❻	$210
☐ 234	7¾"	(CE)	❷	$1500-2000
☐ 234	7¾"	(CE)	❸	$1000-1500
☐ 234	7¾"	(CE)	❹	$300-1000

232 (Old)   235 (Old)

HUM 232
Happy Days, Table Lamp
This lamp was first modeled in 1954 by master sculptor Reinhold Unger and was restyled in 1976. The early model measures 6″ across the base and has a hole for electrical switch at top of base. Had been considered rare but is again in current production with 5 and 6 trademarks. Early models have an incised 1954 copyright date.

HUM 235
Happy Days, Table Lamp
This smaller size lamp was also modeled in 1954 by master sculptor Reinhold Unger and the first sample was painted in October 1954 by artist Georg Mechtold (initials "GM"). Similar to HUM 232 with the exception of having no flower on branch of tree trunk. Older models have an incised 1954 copyright date. Restyled in 1976 and again in current production.

☐ 232 ...... 9¾″ .... (OE) .... ❷ $1000-1500
☐ 232 ...... 9¾″ .... (OE) .... ❺ $240-265
☐ 232 ...... 9¾″ .... (OE) .... ❻ $240

☐ 235 ...... 7¾″ .... (OE) .... ❷ $750-1000
☐ 235 ...... 7¾″ .... (OE) .... ❸ $500-750
☐ 235 ...... 7¾″ .... (OE) .... ❹ $250-500
☐ 235 ...... 7¾″ .... (OE) .... ❺ $210-230
☐ 235 ...... 7¾″ .... (OE) .... ❻ $210

HUM 233 (CN)
Factory records indicate a sample of a "boy feeding birds." Listed as a Closed Number on 7 September 1954. No known examples. Gerhard Skrobek, current master modeler at the factory, stated that this was the first figure he modeled after starting to work at W. Goebel Porzellanfabrik in 1954. Skrobek later restyled this figurine which now appears as HUM 300 "Bird Watcher," issued in 1979.

HUM 236 (ON)
Factory records contain no information at all regarding this number. It has therefore been listed as an Open Number and may be assigned to a future item.

☐ 236 .... (ON) ....

HUM 237
Star Gazer, Wall Plaque (CN)
This plaque was made as a sample only and not produced for sale as an open edition. This white overglaze (unpainted) example was recently located at the Goebel factory and is pictured here for the first time in any book, price guide, or catalogue regarding the subject of "M.I. Hummel" figurines. Was designed in 1954 and apparently rejected by Siessen Convent for production. Note the "M.I. Hummel" signature in the left hand corner. I have not been able to confirm the name of the original modeler of this rare item.

☐ 237 ...... 4¾ x 5" ..... (CN) .... $5000 +

238A   238B   238C

HUM 238 A
Angel With Lute
One of a set of three small angel figures
known as the "Angel Trio." Similar to
HUM 38 except without holder for candle.
Modeled by master sculptor Gerhard
Skrobek in 1967. Has a 1967 incised copy-
right date and only produced with trade-
marks 4, 5 and 6.

HUM 238 B
Angel With Accordion
One of a set of three small angel figures
known as the "Angel Trio." Similar to
HUM 39 except without holder for candle.
Modeled by master sculptor Gerhard
Skrobek in 1967. Has a 1967 incised copy-
right date and only produced with trade-
marks 4, 5 and 6.

HUM 238 C
Angel With Trumpet
One of a set of three small angel figures
known as the "Angel Trio." Similar to
HUM 40 except without holder for candle.
Modeled by master sculptor Gerhard
Skrobek in 1967. Has a 1967 incised copy-
right date and only produced with trade-
marks 4, 5 and 6.

☐ 238 A . . . . . 2 to 2½" . . . . . (OE) . . . . ❹ $25-50
☐ 238 A . . . . . 2 to 2½" . . . . . (OE) . . . . ❺ $23-25
☐ 238 A . . . . . 2 to 2½" . . . . . (OE) . . . . ❻ $23
☐ 238 B . . . . . 2 to 2½" . . . . . (OE) . . . . ❹ $25-50
☐ 238 B . . . . . 2 to 2½" . . . . . (OE) . . . . ❺ $23-25
☐ 238 B . . . . . 2 to 2½" . . . . . (OE) . . . . ❻ $23
☐ 238 C . . . . . 2 to 2½" . . . . . (OE) . . . . ❹ $25-50
☐ 238 C . . . . . 2 to 2½" . . . . . (OE) . . . . ❺ $23-25
☐ 238 C . . . . . 2 to 2½" . . . . . (OE) . . . . ❻ $23

239A   239B   239C

HUM 239 A
Girl With Nosegay
One of a set of three small children figurines known as the "Children Trio." Similar to HUM 115 except without holder for candle. Modeled by master sculptor Gerhard Skrobek in 1967. Has a 1967 incised copyright date and only produced with trademarks 4, 5 and 6.

HUM 239 B
Girl With Doll
One of a set of three small children figurines known as the "Children Trio." Similar to HUM 116 except without holder for candle. Modeled by master sculptor Gerhard Skrobek in 1967. Has a 1967 incised copyright date and only produced with trademarks 4, 5 and 6.

HUM 239 C
Boy With Horse
One of a set of three small children figurines known as the "Children Trio." Similar to HUM 117 except without holder for candle. Modeled by master sculptor Gerhard Skrobek in 1967. Has a 1967 incised copyright date and only produced with trademarks 4, 5 and 6.

☐ 239 A . . . . . 3½" . . . . (OE) . . . . ❹ $30-50
☐ 239 A . . . . . 3½" . . . . (OE) . . . . ❺ $25-30
☐ 239 A . . . . . 3½" . . . . (OE) . . . . ❻ $25
☐ 239 B . . . . . 3½" . . . . (OE) . . . . ❹ $30-50
☐ 239 B . . . . . 3½" . . . . (OE) . . . . ❺ $25-30
☐ 239 B . . . . . 3½" . . . . (OE) . . . . ❻ $25
☐ 239 C . . . . . 3½" . . . . (OE) . . . . ❹ $30-50
☐ 239 C . . . . . 3½" . . . . (OE) . . . . ❺ $25-30
☐ 239 C . . . . . 3½" . . . . (OE) . . . . ❻ $25

HUM 240
Little Drummer
First modeled by master sculptor Reinhold Unger in 1955. Older pieces are usually slightly larger. Has an incised 1955 copyright date. Sometimes listed as "Drummer" even in recent price lists and catalogues. Similar to boy in HUM 50 "Volunteers."

☐ 240	4 to 4¼"	(OE)	❷	$100-150
☐ 240	4 to 4¼"	(OE)	❸	$75-100
☐ 240	4 to 4¼"	(OE)	❹	$60-75
☐ 240	4 to 4¼"	(OE)	❺	$55-60
☐ 240	4 to 4¼"	(OE)	❻	$55

HUM 241
Angel Lights, Candleholder
This number was assigned to this newly designed piece in error. Sometimes referred to as "Angel Bridge." Originally modeled by current master sculptor Gerhard Skrobek in 1976, this is an adaptation of HUM 21 "Heavenly Angel." Usually sold with a round plate which this piece is designed to fit. Found with trademarks 5 and 6 only. Sometimes listed as "241 B" but only the number 241 is incised on this item.

☐ 241 ..... 10⅓ x 8⅓" .... (OE) .... ❺ $142-150
☐ 241 ..... 10⅓ x 8⅓" .... (OE) .... ❻ $142
☐ 241 ..... (Font) .... (CN) ....
☐ 242 ..... (Font) .... (CN) ....

HUM 241
**Holy Water Font, Angel Joyous News
With Lute (CN)**
This font was first modeled by master
sculptor Reinhold Unger in 1955. Made as
a sample only and not produced for sale
as an open edition. Listed as a Closed
Number on 6 April 1955.

HUM 242
**Holy Water Font, Angel Joyous News
With Trumpet (CN)**
This font was first modeled by master
sculptor Reinhold Unger in 1955. Made as
a sample only and not produced for sale
as an open edition. Listed as a Closed
Number on 6 April 1955.

HUM 243
Holy Water Font, Madonna And Child
This font was first modeled by master sculptor Reinhold Unger in 1955. Has an incised 1955 copyright date. Apparently not put on the market until the mid-1960's. Earliest catalogue listing found is 1967. No known variations have been recorded.

☐ 243 . . . . . . 3⅛ x 4" . . . . . . (OE) . . . . ❷ $100-150
☐ 243 . . . . . . 3⅛ x 4" . . . . . . (OE) . . . . ❸ $40-50
☐ 243 . . . . . . 3⅛ x 4" . . . . . . (OE) . . . . ❹ $30-35
☐ 243 . . . . . . 3⅛ x 4" . . . . . . (OE) . . . . ❺ $23-25
☐ 243 . . . . . . 3⅛ x 4" . . . . . . (OE) . . . . ❻ $23

HUM 244 (ON)
Factory records contain no information at all regarding this number. It has therefore been listed as an Open Number and may be assigned to a future item.

☐ 244 . . . . (ON) . . . .

HUM 245 (ON)
Factory records contain no information at all regarding this number. It has therefore been listed as an Open Number and may be assigned to a future item.

☐ 245 . . . . (ON) . . . .

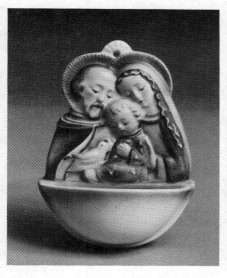

HUM 246
Holy Water Font, Holy Family
Master sculptor Theo R. Menzenbach modeled this font in 1955. Earliest catalogue listing is in 1955 Second Edition Schmid Brothers. Has an incised 1955 copyright date. No known variations have been recorded.

☐ 246 ...... 3⅛ x 4½ " .... (OE)....❷.... $100-150
☐ 246 ...... 3⅛ x 4½ " .... (OE)....❸.... $50-75
☐ 246 ...... 3⅛ x 4½ " .... (OE)....❹.... $30-50
☐ 246 ...... 3⅛ x 4½ " .... (OE)....❺.... $27-30
☐ 246 ...... 3⅛ x 4½ " .... (OE)....❻.... $26.50

HUM 247
Standing Madonna With Child (CN)
This beautiful Madonna with Child was made as a sample only and not produced for sale as an open edition. It was modeled by master sculptor Theo R. Menzenbach in 1961 and apparently was rejected by the Siessen Convent for some unknown reason.

☐ 247 ...... 13 .... (CN) .... $5000 +

248/O

HUM 248
Holy Water Font, Guardian Angel
This font was first modeled by master sculptor Gerhard Skrobek in 1958. Most models have an incised 1959 copyright date. This is a restyled version of HUM 29 which was discontinued at the time HUM 248 was introduced. This font was originally modeled in two sizes (248/0 and 248/I) but to my knowledge the large size was never put on the market. Factory information reveals that in the future it will be made in only the smaller size and "0" size designator will eventually disappear —so far this has not happened.

☐ 248/0	2⅜ x 5⅝"	(OE)	❸	$100-150
☐ 248/0	2⅜ x 5⅝"	(OE)	❹	$30-50
☐ 248/0	2⅜ x 5⅝"	(OE)	❺	$25-30
☐ 248/0	2¼ x 5½"	(OE)	❻	$23
☐ 248/I	2¾ x 6¼"	(CE)	❸	$500-1000

HUM 249
Madonna and Child (in relief)
Wall Plaque (CN)
This wall plaque was made as a sample only and not produced for sale as an open edition. Similar to HUM 48/V except without background or frame. Actually, the piece that I saw and is pictured here was simply a cut-out of HUM 48/V in an unfinished state, with no number or signature on the back—apparently an idea that was rejected or stopped before it was even completed. Possibly the work of master sculptor Reinhold Unger who modeled the first HUM 48 in 1936.

☐ 249	6¾ x 8¾"	(CN)		$5000 +

HUM 250 A
Little Goat Herder, Bookend

HUM 250 B
Feeding Time, Bookend
Factory records indicate these bookends were designed by a team of modelers in 1960. First sold in the U.S. in 1964. The bookends are simply normal figurines affixed to a wooden base. Refer to HUM 199 and HUM 200 for more information.

250 A & B (priced as set)

☐ 250 A & B . 5½" .... (OE).... ❸ $200-250
☐ 250 A & B . 5½" .... (OE).... ❺ $170-190
☐ 250 A & B . 5½" .... (OE).... ❻ $170

HUM 251 A
Good Friends, Bookend

HUM 251 B
She Loves Me, She Loves Me Not!
Bookend
Factory records indicate these bookends were designed by a team of modelers in 1960. First sold in the U.S. in 1964. The bookends are simply normal figurines affixed to a wooden base. Refer to HUM 174 and HUM 182 for more information.

251 A & B (priced as set)

☐ 251 A & B . 5" .... (OE).... ❸ $200-250
☐ 251 A & B . 5" .... (OE).... ❺ $170-190
☐ 251 A & B . 5" .... (OE).... ❻ $170

HUM 252 A
Apple Tree Girl, Bookend

HUM 252 B
Apple Tree Boy, Bookend
Factory records indicate these bookends were designed by a team of modelers in 1962. First sold in the U.S. in 1964. The bookends are simply normal figurines affixed to a wooden base. Refer to HUM 141 and HUM 142 for more information.

252 A & B (priced as set)

☐ 252 A & B . 5" .... (OE).... ❸ $200-250
☐ 252 A & B . 5" .... (OE).... ❺ $170-190
☐ 252 A & B . 5" .... (OE).... ❻ $170

HUM 253 (CN)
Factory records indicate a girl with basket similar to the one in HUM 52 "Going to Grandma's." No known examples.

☐ 253 ...... 4½" .... (CN) ....

HUM 254 (CN)
Factory records indicate a girl playing a mandolin similar to the one in HUM 150 "Happy Days." No known examples.

☐ 254 ...... 4¼" .... (CN) ....

HUM 255
Stitch In Time
First modeled by a combination of sculptors in 1962. Has an incised 1963 copyright date. First sold in the U.S. in 1964. Similar to one of the girls used in HUM 256 "Knitting Lesson" and HUM 177 "School Girls." No unusual variations have been recorded.

☐ 255 ...... 6½ to 6¾" ... (OE).... ❸ $150-250
☐ 255 ...... 6½ to 6¾" ... (OE).... ❹ $105-125
☐ 255 ...... 6½ to 6¾" ... (OE).... ❺ $95-105
☐ 255 ...... 6½ to 6¾" ... (OE).... ❻ $94.50

HUM 256
Knitting Lesson
First modeled by a combination of sculptors in 1962. Has an incised 1963 copyright date. First sold in the U.S. in 1964. Similar to two girls used in HUM 177 "School Girls." No unusual variations have been recorded.

☐ 256 . . . . . . 7½" . . . . (OE) . . . . ❸ $300-350
☐ 256 . . . . . . 7½" . . . . (OE) . . . . ❹ $240-275
☐ 256 . . . . . . 7½" . . . . (OE) . . . . ❺ $220-240
☐ 256 . . . . . . 7½" . . . . (OE) . . . . ❻ $220

HUM 257
For Mother
First modeled by a combination of sculptors in 1962. Has an incised 1963 copyright date. First sold in the U.S. in 1964. No unusual variations have been recorded.

☐ 257 . . . . . . 5 to 5¼" . . . . . (OE) . . . . ❸ $150-250
☐ 257 . . . . . . 5 to 5¼" . . . . . (OE) . . . . ❹ $70-90
☐ 257 . . . . . . 5 to 5¼" . . . . . (OE) . . . . ❺ $65-70
☐ 257 . . . . . . 5 to 5¼" . . . . . (OE) . . . . ❻ $63

HUM 258
Which Hand?
First modeled by a combination of sculptors in 1962. Has an incised 1963 copyright date. First sold in the U.S. in 1964. Similar to girl used in HUM 296 "Telling Her Secret." No unusual variations have been recorded.

□ 258 ......5¼ to 5½".. (OE)....❸.... $150-250
□ 258 ......5¼ to 5½".. (OE)....❹.... $70-90
□ 258 ......5¼ to 5½".. (OE)....❺.... $65-70
□ 258 ......5¼ to 5½".. (OE)....❻.... $63

(Factory sample)

HUM 259
Girl With Accordion (CN)

Modeled by a combination of sculptors in 1962, this figurine depicts a girl playing an accordion as in HUM 218 "Birthday Serenade." This piece was made as a sample only and not produced for sale as an open edition. Listed as a Closed Number on factory records of 8 November 1962.

□ 259 ......4" .... (CN) .... $5000 +

Large size nativity set

HUM 260
Large Nativity Set (with wooden stable)
This large size Nativity set was first modeled in 1968 by current master sculptor Gerhard Skrobek. First sold in the U.S. in the early 1970's. Various styles of wooden stables have been produced through the years. The stable is priced at $290 currently, although it is usually included in the price of the set. This set consists of sixteen pieces, larger and more detailed than the small Nativity set HUM 214. Individual pieces can be purchased separately but are normally sold as a set.

260 A Madonna	260 J Shepherd Boy, kneeling
260 B Saint Joseph	260 K Little Tooter
260 C Infant Jesus	260 L Donkey, standing
260 D Good Night	260 M Cow, lying
260 E Angel Serenade	260 N Moorish King, standing
260 F We Congratulate	260 O King, standing
260 G Shepherd, standing	260 P King, kneeling
260 H Sheep, standing with lamb	260 R One Sheep, lying

☐ 260	SET 16 PIECES	(OE)	❹	$3200-3500	INCLUDES STABLE
☐ 260	SET 16 PIECES	(OE)	❺	$2930-3200	INCLUDES STABLE
☐ 260	SET 16 PIECES	(OE)	❻	$2930	INCLUDES STABLE
☐ 260A	9¾"	(OE)	❹	$320-375	
☐ 260A	9¾"	(OE)	❺	$290-320	
☐ 260A	9¾"	(OE)	❻	$290	
☐ 260B	11¾"	(OE)	❹	$320-375	
☐ 260B	11¾"	(OE)	❺	$290-320	
☐ 260B	11¾"	(OE)	❻	$290	
☐ 260C	5¾"	(OE)	❹	$65-75	
☐ 260C	5¾"	(OE)	❺	$60-65	
☐ 260C	5¾"	(OE)	❻	$60	
☐ 260D	5¼"	(OE)	❹	$85-95	
☐ 260D	5¼"	(OE)	❺	$75-85	
☐ 260D	5¼"	(OE)	❻	$75.50	
☐ 260E	4¼"	(OE)	❹	$75-85	
☐ 260E	4¼"	(OE)	❺	$66-75	
☐ 260E	4¼"	(OE)	❻	$66	
☐ 260F	6¼"	(OE)	❹	$220-275	
☐ 260F	6¼"	(OE)	❺	$200-220	
☐ 260F	6¼"	(OE)	❻	$200	
☐ 260G	11¾"	(OE)	❹	$345-395	
☐ 260G	11¾"	(OE)	❺	$315-345	
☐ 260G	11¾"	(OE)	❻	$315	
☐ 260H	3¾"	(OE)	❹	$60-70	
☐ 260H	3¾"	(OE)	❺	$55-60	
☐ 260H	3¾"	(OE)	❻	$55	
☐ 260J	7"	(OE)	❹	$190-215	
☐ 260J	7"	(OE)	❺	$174-190	
☐ 260J	7"	(OE)	❻	$174	
☐ 260K	5⅛"	(OE)	❹	$95-105	
☐ 260K	5⅛"	(OE)	❺	$84-95	
☐ 260K	5⅛"	(OE)	❻	$84	
☐ 260L	7½"	(OE)	❹	$75-85	
☐ 260L	7½"	(OE)	❺	$66-75	
☐ 260L	7½"	(OE)	❻	$66	
☐ 260M	6 x 11"	(OE)	❹	$95-105	
☐ 260M	6 x 11"	(OE)	❺	$84-95	
☐ 260M	6 x 11"	(OE)	❻	$84	
☐ 260N	12¾"	(OE)	❹	$320-375	
☐ 260N	12¾"	(OE)	❺	$290-320	
☐ 260N	12¾"	(OE)	❻	$290	
☐ 260O	12"	(OE)	❹	$320-375	
☐ 260O	12"	(OE)	❺	$290-320	
☐ 260O	12"	(OE)	❻	$290	
☐ 260P	9"	(OE)	❹	$300-340	
☐ 260P	9"	(OE)	❺	$273-300	
☐ 260P	9"	(OE)	❻	$273	
☐ 260R	3¼ x 4"	(OE)	❹	$30-35	
☐ 260R	3¼ x 4"	(OE)	❺	$28-30	
☐ 260R	3¼ x 4"	(OE)	❻	$27.50	

261   193   261   193

HUM 261   Angel Duet

Same name and same design as HUM 193 but without holder for candle. Modeled by master sculptor Gerhard Skrobek in 1968. Has an incised copyright date of 1968 on the bottom of each piece. Notice position of angel's arm in rear view. HUM 193 candle-holder can be found with arms in either position while HUM 261 is found with arm in lower position only. Difficult to find with 4 trademark.

☐ 261 ...... 5" .... (OE).... ❹ $300-350
☐ 261 ...... 5" .... (OE).... ❺ $90-100
☐ 261 ...... 5" .... (OE).... ❻ $88

HUM 262
Heavenly Lullaby

This is the same design as HUM 24/I "Lullaby" without the hole for candle. Modeled by master sculptor Gerhard Skrobek in 1968. Has an incised copyright date of 1968 on the bottom of each piece. Difficult to find with 4 trademark.

☐ 262 ...... 3½ x 5" ..... (OE).... ❹ $300-350
☐ 262 ...... 3½ x 5" ..... (OE).... ❺ $80-90
☐ 262 ...... 3½ x 5" ..... (OE).... ❻ $80

HUM 263 (CN)
Merry Wanderer, Wall Plaque (in relief)
This wall plaque, modeled by master sculptor Gerhard Skrobek in 1968, was made as a sample only and not produced for sale as an open edition. It is simply a "Merry Wanderer" figurine made without a base, slightly flattened on the back side with a hole provided for hanging. The example in our collection has trademark 4.

☐ 263 ...... 4 x 5⅜" ...... (CN) ... ❹ ... $5000 +

HUM 264
Annual Plate, 1971
Heavenly Angel (CE)
1971 was the 100th anniversary of W. Goebel Porzellanfabrik. The annual plate was issued in commemoration of that occasion. Each employee of the company was presented with a 1971 Annual Plate bearing a special inscription on the back. These plates with the special inscription have become a highly sought-after col-

lector's item because of the very limited production. Produced with the 4 trademark only.

HUM 265
Annual Plate, 1972
Hear Ye, Hear Ye (CE)
Produced with 4 and 5 trademarks. Change was made in mid-production year.

264	...... 7½"	.... (CE)	....	....	$25 issue price
☐ 264	...... 7½"	.... (CE)	.... ❹	....	$700-950
265	...... 7½"	.... (CE)	....	....	$30 issue price
☐ 265	...... 7½"	.... (CE)	.... ❹	....	$75-100
☐ 265	...... 7½"	.... (CE)	.... ❺	....	$75-100

HUM 266
Annual Plate, 1973
Globe Trotter (CE)

HUM 267
Annual Plate, 1974
Goose Girl (CE)

266	7½"	(CE)		$32.50 issue price
☐ 266	7½"	(CE)	❺	$150-250
267	7½"	(CE)		$40 issue price
☐ 267	7½"	(CE)	❺	$100-125

HUM 268
Annual Plate, 1975
Ride Into Christmas (CE)

HUM 269
Annual Plate, 1976
Apple Tree Girl (CE)

268	7½"	(CE)		$50 issue price
☐ 268	7½"	(CE)	❺	$100-125
269	7½"	(CE)		$50 issue price
☐ 269	7½"	(CE)	❺	$75-100

Early sample

Restyled version

HUM 270   Annual Plate, 1977 Apple Tree Boy (CE)

Note the picture on the 1977 plate. The one shown here is an early sample piece. Before production commenced, the boy's shoes were changed to a slightly different angle and the boy's stockings were reversed (his right one is higher than the left in most known examples). If your plate is exactly like this picture, you have a rare plate!

270	7½"	(CE)			$52.50 issue price
☐ 270	7½"	(CE)	❺		$100-150

HUM 271
Annual Plate, 1978
Happy Pastime (CE)

HUM 272
Annual Plate, 1979
Singing Lesson (CE)

271	7½"	(CE)			$65 issue price
☐ 271	7½"	(CE)	❺		$100-125
271	7½"	(CE)			$90 issue price
☐ 272	7½"	(CE)	❻		$90-125

HUM 273
Annual Plate, 1980
School Girl (CE)

HUM 274
Annual Plate, 1981
Umbrella Boy (CE)

273	7½"	(CE)		$100 issue price
☐ 273	7½"	(CE)	❻	$100
274	7½"	(CE)		$100 issue price
☐ 274		(CE)	❻	$100

HUM 275
Annual Plate, 1982
• Umbrella Girl (CE)

HUM 276
Annual Plate, 1983
Postman

275	7½"	(CE)		$100 issue price
☐ 275	7½"	(CE)		$100
276	7½"	(OE)		$108 issue price
☐ 276	7½"	(OE)		$108

HUM 277
Annual Plate, 1984
Little Helper

HUM 278
Annual Plate, 1985
Chick Girl

☐ 277 ...... 7½" .... (ON) ....
☐ 278 ...... 7½" .... (ON) ....

HUM 279
Annual Plate, 1986
Playmates

HUM 280
Anniversary Plate, 1975
Stormy Weather (CE)

☐ 279 ...... 7½" .... (ON) ....
   280 ...... 10" .... (CE) .... $100 issue price
☐ 280 ...... 10" .... (CE).... ❺ $250-350

HUM 281
Anniversary Plate, 1980
Ring Around The Rosie (two girls only)
All plates labeled "Spring Dance" on back.

281	10"	(OE)			$225 issue price
☐ 281	10"	(OE)	... ⑥ ...		$225

282-299 Open Numbers
Open Number (ON): An identification number, which in W. Goebel's numerical identification system has not yet been used, but which may be used to identify new "M.I. Hummel" figurines as they are released in the future.

Offered here is a hypothetical example of how these eighteen Open Numbers (ON) might possibly be used in the coming years.

HUM 282—1985 Anniversary Plate
HUM 283—1987 Annual Plate
HUM 284—1988 Annual Plate

HUM 285—1989 Annual Plate
HUM 286—1990 Annual Plate
HUM 287—1990 Anniversary Plate
HUM 288—1991 Annual Plate
HUM ^39—1992 Annual Plate
HUM 290—1993 Annual Plate
HUM 291—1994 Annual Plate
HUM 292—1995 Annual Plate
HUM 293—1995 Anniversary Plate
HUM 294—1996 Annual Plate
HUM 295—1997 Annual Plate
HUM 296—1998 Annual Plate
HUM 297—1999 Annual Plate
HUM 298—2000 Annual Plate
HUM 299—2000 Anniversary Plate

HUM 300
Bird Watcher
First sold in the U.S. in 1979. At one time called "Tenderness." Has an incised 1956 copyright date. An early sample of this figure was modeled in 1954 by Gerhard Skrobek and was assigned the number HUM 233 (CN). Skrobek stated that this was the first figure he modeled after starting to work at the Goebel factory in 1954. An early sample model with the full bee trademark, incised 1954 date, is in the Robert L. Miller collection.

☐ 300	5"	(OE)	❷	$1500-2500
☐ 300	5"	(OE)	❺	$100-125
☐ 300	5"	(OE)	❻	$100

HUM 301
Christmas Angel (PFE)
Originally called: "Delivery Angel." An early sample model of this figure was modeled by Theo R. Menzenbach in 1957. Menzenbach stated that it was not approved by the Siessen Convent for production. The sample model in our collection has an early stylized trademark 3 and 1957 incised copyright date. Listed here as (PFE) Possible Future Edition: pieces that have been designed and approved for production and possible release in future years.

☐ 301 ...... 6¼" .... (PFE) ....

HUM 302
Concentration (PFE)
First modeled by master sculptor Arthur Moeller in 1955. Originally called "Knit One, Purl Two." Girl is similar to HUM 255 "Stitch in Time."

☐ 302 ...... 5" .... (PFE) ....

HUM 303
Arithmetic Lesson (PFE)
Originally called "School Lesson." Modeled by master sculptor Arthur Moeller in 1955. Notice similarity to middle boy in HUM 170 "School Boys" and girl from HUM 177 "School Girls."

☐ 303 . . . . . . 5¼" . . . . (PFE) . . . .

HUM 304
The Artist
Originally modeled by master sculptor Karl Wagner in 1955 and later restyled by master sculptor Gerhard Skrobek in 1970. First introduced in the U.S. market in 1971. Has an incised 1955 copyright date. Could possibly be found in trademarks 2 and 3, but would be considered extremely rare. Would have trademark 4 when first issued in quantity in 1971. Note: artist Karl Wagner is no longer living.

☐ 304 . . . . . . 5½" . . . . (OE) . . . . ❷ 1500-2500
☐ 304 . . . . . . 5½" . . . . (OE) . . . . ❸ . . . $1000-1500
☐ 304 . . . . . . 5½" . . . . (OE) . . . . ❹ . . . $250-300
☐ 304 . . . . . . 5½" . . . . (OE) . . . . ❺ . . . $95-105
☐ 304 . . . . . . 5½" . . . . (OE) . . . . ❻ . . . $94.50

HUM 305
The Builder

First introduced in the U.S. market in 1963, this figurine was originally modeled in 1955 by master sculptor Gerhard Skrobek. Has an incised 1955 copyright date. An example with trademark 2 would be considered rare.

☐ 305	5½"	(OE)	❷	$1500-2500
☐ 305	5½"	(OE)	❸	$200-250
☐ 305	5½"	(OE)	❹	$105-125
☐ 305	5½"	(OE)	❺	$95-105
☐ 305	5½"	(OE)	❻	$94.50

HUM 306
The Little Bookkeeper

First introduced in the U.S. market in 1962, this figurine was originally modeled in 1955 by master sculptor Arthur Moeller. Has an incised 1955 copyright date. A "Little Bookkeeper" with a full bee, trademark 2, was recently purchased at auction in New York at a fraction of the true value. An example with trademark 2 would be considered rare.

☐ 306	4¾"	(OE)	❷	$1500-2500
☐ 306	4¾"	(OE)	❸	$200-250
☐ 306	4¾"	(OE)	❹	$130-150
☐ 306	4¾"	(OE)	❺	$120-130
☐ 306	4¾"	(OE)	❻	$115.50

New style

HUM 307
Good Hunting
First introduced in the U.S. market in 1962, this figurine was originally modeled by master sculptor Reinhold Unger and sculptor Helmut Wehlte in 1955. Has an incised 1955 copyright date. Hat, brush, collar, hair and position of binoculars have some variations. An example with trademark 2 would be considered rare.

☐ 307	5"	(OE)	❷	$1500-2500
☐ 307	5"	(OE)	❸	$200-250
☐ 307	5"	(OE)	❹	$105-175
☐ 307	5"	(OE)	❺	$95-105
☐ 307	5"	(OE)	❻	$94.50

New   **Old**

HUM 308
Little Tailor
First introduced in the U.S. market in 1972. Originally modeled by master sculptor Horst Ashermann in 1955. Later restyled by current master sculptor Gerhard Skrobek in 1972. Early model on the right has an incised 1955 copyright date while the restyled version on the left has an incised 1972 copyright date. Both styles can be found in trademark 5.

☐ 308	5¼ to 5¾"	(CE)	❷	$1500-2500
☐ 308	5¼ to 5¾"	(CE)	❹	$400-500
☐ 308	5¼ to 5¾"	(CE)	❺	$350-400 (Old style)
☐ 308	5¼ to 5¾"	(OE)	❺	$105-115 (New style)
☐ 308	5¼ to 5¾"	(OE)	❻	$105

HUM 309
With Loving Greetings

First released in the U.S. market in 1983. Modeled in 1955 by master sculptor Karl Wagner. Originally called "Greetings From" on old factory records, but later changed to "With Loving Greetings." The original issue price was $80 in 1983. This figurine was listed as a (PFE) in our 1979 "M.I. Hummel" book.

☐ 309 ...... 3¼ to 3½" ... (OE).... ❻ $80

HUM 310
Searching Angel, Wall Plaque

First introduced in the U.S. market in 1979 along with two other "M.I. Hummel" items. This plaque was originally called "Angelic Concern" on factory records, but later changed to above name. Has an incised 1955 copyright date and was modeled by master sculptor Gerhard Skrobek in 1955. Some catalogues list this piece as number 310 A in error; the incised number is 310 only.

☐ 310 ...... 4¼ x 3¼" ... (OE).... ❺ $65-75
☐ 310 ...... 4¼ x 3¼" ... (OE).... ❻ $63

New   **Old**

HUM 311
Kiss Me
First introduced in the U.S. market in 1961. Originally modeled by master sculptor Reinhold Unger in 1955. Later restyled in 1963 by master sculptor Gerhard Skrobek at the request of the Convent. The doll was redesigned to look more like a doll instead of a child. Has an incised 1955 copyright date. Both styles can be found with 3 and 4 trademarks.

☐ 311	6 to 6¼"	(OE)	❸	$350-500
☐ 311	6 to 6¼"	(OE)	❹	$105-350
☐ 311	6 to 6¼"	(OE)	❺	$95-105
☐ 311	6 to 6¼"	(OE)	❻	$94.50

HUM 312
Honey Lover (PFE)
First modeled by master sculptor Helmut Wehlte in 1955. This figurine was originally called "In the Jam Pot" on factory records, but later changed to the above name. Listed on factory records as a Possible Future Edition (PFE) and may be released at some future date.

☐ 312 ...... 3¾" .... (PFE) ....

HUM 313
Sunny Morning (PFE)
This figurine was originally called "Slumber Serenade" on factory records, but later changed to "Sunny Morning." Modeled in 1955 by master sculptor Arthur Moeller. Listed on factory records as a Possible Future Edition (PFE) and may be released at some future date.

☐ 313 ...... 3¾" .... (PFE) ....

Early sample model   *Old*   *New*

HUM 314 Confidentially

First introduced in the U.S. market in 1972. Originally modeled by master sculptor Horst Ashermann in 1955. Later restyled by master sculptor Gerhard Skrobek in 1972. Skrobek completely restyled it by changing the stand, adding a tie to the boy and giving it the new textured finish. The early models have an incised 1955 copyright date while the restyled version has an incised 1972 copyright date. When first put on the market in 1972 it was in the old style and had the 4 trademark. Older trademarks such as 2 and 3 would be considered rare. The original issue price in 1972 was $22.50.

☐ 314 ...... 5¼ to 5¾" ... (CE) .... ❷ $1500-2500
☐ 314 ...... 5¼ to 5¾" ... (CE) .... ❹ $400-600
☐ 314 ...... 5¼ to 5¾" ... (CE) .... ❺ .... $350-500 (OLD STYLE)
☐ 314 ...... 5¼ to 5¾" ... (OE) .... ❺ .... $95-105 (NEW STYLE)
☐ 314 ...... 5¼ to 5¾" ... (OE) .... ❻ $94.50

HUM 315
Mountaineer
First introduced in the U.S. market at the N.Y. World's Fair in 1964. Has an incised 1955 copyright date. Originally modeled by master sculptor Gerhard Skrobek in 1955. Older models are slightly smaller and have a green stick rather than the dark gray stick found on the newer models. If found with trademark 2 would be considered rare.

☐ 315 ...... 5" .... (OE) .... ❷ $1500-2500
☐ 315 ...... 5" .... (OE) .... ❸ $250-300
☐ 315 ...... 5" .... (OE) .... ❹ $105-125
☐ 315 ...... 5" .... (OE) .... ❺ $95-105
☐ 315 ...... 5" .... (OE) .... ❻ $94.50

HUM 316
Relaxation (PFE)
This figurine was originally called "Nightly Ritual" on factory records, but later changed to "Relaxation." Modeled by master sculptor Karl Wagner in 1955. Listed on factory records as a Possible Future Edition (PFE) and may be released at some future date.

☐ 316 ...... 4" .... (PFE) ....

HUM 317
Not For You!
First introduced in the U.S. market in 1961. Has an incised 1955 copyright date. Originally modeled by master sculptor Arthur Moeller in 1955. Some catalogues and price lists incorrectly show size as 6". The collector should not rely on the measurements in price lists and catalogues as being absolutely accurate, as there have been many typographical errors in them throughout the years. In this book, we used the "bracket" system and show the smallest to the largest size known, verified by actual measurement.

☐ 317 ...... 5½" .... (OE).... ❷ $500-750
☐ 317 ...... 5½" .... (OE).... ❸ $250-300
☐ 317 ...... 5½" .... (OE).... ❹ $105-125
☐ 317 ...... 5½" .... (OE).... ❺ $95-105
☐ 317 ...... 5½" .... (OE).... ❻ $94.50

HUM 318
Art Critic (PFE)
First modeled by master sculptor Horst Ashermann in 1955. Listed on factory records as a Possible Future Edition (PFE) and may be released at some future date.

☐ 318 ...... 5½" .... (PFE) ....

HUM 319
Doll Bath
First introduced in the U.S. market in 1962. Has an incised 1956 copyright date. Originally modeled by master sculptor Gerhard Skrobek in 1956 and was restyled with the new textured finish in the early 1970's.

□ 319	5"	(OE)	❷	$1500-2500
□ 319	5"	(OE)	❸	$250-300
□ 319	5"	(OE)	❹	$125-150
□ 319	5"	(OE)	❺	$95-105
□ 319	5"	(OE)	❻	$94.50

Front view

Back view

HUM 320
The Professor (PFE)
Originally modeled in 1955 by master sculptor Gerhard Skrobek. Listed on factory records as a Possible Future Edition (PFE) and may be released at some future date.

□ 320 . . . . . . 5¾" . . . . (PFE) . . . .

Current style

Early sample model

HUM 321
Wash Day
First introduced in the U.S. market in 1963. Has an incised 1957 copyright date. Originally modeled in 1955 by master sculptor Reinhold Unger and Helmut Wehlte. Notice early sample model pictured here. Older pieces are usually slightly larger in size.

☐ 321 ...... 5½ to 6" ..... (OE).... ❷ $1500- 2500
☐ 321 ...... 5½ to 6" ..... (OE).... ❸ $250-300
☐ 321 ...... 5½ to 6" ..... (OE).... ❹ $105-125
☐ 321 ...... 5½ to 6" ..... (OE).... ❺ $95-105
☐ 321 ...... 5½ to 6" ..... (OE).... ❻ $94.50

German   **English**

HUM 322
Little Pharmacist
First introduced in the U.S. market in 1962. Originally modeled by master sculptor Karl Wagner in 1955. Most examples have an incised 1955 copyright date. Older models are slightly larger in size. Several variations on label of bottle; "Rizinusol" (German for Castor Oil) and "Vitamins" are most common. Also found with "Castor Bil."

☐ 322 ...... 5¾ to 6" ..... (OE).... ❷ $1500-2500
☐ 322 ...... 5¾ to 6" ..... (OE).... ❸ $250-300
☐ 322 ...... 5¾ to 6" ..... (OE).... ❹ $125-150
☐ 322 ...... 5¾ to 6" ..... (OE).... ❺ $100-110
☐ 322 ...... 5¾ to 6" ..... (OE).... ❻ $100

HUM 323
Merry Christmas, Wall Plaque
First introduced in the U.S. market in 1979 along with two other "M.I. Hummel" items, HUM 310 "Searching Angel" plaque and HUM 300 "Bird Watcher." Has an incised 1955 copyright date. Originally modeled by master sculptor Gerhard Skrobek in 1955.

☐ 323 ...... 5¼ x 3½" ... (OE) .... ⑤ $65-75
☐ 323 ...... 5½ x 3½" ... (OE) .... ⑥ $63

HUM 324
At The Fence (PFE)
Originally called "The Other Side of the Fence" on factory records, but later changed to "At The Fence." Modeled in 1955 by master sculptor Arthur Moeller. Listed on factory records as a Possible Future Edition (PFE) and may be released at some future date.

☐ 324 ...... 4¾" .... (PFE) ....

HUM 325
Helping Mother (PFE)
This figurine was originally modeled by master sculptor Arthur Moeller in August 1955 and the first sample was painted in July 1956 by artist "F/K"—the initials used by Franz Kirchner. Originally called "Mother's Aid" on old factory records but later changed to "Helping Mother." Similar in design to HUM 133 "Mother's Helper" and when released will only be the second "M.I. Hummel" figurine designed with a cat. This early sample model pictured here has the full bee trademark and is in the Robert L. Miller collection.

☐ 325 . . . . . . 5" . . . . (PFE) . . . .

HUM 326
Being Punished, Wall Plaque (PFE)
This figurine was originally modeled by master sculptor Gerhard Skrobek in July 1957 and the first sample was painted by artist Franz Kirchner in August 1957. Originally called "Naughty Boy" on old factory records but later changed to "Being Punished." This piece has a hole on the back for hanging as a plaque or will sit upright on base. Has an incised 1955 copyright date on back. This early sample model pictured here has the full bee trademark and is part of the Robert L. Miller collection.

☐ 326 . . . . . . 4 x 5" . . . . (PFE) . . . .

New   **Old**

HUM 327   The Run-A-Way

First introduced in the U.S. market in 1972. Originally modeled by master sculptor Helmut Wehlte in 1955 and later restyled by current master sculptor Gerhard Skrobek in 1972. Skrobek completely restyled this figure with the new textured finish and variations in the location of basket, hat and shoes. Slight color variations also. The early models have an incised 1955 copyright date while the restyled version has an incised 1972 copyright date. When first put on the market in 1972 it was in the old style and had the 4 trademark. Older trademarks such as 2 and 3 would be considered rare. The original issue price in 1972 was $28.50.

☐ 327 . . . . . . 5¼" . . . . (CE) . . . . ❷ $1500-2500
☐ 327 . . . . . . 5¼" . . . . (CE) . . . . ❸ $750-1000
☐ 327 . . . . . . 5¼" . . . . (CE) . . . . ❹ $500-750
☐ 327 . . . . . . 5¼" . . . . (CE) . . . . ❺ . . . . $350-500 (Old style)
☐ 327 . . . . . . 5¼" . . . . (OE) . . . . ❺ . . . . $120-130 (New style)
☐ 327 . . . . . . 5¼" . . . . (OE) . . . . ❻ $115.50

HUM 328
Carnival
First introduced in the U.S. market in 1963. Originally modeled by master sculptors Reinhold Unger and Helmut Wehlte in 1955. Early sample model with full bee trademark has a 1955 incised copyright date. Later models have a 1957 incised copyright date. Older examples are slightly larger with only minor variations. The object under the child's arm is a noise maker or "slapstick," a device generally made of wood and paper or cloth—popular with stage comedians.

☐ 328 ...... 5¾ to 6" ..... (OE).... ❷ $1000-2000
☐ 328 ...... 5¾ to 6" ..... (OE).... ❸ $250-300
☐ 328 ...... 5¾ to 6" ..... (OE).... ❹ $100-125
☐ 328 ...... 5¾ to 6" ..... (OE).... ❺ $80-90
☐ 328 ...... 5¾ to 6" ..... (OE).... ❻ $77.50

HUM 329
Off To School (PFE)
Originally called "Kindergarten Romance" on factory records, but later changed to "Off To School." Modeled by master sculptor Arthur Moeller in 1955. The boy is quite similar to HUM 82 "School Boy" while the girl is completely new. Listed on factory records as a Possible Future Edition (PFE) and may be released at some future date.

☐ 329 . . . . . . 5" . . . . (PFE) . . . .

HUM 330
Baking Day (PFE)
Originally called "Kneading Dough" on old factory records, but later changed to "Baking Day." Modeled by master sculptor Gerhard Skrobek in 1955. Listed on factory records as a Possible Future Edition (PFE) and may be released at some future date.

☐ 330 ...... 5¼" .... (PFE) ....

| Old | New |

| Old | New |

HUM 331 Crossroads
First introduced in the U.S. market in 1972. Has an incised 1955 copyright date. Modeled by master sculptor Arthur Moeller in 1955. This early sample model has the trombone reversed. Research at the factory indicated this was probably an accident in assembling the separate clay molds and possibly this is the only one made that way. We are unaware of any others having been found. The full bee example in our collection has the trombone in the normal position. The original issue price in 1972 was $45.00.

☐ 331 ...... 6¾" .... (OE).... ❷ $1500-2500
☐ 331 ...... 6¾" .... (OE).... ❸ $750-1000
☐ 331 ...... 6¾" .... (OE).... ❹ $500-750
☐ 331 ...... 6¾" .... (OE).... ❺ $185-200
☐ 331 ...... 6¾" .... (OE).... ❻ $185

HUM 332
Soldier Boy
First introduced in the U.S. market in 1963.
Modeled by master sculptor Gerhard Skrobek in 1955. The early prototype model in
our collection has a full bee trademark
and a 1955 incised copyright date. Later
models have a 1957 incised copyright
date. Older pieces are slightly larger and
usually have a red ornament on hat while
the newer pieces have a blue one.

☐ 332	5¾ to 6"	(OE)	❷	$1000-2000
☐ 332	5¾ to 6"	(OE)	❸	$150-250
☐ 332	5¾ to 6"	(OE)	❹	$80-150
☐ 332	5¾ to 6"	(OE)	❺	$75-80
☐ 332	5¾ to 6"	(OE)	❻	$72

HUM 333
Blessed Event
First introduced in the U.S. market at the
N.Y. World's Fair in 1964. Originally modeled by master sculptor Arthur Moeller in
1955. Found with either 1955 or 1957 incised copyright dates.

☐ 333	5¼ to 5½"	(OE)	❷	$1000-2000
☐ 333	5¼ to 5½"	(OE)	❸	$350-500
☐ 333	5¼ to 5½"	(OE)	❹	$175-200
☐ 333	5¼ to 5½"	(OE)	❺	$150-165
☐ 333	5¼ to 5½"	(OE)	❻	$147

Old   New

HUM 334
Homeward Bound

First introduced in the U.S. market in 1971 along with three other new releases: HUM 304 "Artist," HUM 340 "Letter to Santa Claus" and HUM 347 "Adventure Bound." "Homeward Bound" was originally modeled by master sculptor Arthur Moeller in 1956 and later restyled by master sculptor Gerhard Skrobek in 1974. Found with either 1955 or 1956 incised copyright dates in early models. The restyled version has the new textured finish and no support pedestal under the goat. Current model has an incised 1975 copyright date.

☐ 334 ...... 5¼" .... (OE).... ❸ ... $750-1000
☐ 334 ...... 5¼" .... (CE).... ❹ ... $350-500
☐ 334 ...... 5¼" .... (CE).... ❺ ... $250-350 (Old style)
☐ 334 ...... 5¼" .... (OE).... ❺ ... $160-250 (New style)
☐ 334 ...... 5¼" .... (OE).... ❻ ... $157.50

HUM 335
Lucky Boy (PFE)

Originally called "Fair Prizes" on old factory records, but later changed to "Lucky Boy." Modeled by master sculptor Arthur Moeller in 1956. Now listed on factory records as a Possible Future Edition (PFE) and may be released at some future date.

☐ 335 ...... 5¾ to 6" ..... (PFE) ....

New   *Old*

New   *Old*

HUM 336
Close Harmony
First introduced in the U.S. market in 1963. Found with either 1955, 1956 or 1957 copyright dates. Originally modeled in 1956 by master modeler Gerhard Skrobek and in 1962 he also restyled it. The current production has been restyled but bears the 1955 incised copyright date. Older models have variations in girl's hairstyle and position of stockings.

HUM 337
Cinderella
First introduced in the U.S. market in 1972.

First modeled by master sculptor Arthur Moeller in March 1956. First sample painted by artist Franz Kirchner in July 1956. Later restyled by master sculptor Gerhard Skrobek in 1972. Early models have a 1958 incised copyright date while the restyled version has a 1972 copyright date. Completely restyled with Skrobek's new textured finish and girl's eyes looking down. The older models have eyes open. When first put on the market in 1972 it was in the old style and had the 4 trademark. Older trademarks such as 2 and 3 would be considered rare. The original issue price in 1972 was $26.50.

☐ 336	5¼ to 5½ "	(OE)	❸	$350-500
☐ 336	5¼ to 5½ "	(OE)	❹	$150-350
☐ 336	5¼ to 5½ "	(OE)	❺	$125-140
☐ 336	5¼ to 5½ "	(OE)	❻	$125
☐ 337	4½ "	(CE)	❹	$500-750
☐ 337	4½ "	(CE)	❺	$350-500 (Old style)
☐ 337	4½ "	(OE)	❺	$120-130 (New style)
☐ 337	4½ "	(OE)	❻	$115.50

HUM 338
Birthday Cake, Candleholder (PFE)
Originally called "A Birthday Wish" on old factory records, but later changed to "Birthday Cake." Modeled by master sculptor Gerhard Skrobek in March 1956. First sample painted by Harald Sommer in July 1956. This early prototype model pictured here has the full bee trademark and is part of the Robert L. Miller collection. This figurine is now listed on factory records as a Possible Future Edition (PFE) and may be released at some future date.

☐ 338	3¾ "	(PFE)	

HUM 339
Behave! (PFE)

Originally called "Walking Her Dog" on old factory records, but later changed to "Behave!" Modeled by master sculptor Helmut Wehlte in 1956. Now listed on factory records as a Possible Future Edition (PFE) and may be released at some future date.

☐ 339 . . . . . . 5⅓ to 5¾" . . . (PFE) . . . .

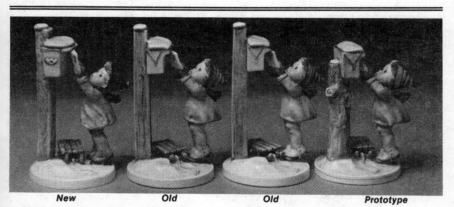

New   **Old**   **Old**   **Prototype**

HUM 340   Letter to Santa Claus

First introduced in the U.S. market in 1971. Originally modeled by master sculptor Helmut Wehlte in April 1956. Early sample was painted in September 1957 by artist Guenther Neubauer (now Chief Sample Painter at Goebel). Completely restyled by current master sculptor Gerhard Skrobek in 1970. The prototype mailbox on a tree trunk apparently was rejected in favor of the wooden post style. This piece has a full bee trademark, stamped 1956 copyright date and artist initials "HS" (probably Harald Sommer) along with a June 1956 date. The current production has new textured finish and color variations on girl's hats and leggings.

☐ 340 . . . . . . 7¼" . . . . (CE) . . . . ❷ $1500-2500
☐ 340 . . . . . . 7¾" . . . . (CE) . . . . ❸ $1500-2000
☐ 340 . . . . . . 7¼" . . . . (OE) . . . . ❹ $350-500
☐ 340 . . . . . . 7¼" . . . . (OE) . . . . ❺ $140-165
☐ 340 . . . . . . 7¼" . . . . (OE) . . . . ❻ $137

HUM 341
Birthday Present (PFE)
Originally called "The Birthday Present" on old factory records, but later changed to just "Birthday Present." First modeled by master sculptor Gerhard Skrobek in 1956. Now listed on factory records as a Possible Future Edition (PFE) and may be released at some future date.

HUM 342
Mischief Maker
First introduced in the U.S. market in 1972. Originally modeled by master sculptor Arthur Moeller in 1956. Found with either 1958 or 1960 copyright dates. No major variations have been recorded in size, color or design. The original issue price in 1972 was $26.50.

☐ 341 ...... 5 to 5⅓" ..... (PFE) ....

☐ 342 ...... 5" .... (OE).... ➍ $250-350
☐ 342 ...... 5" .... (OE).... ➎ $110-120
☐ 342 ...... 5" .... (OE).... ➏ $110

HUM 343
Christmas Song
First introduced in the U.S. market in 1981. Originally called "Singing Angel" on old factory records, but later changed to "Christmas Song." Modeled by master sculptor Gerhard Skrobek in 1956. Original issue price of $85.00 in 1981. This figurine was listed as a (PFE) in our 1979 "M.I. Hummel" book.

☐ 343 ...... 6½" .... (OE).... ➏ $90

HUM 344
Feathered Friends

First introduced in the U.S. market in 1972. Modeled by master sculptor Gerhard Skrobek in 1956. Has an incised 1956 copyright date on the base. Full bee and early stylized examples have appeared on the market. The original issue price in 1972 was $27.50.

☐ 344	4¾"	(OE)	❷	$1500-2500
☐ 344	4¾"	(OE)	❸	$1000-1500
☐ 344	4¾"	(OE)	❹	$250-350
☐ 344	4¾"	(OE)	❺	$110-120
☐ 344	4¾"	(OE)	❻	$110

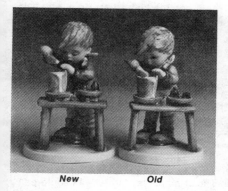

New   *Old*

HUM 345
A Fair Measure

First introduced in the U.S. market in 1972. Originally modeled by master sculptor Helmut Wehlte in August 1956. First sample was painted by artist "W/Ha" Werner Hausschild in August 1957. Later restyled by master sculptor Gerhard Skrobek in 1972. Early full bee prototype has a stamped 1957 copyright date. Early production models have 1956 incised copyright date. Completely restyled with new textured finish, boy's eyes looking down and weights on scale reversed. Current model has a 1972 incised copyright date. Original issue price in 1972 was $27.50.

☐ 345	5½ to 5¾"	(CE)	❷	$1500-2500
☐ 345	5½ to 5¾"	(CE)	❸	$1000-1500
☐ 345	5½ to 5¾"	(CE)	❹	$350-500
☐ 345	5½ to 5¾"	(CE)	❺	$300-350 OLD STYLE
☐ 345	5½ to 5¾"	(OE)	❺	$120-130 NEW STYLE
☐ 345	5½ to 5¾"	(OE)	❻	$115.50

HUM 346
Smart Little Sister
First introduced in the U.S. market in 1962. Originally modeled by master sculptor Gerhard Skrobek in 1956. Has an incised 1956 copyright date on the bottom. No unusual variations have been recorded.

☐ 346	4¾"	(OE)	❸	$350-500
☐ 346	4¾"	(OE)	❹	$105-125
☐ 346	4¾"	(OE)	❺	$95-105
☐ 346	4¾"	(OE)	❻	$94.50

HUM 347
Adventure Bound
First introduced in the U.S. market in 1971. Sometimes known as the "Seven Swabians." Has an incised 1957 copyright date. The original clay model was sculpted by Theo R. Menzenbach. Menzenbach began working at the Goebel factory in October 1948, at the age of 18. He left the factory in October 1961 to start his own business as a commercial artist. He is still living and resides in Germany, near Coburg. An early prototype with full bee trademark was painted in October 1957 and is now part of the Robert L. Miller collection.

☐ 347	7½ x 8¼"	(OE)	❷	$5000 +
☐ 347	7½ x 8¼"	(OE)	❸	$2500-3000
☐ 347	7½ x 8¼"	(OE)	❹	$2000-2500
☐ 347	7½ x 8¼"	(OE)	❺	$1800-1850
☐ 347	7½ x 8¼"	(OE)	❻	$1790

HUM 348
Ring Around The Rosie
The original clay model was sculpted by Gerhard Skrobek, current master modeler at the factory, in 1957. First introduced in the U.S. market in the early 1960's. Incised on the bottom: "© by W. Goebel, Oeslau 1957." Older models are usually slightly larger. So far, no early full bee prototype examples have been located. Originally sold for less than $100 when first introduced for sale.

☐ 348	6¾"	(OE)	❷	$5000 +
☐ 348	6¾"	(OE)	❸	$1750-2000
☐ 348	6¾"	(OE)	❹	$1500-1750
☐ 348	6¾"	(OE)	❺	$1310-1500
☐ 348	6¾"	(OE)	❻	$1310

HUM 349
The Florist (PFE)
Originally called "Flower Lover" on old factory records, but later changed to "The Florist." First modeled by master sculptor Gerhard Skrobek in 1957. Now listed on factory records as a Possible Future Edition (PFE) and may be released at some future date.

☐ 349 ...... 7 to 7½" ..... (PFE) ....

HUM 350
On Holiday
First introduced in the U.S. market in 1981. Originally called "Holiday Shopper" on old factory records, but later changed to "On Holiday." Modeled by master sculptor Gerhard Skrobek in 1964. Original issue price was $85 in 1981. This figurine was listed as a PFE in our 1979 "M.I. Hummel" book. Has an incised 1965 copyright date.

☐ 350 ...... 4¼" .... (OE) .... ❻ $90

HUM 351
The Botanist
First introduced in the U.S. market in the fall of 1982. Originally called "Remembering" on old factory records, but later changed to "The Botanist." First modeled by master sculptor Gerhard Skrobek in 1965. Has an incised 1972 copyright date on the bottom. The original issue price was $84 in 1982. This figurine was listed as a PFE in our 1979 "M.I. Hummel" book.

☐ 351 ...... 4 to 4¼" ..... (OE).... ❻ $88

HUM 352
Sweet Greetings
First released in the U.S. market in 1981. Originally called "Musical Morning" on old factory records, but later changed to "Sweet Greetings." Modeled by master sculptor Gerhard Skrobek in 1964. Has an incised 1964 copyright date on the bottom of the base. The original issue price was $85 in 1981. This figurine was listed as a PFE in our 1979 "M.I. Hummel" book.

☐ 352 ...... 4¼" .... (OE).... ❻ $90

353/I 353/O

HUM 353
Spring Dance
First introduced in the U.S. market in 1964.

According to factory records, this was first modeled in 1962 by a combination of modelers. Until recently, "Spring Dance" was the highest numbered figurine made in two sizes; HUM 396 "Ride Into Christmas" now has that distinction. The small size 353/O has been considered rare, having been produced in very limited quantities in 1964 and then not produced again until 1978. Some of the early pieces have sold for as high as $2,000. It is again in current production with the 5 and 6 trademarks. Both sizes have an incised 1963 copyright date. In 1982 the large size 353/I was listed as a "temporary withdrawal" on company records, to be possibly reinstated at a future date. The "Spring Dance" design consists of two of the four girls from HUM 348 "Ring Around The Rosie."

☐ 353/0	5¼"	(OE)	❹	$1000-1500
☐ 353/0	5¼"	(OE)	❺	$120-150
☐ 353/0	5¼"	(OE)	❻	$115.50
☐ 353/I	6¾"	(OE)	❸	$350-500
☐ 353/I	6¾"	(OE)	❹	$300-350
☐ 353/I	6¾"	(OE)	❺	$275-300
☐ 353/I	6¾"	(OE)	❻	$265

HUM 354 A   Holy Water Font, Angel With Lantern (CN)
This early prototype font has the incised number 354 only, on the back. According to factory information, this design was not approved by the Siessen Convent as a font. It was then restyled into a figurine and approved as HUM 357 "Guiding Angel." Now listed on factory records as a Closed Number.

HUM 354 B   Holy Water Font, Angel With Trumpet (CN)
This early prototype font has the incised number 355 only, on the back. According to factory information, this design was not approved by the Siessen Convent as a font. It was then restyled into a figurine and approved as HUM 359 "Tuneful Angel." Now listed on factory records as a Closed Number.

HUM 354 C   Holy Water Font, Angel With Bird (CN)
This early prototype font has the incised number 356 only, on the back. According to factory information, this design was not approved by the Siessen Convent as a font. It was then restyled into a figurine and approved as HUM 358 "Shining Light." Now listed on factory records as a Closed Number.

☐ 354A ..... 3¼ x 5" ..... (CN) ....
☐ 354B ..... 3¼ x 5" ..... (CN) ....
☐ 354C ..... 3¼ x 5" ..... (CN) ....

HUM 355
Autumn Harvest
First introduced in the U.S. market in 1972. Originally modeled by master sculptor Gerhard Skrobek in 1963. Has an incised 1964 copyright date on the bottom. No major variations have been recorded in size, color or design. The original issue price in 1972 was $22.50.

☐ 355 ...... 5" .... (OE).... ❹ $300-350
☐ 355 ...... 5" .... (OE).... ❺ $90-100
☐ 355 ...... 5" .... (OE).... ❻ $88

HUM 356
Gay Adventure
First released in the U.S. market in 1972. Originally modeled by master sculptor Gerhard Skrobek in 1963. It has an incised 1971 copyright date on the bottom. Slightly restyled with the new textured finish on current models. Early models have slightly different construction on the underside of base. Was called "Joyful Adventure" in some catalogues. The original issue price in 1972 was $22.50.

☐ 356 ...... 4¾" .... (OE).... ❹ $300-350
☐ 356 ...... 4¾" .... (OE).... ❺ $75-85
☐ 356 ...... 4¾" .... (OE).... ❻ $75

357   358   359

HUM 357   Guiding Angel

First released in the U.S. market in 1972. Originally modeled by master sculptor Reinhold Unger in 1958. Has an incised 1960 copyright date. The original issue price in 1972 was $11. Usually offered, along with HUM 358 and HUM 359, as a set of three angels, although priced separately.

HUM 358   Shining Light

First released in the U.S. market in 1972. Originally modeled by master sculptor Reinhold Unger in 1958. Has an incised 1960 copyright date. The original issue price in 1972 was $11. Usually offered, along with HUM 357 and HUM 359, as a set of three angels, although priced separately.

HUM 359   Tuneful Angel

First released in the U.S. market in 1972. Originally modeled by master sculptor Reinhold Unger in 1958. Has an incised 1960 copyright date. Usually offered, along with HUM 357 and HUM 358, as a set of three angels, although priced separately. The original issue price in 1972 was $11.

☐ 357	2¾"	(OE)	❹	$60-75
☐ 357	2¾"	(OE)	❺	$45-50
☐ 357	2¾"	(OE)	❻	$42
☐ 358	2¾"	(OE)	❹	$60-75
☐ 358	2¾"	(OE)	❺	$45-50
☐ 358	2¾"	(OE)	❻	$42
☐ 359	2¾"	(OE)	❹	$60-75
☐ 359	2¾"	(OE)	❺	$45-50
☐ 359	2¾"	(OE)	❻	$42

360B

360A

360C

HUM 360/A   Wall Vase, Boy and Girl
One of a set of three wall vases that had been considered rare but is again in current production with the 5 and 6 trademarks. According to factory records, this vase was modeled by master sculptor Gerhard Skrobek in 1959. Early models incised on back: " © by W. Goebel 1958." The new model reissued in 1979 has been slightly restyled and has copyright date 1958 only incised on back.

HUM 360/B   Wall Vase, Boy
One of a set of three wall vases that had been considered rare but is again in current production with the 5 and 6 trademarks. According to factory records, this vase was modeled by master sculptor Gerhard Skrobek in 1959. Early models incised on back: " © by W. Goebel 1958." The new model reissued in 1979 has been slightly restyled and has copyright date 1958 only incised on back.

HUM 360/C   Wall Vase, Girl
One of a set of three wall vases that had been considered rare but is again in current production with the 5 and 6 trademarks. According to factory records, this vase was modeled by master sculptor Gerhard Skrobek in 1959. Early models incised on back: "© by W. Goebel 1958." The new model reissued in 1979 has the trunk of the tree slightly restyled and has copyright date 1958 only incised on back.

☐ 360A	4½ x 6"	(OE)	❸	$350-500
☐ 360A	4½ x 6"	(OE)	❺	$65-70
☐ 360A	4½ x 6"	(OE)	❻	$63
☐ 360B	4½ x 6"	(OE)	❸	$350-500
☐ 360B	4½ x 6"	(OE)	❺	$65-70
☐ 360B	4½ x 6"	(OE)	❻	$63
☐ 360C	4½ x 6"	(OE)	❸	$350-500
☐ 360C	4½ x 6"	(OE)	❺	$65-70
☐ 360C	4½ x 6"	(OE)	❻	$63

HUM 361
Favorite Pet
First released in the U.S. market at the N.Y. World's Fair in 1964. Originally modeled by master sculptor Theo R. Menzenbach in 1959. Has an incised 1960 copyright date. No unusual variations have been recorded.

☐ 361	4½"	(OE)	❸	$250-300
☐ 361	4½"	(OE)	❹	$110-125
☐ 361	4½"	(OE)	❺	$100-110
☐ 361	4½"	(OE)	❻	$100

HUM 362
I Forgot (PFE)
Originally called "Thoughtful" on old factory records, but later changed to "I Forgot." First modeled by master sculptor Theo R. Menzenbach in 1959. Now listed on factory records as a Possible Future Edition (PFE) and may be released at some future date.

☐ 362	5½"	(PFE)	....

HUM 363
Big Housecleaning
First introduced in the U.S. market in 1972. Originally modeled by master sculptor Gerhard Skrobek in 1959. Has an incised 1960 copyright date on the bottom. No major variations have been recorded in size, color or design. The original issue price in 1972 was $28.50.

□ 363	...... 4"	.... (OE)....	❹	$250-350
□ 363	...... 4"	.... (OE)....	❺	$120-130
□ 363	...... 4"	.... (OE)....	❻	$115.50

HUM 364
Supreme Protection (PFE)
Originally called "Blessed Madonna and Child" on old factory records, but later changed to "Supreme Protection." First modeled by master sculptor Gerhard Skrobek in 1963. Now listed on factory records as a Possible Future Edition (PFE) and may be released at some future date.

□ 364 ...... 8¾ to 9" ..... (PFE) ....

HUM 365
Littlest Angel (PFE)
Originally called "The Wee Angel" on old factory records, but later changed to "Littlest Angel." Modeled by master sculptor Gerhard Skrobek in 1963. Now listed on factory records as a Possible Future Edition (PFE) and may be released at some future date.

□ 365 ...... 2¼ to 2¾" ... (PFE) ....

HUM 366
Flying Angel
First modeled by master sculptor Gerhard Skrobek in 1963, this piece was designed as an addition to the small Nativity Set, HUM 214. It is produced in color and in white overglaze. Makes an excellent decoration or ornament for hanging on the Christmas tree. See photo of HUM 214 Nativity Set for application.

□ 366	...... 3½"	.... (OE)....	❹	$60-75
□ 366	...... 3½"	.... (OE)....	❺	$55-60
□ 366	...... 3½"	.... (OE)....	❻	$55

HUM 367
Busy Student
First released in the U.S. market in 1964.
Originally modeled in 1962 by a combination of modelers. Has an incised 1963
copyright date. Similar to the little girl in
HUM 346 "Smart Little Sister." No major
variations have been reported in size, col-
or or design.

☐ 367 . . . . . . 4¼" . . . . (OE) . . . . ❸ $125-250
☐ 367 . . . . . . 4¼" . . . . (OE) . . . . ❹ $80-100
☐ 367 . . . . . . 4¼" . . . . (OE) . . . . ❺ $75-80
☐ 367 . . . . . . 4¼" . . . . (OE) . . . . ❻ $72

HUM 368
Lute Song (PFE)
Originally called "Lute Player" on old factory records, but later changed to "Lute
Song." First modeled by master sculptor
Gerhard Skrobek in July 1964. Notice the
similarity between this figure and the girl
in HUM 336 "Close Harmony." Now listed
on factory records as a Possible Future
Edition (PFE) and may be released at
some future date.

☐ 368 . . . . . . 5" . . . . (PFE) . . . .

HUM 369
Follow The Leader
First introduced in the U.S. market in 1972. This figurine was first modeled by master sculptor Gerhard Skrobek in February 1964. It has an incised 1964 copyright date on the bottom. The original issue price in 1972 was $110. No major variations have been recorded in size, color or design.

☐ 369 ..... 7" .... (OE).... ❹ $500-750
☐ 369 ..... 7" .... (OE).... ❺ $450-500
☐ 369 ..... 7" .... (OE).... ❻ $450

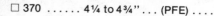

HUM 370
Companions (PFE)
Originally called "Brotherly Love" on old factory records, but later changed to "Companions." Originally modeled by master sculptor Gerhard Skrobek in May 1964. Now listed on factory records as a Possible Future Edition (PFE) and may be released at some future date.

☐ 370 ..... 4¼ to 4¾" ... (PFE) ....

HUM 371
Daddy's Girls (PFE)
Originally called "Sisterly Love" on old factory records, but later changed to "Daddy's Girls." Modeled by master sculptor Gerhard Skrobek in May 1964. Now listed on factory records as a Possible Future Edition (PFE) and may be released at some future date.

☐ 371 ..... 4¾" .... (PFE) ....

HUM 372
Blessed Mother (PFE)
Originally called "Virgin Mother and Child" on old factory records, but later changed to "Blessed Mother." Modeled by master sculptor Gerhard Skrobek in May 1964. Now listed on factory records as a Possible Future Edition (PFE) and may be released at some future date.

☐ 372 . . . . . . 10¼" . . . . (PFE) . . . .

HUM 373
Just Fishing (PFE)
Originally called "The Fisherman" on old factory records, but later changed to "Just Fishing." First modeled by present master sculptor Gerhard Skrobek in 1964. Now listed on factory records as a Possible Future Edition (PFE) and may be released at some future date.

☐ 373 . . . . . . 4¼ to 4½" . . . (PFE) . . . .

HUM 374
Lost Stocking
This figurine was one of twenty-four new motifs first released in the U.S. market in 1972. Originally modeled by master sculptor Gerhard Skrobek in 1965. It has an incised 1965 copyright date. No major variations have been recorded in size, color or design. The original issue price in 1972 was $17.50.

☐ 374 ...... 4½" .... (OE).... ❹ $250-350
☐ 374 ...... 4½" .... (OE).... ❺ $65-70
☐ 374 ...... 4½" .... (OE).... ❻ $63

HUM 375
Morning Stroll (PFE)
Originally called "Walking the Baby" on old factory records, but later changed to "Morning Stroll." This figurine was first modeled by master sculptor Gerhard Skrobek in November 1964. It is now listed on factory records as a Possible Future Edition (PFE) and may be released at some future date.

☐ 375 ...... 4¼" .... (PFE) ....

HUM 376
Little Nurse
This figurine was first released in the U.S. market in the fall of 1982. Originally called "First Aid" on old factory records, but later changed to "Little Nurse." Modeled by master sculptor Gerhard Skrobek in April 1965. It has an incised 1972 copyright date on the bottom. The original issue price was $95 in 1982. This figurine was listed as a (PFE) in our 1979 "M.I. Hummel" book.

☐ 376 ...... 4" .... (OE).... ❻ $100

HUM 377
Bashful!
First released in the U.S. market in 1972. Originally modeled by master sculptor Gerhard Skrobek in January 1966. It usually was found with an incised 1966 copyright date, but occasionally found with a 1971 incised date. Models in current production have no incised date at all. No major variations have been recorded in size, color or design. The original issue price was $17.50 in 1972.

☐ 377	4¾"	(OE)	❹	$250-350
☐ 377	4¾"	(OE)	❺	$80-90
☐ 377	4¾"	(OE)	❻	$77.50

HUM 378
Easter Greetings!
First released in the U.S. market in 1972 as one of twenty-four new motifs released that year. Originally modeled by master sculptor Gerhard Skrobek in January 1966. It has an incised 1971 copyright date on the bottom. No major variations have been found in size, color or design. The original issue price was $24 in 1972.

☐ 378	5"	(OE)	❹	$250-350
☐ 378	5"	(OE)	❺	$90-100
☐ 378	5"	(OE)	❻	$88

HUM 379
Don't Be Shy (PFE)
Originally called "One For You—One For Me" on old factory records, but later changed to "Don't Be Shy." This figurine was first modeled by master sculptor Gerhard Skrobek in February 1966. It is now listed on factory records as a Possible Future Edition (PFE) and may be released at some future date.

☐ 379 . . . . . . 4¼ to 4½" . . . (PFE) . . . .

HUM 380
Daisies Don't Tell (CE)
First introduced in 1981 for members of the Goebel Collector's Club only as "Special Edition No. 5." Was not sold as an open edition but can be purchased on the secondary market at premium prices. The original issue price was $80 in the U.S. and $95 in Canada. It has an incised 1972 copyright date and the 6 trademark. The original name was "Does He?" on old factory records. Modeled by master sculptor Gerhard Skrobek in February 1966. This figurine was listed as a PFE in our 1979 "M.I. Hummel" book.

☐ 380 . . . . . . 4½ to 5" . . . . . (CE) . . . . ➏ $100-125

HUM 381
Flower Vendor
First introduced in the U.S. market in 1972. Originally modeled by master sculptor Gerhard Skrobek in October 1966. It has an incised 1971 copyright date on the underside of the base. No major variations have been found in size, color or design. The original issue price was $24 in 1972.

☐ 381 ...... 5¼" .... (OE).... ❹ $250-350
☐ 381 ...... 5¼" .... (OE).... ❺ $100-110
☐ 381 ...... 5¼" .... (OE).... ❻ $100

HUM 382
Visiting An Invalid
First released in the U.S. market in 1972. Originally modeled by master sculptor Gerhard Skrobek in October 1966. It has an incised 1971 copyright date on the underside of the base. No major variations have been noticed in size, color or design. The original issue price was $26.50 in 1972.

☐ 382 ...... 5" .... (OE).... ❹ $250-350
☐ 382 ...... 5" .... (OE).... ❺ $95-105
☐ 382 ...... 5" .... (OE).... ❻ $94.50

HUM 383
Going Home (PFE)
Originally called "Fancy Free" in old factory records, but later changed to "Going Home." This figurine was first modeled by master sculptor Gerhard Skrobek in November 1966. It is now listed on factory records as a Possible Future Edition (PFE) and may be released at some future date.

☐ 383 ...... 4¼ to 4¾" ... (PFE) ....

HUM 384
Easter Time
First introduced in the U.S. market in 1972. Originally modeled by master sculptor Gerhard Skrobek in January 1967. It has an incised 1971 copyright date on the underside of the base. No major variations have been recorded in size, color or design. The original issue price was $27.50 in 1972. Also called "Easter Playmates" in some catalogues.

☐ 384 ...... 4" .... (OE).... ❹ $250-350
☐ 384 ...... 4" .... (OE).... ❺ $125-140
☐ 384 ...... 4" .... (OE).... ❻ $125

HUM 385
Chicken-Licken
First introduced in the U.S. market in 1972 as one of twenty-four new motifs released that year. Originally modeled by master sculptor Gerhard Skrobek in June 1967. It has an incised 1971 copyright date on the bottom of the base. No major variations have been recorded in size, color or design. The original issue price was $28.50 in 1972.

□ 385 ...... 4¾" .... (OE) .... ❹ $250-350
□ 385 ...... 4¾" .... (OE) .... ❺ $125-140
□ 385 ...... 4¾" .... (OE) .... ❻ $125

HUM 386
On Secret Path
First introduced in the U.S. market in 1972. Originally modeled by master sculptor Gerhard Skrobek in July 1967. It has an incised 1971 copyright date on the bottom of the base. No major variations have been found in size, color or design. The original issue price was $26.50 in 1972.

□ 386 ...... 5¼" .... (OE) .... ❹ $250-350
□ 386 ...... 5¼" .... (OE) .... ❺ $120-130
□ 386 ...... 5¼" .... (OE) .... ❻ $115.50

HUM 387
Valentine Gift (CE)
This figurine was first introduced in 1977 for members of the Goebel Collectors' Club only and not sold in Open Edition. Originally modeled by master sculptor Gerhard Skrobek in July 1967. It has an incised 1972 copyright date along with the 5 trademark. Also bears the inscription "EXCLUSIVE SPECIAL EDITION No. 1 FOR MEMBERS OF THE GOEBEL COLLECTORS' CLUB" applied by blue decal. The original issue price was $45 in addition to the member's redemption card. Translation of message on heart: "I Love You Very Much" or "I Like You." Several examples without the special inscription but with trademark 4 only have appeared on the market. Some have 1968 copyright date and usually sell for $750 to $1,000.

☐ 387 ...... 5¾" .... (CE).... ❹ $750-1000
☐ 387 ...... 5¾" .... (CE).... ❺ $250-350

HUM 388
Little Band, Candleholder
This piece is a candleholder with three figurines, HUM 389, HUM 390 and HUM 391, attached to a round ceramic base. Modeled by master sculptor Gerhard Skrobek in December 1967. It has an incised 1968 copyright date.

HUM 388 M
Little Band, Candleholder on Music Box
Same as HUM 388 but fastened on a music box. There are variations in type of music box as well as tunes played. The music box is usually Swiss-made and not produced by Goebel.

☐ 388	3 x 4¾"	(OE)	❹	$150-175
☐ 388	3 x 4¾"	(OE)	❺	$135-140
☐ 388	3 x 4¾"	(OE)	❻	$132
☐ 388M	3 x 4¾"	(OE)	❹	$210-225
☐ 388M	3 x 4¾"	(OE)	❺	$204-210
☐ 388M	3 x 4¾"	(OE)	❻	$204

389   390   391

HUM 389   Girl With Sheet of Music
One of a set of three sometimes referred to as the "Little Band." Originally modeled by master sculptor Gerhard Skrobek in May 1968. It has an incised 1968 copyright date and only found in trademarks 4, 5 and 6.

HUM 390   Boy With Accordion
One of a set of three sometimes referred to as the "Little Band." Originally modeled by master sculptor Gerhard Skrobek in May 1968. It has an incised 1968 copyright date and only found in trademarks 4, 5 and 6.

HUM 391   Girl With Trumpet
One of a set of three sometimes referred to as the "Little Band." Originally modeled by master sculptor Gerhard Skrobek in May 1968. It has an incised 1968 copyright date and only found in trademarks 4, 5 and 6.

☐ 389 ...... 2½" .... (OE).... ❹ $35-50
☐ 389 ...... 2½" .... (OE).... ❺ $32-35
☐ 389 ...... 2½" .... (OE).... ❻ $31.50

☐ 390 ...... 2½" .... (OE).... ❹ $35-50
☐ 390 ...... 2½" .... (OE).... ❺ $32-35
☐ 390 ...... 2½" .... (OE).... ❻ $31.50

☐ 391 ...... 2½" .... (OE).... ❹ $35-50
☐ 391 ...... 2½" .... (OE).... ❺ $32-35
☐ 391 ...... 2½" .... (OE).... ❻ $31.50

392 392M

HUM 392
Little Band (on base)
Same as HUM 388 but without socket for
candle. Modeled by master sculptor Gerhard Skrobek in May 1968. It has an incised 1968 copyright date.

HUM 392 M
Little Band on Music Box
Same as HUM 392 but fastened on a
music box. There are variations in type of
music box as well as in tunes played. The
music box is usually Swiss-made and not
produced by Goebel.

☐ 392 ...... 3 x 4¾" ..... (OE).... ❹ $150-175
☐ 392 ...... 3 x 4¾" ..... (OE).... ❺ $135-140
☐ 392 ...... 3 x 4¾" ..... (OE).... ❻ $132

☐ 392M ..... 3 x 4¾" ..... (OE).... ❹ $210-225
☐ 392M ..... 3 x 4¾" ..... (OE).... ❺ $204-210
☐ 392M ..... 3 x 4¾" ..... (OE).... ❻ $204

HUM 393
Holy Water Font, Dove (PFE)
This holy water font was modeled by master sculptor Gerhard Skrobek in June 1968. The inscription reads: "Come Holy Spirit." Now listed on factory records as a Possible Future Edition (PFE) and may be released at some time in the future.

☐ 393 . . . . . . 2¾ x 4¼" . . . (PFE) . . . .

HUM 394
Timid Little Sister
First released in the U.S. market in 1981 along with five other figurines. Originally modeled by master sculptor Gerhard Skrobek in February 1972. It has an incised 1972 copyright date on the underside of the base. The original issue price was $190 in 1981. The figurine was listed as a PFE in our 1979 "M.I. Hummel" book.

☐ 394 . . . . . . 7" . . . . (OE) . . . . ❻ $200

HUM 395
Shepherd Boy (PFE)
Originally named "Young Shepherd" on old factory records, but later changed to "Shepherd Boy." This figurine was modeled by master sculptor Gerhard Skrobek in February 1971. It is now listed as a Possible Future Edition (PFE) on factory records and may be released at some future date.

☐ 395 . . . . . . 6 to 6½" . . . . . (PFE) . . . .

HUM 396
Ride Into Christmas
This design was first introduced in the U.S. market in 1972. First modeled by master sculptor Gerhard Skrobek in December 1970. It has an incised 1971 copyright date. The original issue price was $48.50 on the 1972 price list. A smaller model was released in 1982 with the incised number 396 2/0 and incised 1981 copyright date. The small version was also modeled by Gerhard Skrobek but in 1980. The original issue price was $95 in 1982. According to factory information, the large size will eventually be changed to 396/I. This same motif is used on the 1975 Annual Plate, HUM 268.

☐ 396	. . . . . . 5¾"	. . . . (CE)	. . . . ❹	$500-750
☐ 396	. . . . . . 5¾"	. . . . (CE)	. . . . ❺	$185-225
☐ 396	. . . . . . 5¾"	. . . . (CE)	. . . . ❻	$185
☐ 396 2/0	. . . . 4¼"	. . . . (OE)	. . . . ❻	$100
☐ 396/I	. . . . . 5¾"	. . . . (OE)	. . . . ❻	$185

HUM 397
The Poet (PFE)
This figurine was first modeled by master sculptor Gerhard Skrobek in 1973. Presently listed on factory records as a Possible Future Edition (PFE) and may be released at some future date.

☐ 397 ...... 6" .... (PFE) ....

HUM 398 (PFE)
Spring Bouquet
This figurine was first modeled by master sculptor Gerhard Skrobek in 1973. Presently listed on factory records as a Possible Future Edition (PFE) and may be released at some future date.

☐ 398 ...... 6¼" .... (PFE) ....

HUM 399
Valentine Joy (CE)
This figurine was first introduced in 1980 for members of the Goebel Collectors' Club only and not sold as an Open Edition. Originally modeled by master sculptor Gerhard Skrobek from an original drawing by Sister M.I. Hummel. It has an incised 1979 copyright date along with the 6 trademark. Also bears the inscription "EXCLUSIVE SPECIAL EDITION No. 4 FOR MEMBERS OF THE GOEBEL COLLECTORS' CLUB" applied by blue decal. The original issue price was $95 in the U.S. and $105 in Canada, in addition to the member's redemption card. Translation of message on heart: "I Like You." This figurine can be purchased on the secondary market at premium prices.

□ 399 . . . . . . 5¾" . . . . (CE) . . . . ❻ $95-150

HUM 400
Well Done! (PFE)
This figurine was first modeled by master sculptor Gerhard Skrobek in 1973. Presently listed on factory records as a Possible Future Edition (PFE) and may be released at some future date.

□ 400 . . . . . . 6¼" . . . . (PFE) . . . .

HUM 401
Forty Winks (PFE)
This figurine was first modeled by master sculptor Gerhard Skrobek in 1973. Presently listed on factory records as a Possible Future Edition (PFE) and may be released at some future date.

☐ 401 ...... 5¼" .... (PFE) ....

HUM 402
True Friendship (PFE)
This figurine was first modeled by master sculptor Gerhard Skrobek in 1973. Presently listed on factory records as a Possible Future Edition (PFE) and may be released at some future date.

☐ 402 ...... 4¾" .... (PFE) ....

HUM 403
An Apple A Day (PFE)
This figurine was first modeled by master sculptor Gerhard Skrobek in 1973. Presently listed on factory records as a Possible Future Edition (PFE) and may be released at some future date.

☐ 403 . . . . . . 6½" . . . . (PFE) . . . .

HUM 404
Sad Song (PFE)
This figurine was first modeled by master sculptor Gerhard Skrobek in 1973. Presently listed on factory records as a Possible Future Edition (PFE) and may be released at some future date.

☐ 404 . . . . . . 6¼" . . . . (PFE) . . . .

HUM 405
Sing With Me (PFE)
This figurine was first modeled by master sculptor Gerhard Skrobek in 1973. Presently listed on factory records as a Possible Future Edition (PFE) and may be released at some future date.

☐ 405 . . . . . . 5" . . . . (PFE) . . . .

HUM 406
Pleasant Journey (PFE)
This figurine was first modeled by master sculptor Gerhard Skrobek in 1974. Presently listed on factory records as a Possible Future Edition (PFE) and may be released at some future date.

☐ 406 . . . . . . 7⅛ x 6½" . . . . (PFE) . . . .

HUM 407
Flute Song (PFE)
This figurine was first modeled by master sculptor Gerhard Skrobek in 1974. Presently listed on factory records as a Possible Future Edition (PFE) and may be released at some future date.

☐ 407 ...... 6" .... (PFE) ....

HUM 408 (ON)
This figurine is still in the development stage and needs some minor revisions, pending final approval by Siessen Convent.

HUM 409
Coffee Break (PFE)
This figurine was first modeled by master sculptor Gerhard Skrobek in 1976. Presently listed on factory records as a Possible Future Edition (PFE) and may be released at some future date.

☐ 409 ...... 4" .... (PFE) ....

HUM 410
Truant (PFE)
This figurine was first modeled by master sculptor Gerhard Skrobek in 1978. Presently listed on factory records as a Possible Future Edition (PFE) and may be released at some future date.

□ 410 ...... 6" .... (PFE) ....

HUM 411
Do I Dare? (PFE)
This figurine was first modeled by master sculptor Gerhard Skrobek in 1978. Presently listed on factory records as a Possible Future Edition (PFE) and may be released at some future date.

□ 411 ...... 6" .... (PFE) ....

HUM 412
Bath Time (PFE)
This figurine was first modeled by master sculptor Gerhard Skrobek in 1978. Presently listed on factory records as a Possible Future Edition (PFE) and may be released at some future date.

☐ 412 ...... 6¼" .... (PFE) ....

HUM 413
Whistler's Duet (PFE)
This figurine was first modeled by master sculptor Gerhard Skrobek in 1979. Presently listed on factory records as a Possible Future Edition (PFE) and may be released at some future date.

☐ 413 ...... 4¼" .... (PFE) ....

HUM 414
In Tune
First released in the U.S. market in 1981.
Modeled by Gerhard Skrobek in 1979.
This figurine was designed to match the
fourth edition of the annual bell series,
HUM 703 "In Tune" 1981 Annual. The figurine
has an incised 1979 copyright date
on the bottom of the base and is found
only in 6 trademark. The original issue
price was $115 in 1981.

☐ 414 ...... 4" .... (OE).... ❻ $120

HUM 415
Thoughtful
First released in the U.S. market in 1981.
Modeled by Gerhard Skrobek in 1979.
This figurine was designed to match the
third edition of the annual bell series,
HUM 702 "Thoughtful" 1980 Annual. The
figurine has an incised 1980 copyright
date on the bottom of the base and is
found only in 6 trademark. The original
issue price was $105 in 1981.

☐ 415 ...... 4½" .... (OE).... ❻ $110

HUM 416 (ON)
This figurine is still in the development stage and needs some minor revisions, pending final approval by Siessen Convent.

HUM 417 (ON)
This figurine is still in the development stage and needs some minor revisions, pending final approval by Siessen Convent.

HUM 418
What's New? (PFE)
This figurine was first modeled by master sculptor Gerhard Skrobek in 1980. Presently listed on factory records as a Possible Future Edition (PFE) and may be released at some future date.

☐ 418 . . . . . . 5¼" . . . . (PFE) . . . .

HUM 419
Good Luck! (PFE)
This figurine was first modeled by master sculptor Gerhard Skrobek in 1981. Presently listed on factory records as a Possible Future Edition (PFE) and may be released at some future date.

☐ 419 . . . . . . 6¼" . . . . (PFE) . . . .

HUM 420
Is It Raining? (PFE)
This figurine was first modeled by master sculptor Gerhard Skrobek in 1981. Presently listed on factory records as a Possible Future Edition (PFE) and may be released at some future date.

☐ 420 . . . . . . 6¼" . . . . (PFE) . . . .

HUM 421
It's Cold
This figurine was first introduced in 1982 for members of the Goebel Collectors' Club only and not sold as an Open Edition. Originally modeled by master sculptor Gerhard Skrobek from an original drawing by Sister M.I. Hummel. It has an incised 1981 copyright date along with the 6 trademark. Also bears the inscription "EXCLUSIVE SPECIAL EDITION No. 6 FOR MEMBERS OF THE GOEBEL COLLECTORS' CLUB" applied by blue decal. The official issue price was $80 in the U.S. and $95 in Canada, in addition to the member's redemption card. This figurine can be purchased in the secondary market at premium prices.

☐ 421 . . . . . . 5-5¼" . . . . (OE) . . . . ⊙ $80

HUM 422
What Now?
This is the latest edition produced for members of the Goebel Collectors' Club for the 1983-1984 year. The "EXCLUSIVE SPECIAL EDITION No. 7" is for members only and will not be sold as an Open Edition. Originally modeled by master sculptor Gerhard Skrobek from an original drawing by Sister M.I. Hummel. It has an incised 1982 copyright date along with the 6 trademark. Also bears the inscription "EXCLUSIVE SPECIAL EDITION No. 7 FOR MEMBERS OF THE GOEBEL COLLECTORS' CLUB" applied by blue decal. The official issue price is $90 in the U.S. and $110 in Canada, in addition to the member's redemption card. There is still time for you to join the club and receive your redemption card for the purchase of this figurine.

☐ 422 . . . . . . 5¼" . . . . (OE) . . . . ⊙ $90

HUM 432
Knit One, Purl One
First released in the U.S market in 1983.
Modeled by master sculptor Gerhard
Skrobek in 1982. This figurine was designed especially to match the sixth edition of the annual bell series, HUM 705
"Knit One" 1983 annual. The figurine has
an incised 1982 copyright date on the bottom of the base and is found only in 6
trademark. The original issue price was
$52 in 1983.

☐ 432 . . . . . . 3" . . . . (OE) . . . . ❻ $52

HUM 690   Smiling Through, Plaque (CE)
This round plaque was first issued in 1978 for members of the Goebel Collectors' Club
only and not sold as an Open Edition. Originally modeled by master sculptor Gerhard
Skrobek from an original drawing by Sister M.I. Hummel. There is nothing incised on
the back but the inscription "EXCLUSIVE SPECIAL EDITION No. 2 HUM 690 FOR
MEMBERS OF THE GOEBEL COLLECTORS' CLUB" is applied by blue decal. Also has
5 trademark and W. Germany 1978. No holes are provided for hanging. The original
issue price was $50 in the U.S. and $55 in Canada, in addition to the member's redemption card. This plaque can be purchased on the secondary market at premium prices.

☐ 690 . . . . . . 5¾" . . . . (CE) . . . . ❺ $50-75

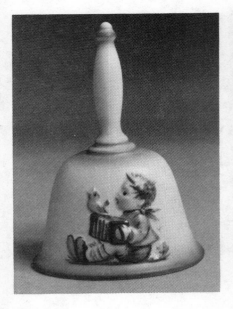

HUM 700
Annual Bell 1978, Let's Sing (CE)
First edition in a series of annual bells.
The motif of HUM 110 "Let's Sing" is in
bas-relief on the front, and 1978 is embossed in red on the reverse side along
with the "M.I. Hummel" signature. "HUM
700" is affixed by blue decal along with
the 5 trademark on the inside of bell.

HUM 701
Annual Bell 1979, Farewell (CE)
Second edition in a series of annual bells.
The motif of HUM 65 "Farewell" is in bas-
relief on the front, and 1979 is embossed
in red on the reverse side along with the
"M.I. Hummel" signature. "HUM 701" is
affixed by blue decal along with the 5
trademark on the inside of bell.

☐ 700 ..... 6" .... (CE) .... $50 issue price
☐ 700 ..... 6" .... (CE) .... ❺ $100-150

☐ 701 ..... 6" .... (CE) .... $70 issue price
☐ 701 ..... 6" .... (CE) .... ❺ $70-85

HUM 702
Annual Bell 1980, Thoughtful (CE)
Third edition in a series of annual bells. The motif of HUM 415 "Thoughtful" is in bas-relief on the front, and 1980 is embossed in red on the reverse side along with the "M.I. Hummel" signature. "HUM 702" is affixed by blue decal along with the 6 trademark on the inside of bell.

HUM 703
Annual Bell 1981, In Tune (CE)
Fourth edition of the annual bell series. The motif of HUM 414 "In Tune" is in bas-relief on the front, and 1981 is embossed in red on the reverse side along with the "M.I. Hummel" signature. "HUM 703" is affixed by blue decal along with the 6 trademark on the inside of bell.

☐ 702 ...... 6" .... (CE) .... $85 issue price
☐ 702 ...... 6" .... (CE).... ⑥ $85

☐ 703 ...... 6" .... (OE) .... $85 issue price
☐ 703 ...... 6" ...·..... (OE).... ⑥ $85

HUM 704
Annual Bell 1982, She Loves Me (CE)
Fifth edition of the annual bell series. The motif of HUM 174 "She Loves Me, She Loves Me Not!" is in bas-relief on the front, and 1982 is embossed in red on the reverse side along with the "M.I. Hummel" signature. "HUM 704" is affixed by blue decal along with the 6 trademark on the inside of bell.

HUM 705
Annual Bell 1983, Knit One
Sixth edition of the annual bell series. The motif of HUM 432 "Knit One, Purl Two" is in bas-relief on the front, and 1983 is embossed in red on the reverse side along with the "M.I. Hummel" signature. "HUM 705" is affixed by blue decal along with the 6 trademark on the inside of bell.

☐ 704 . . . . . . 6" . . . . (CE) . . . . ❻ . . . . $85 issue price
☐ 704 . . . . . . 6" . . . . (CE) . . . . ❻ $85

☐ 705 . . . . . . 6" . . . . (OE) . . . . ❻ . . . . $90 issue price
☐ 705 . . . . . . 6" . . . . (OE) . . . . ❻ $90

HUM 706
Annual Bell 1984, Mountaineer
Seventh edition of the annual bell series.
The motif of HUM 315 "Mountaineer" is
in bas-relief on the front, and 1984 is embossed in red on the reverse side along
with the "M.I. Hummel" signature.
"HUM 706" is affixed by blue decal along
with the 6 trademark on the inside of bell.

☐ 706 ...... 6" .... (ON) .....   **HUM 707-799 OPEN NUMBERS**

International "M.I. Hummel" Figurines

The following eight "M.I. Hummel" figurines are the original "Hungarian" figurines discovered in 1976 by a man in Vienna, Austria. He had acquired them from a lady in Budapest, who had purchased them at the weekly flea market —one at a time, over a six-month period. He in turn sold them to (this author) collector Robert L. Miller, a supermarket owner in Eaton, Ohio, as a gift for his wife, Ruth.

"M.I. Hummel" figurines have always been typically German, with German-style dress or costumes. In 1940 the W. Goebel company decided to produce a line of "M.I. Hummel" figurines in the national dress of other countries. Sister M.I. Hummel made many sketches of children in their native costumes. Master modelers Reinhold Unger and Arthur Moeller then turned the sketches into the adorable figurines you see on the following pages. Due to the events of World War II, production of the International Figurines series was not started. After the discovery in 1976 of the "Hungarian" figurines, a thorough search of the factory was conducted, including the checking and re-checking of old records. Twenty-four prototypes were found and are pictured here. Most of the people involved in the original project are no longer living; therefore the information contained here may not be absolutely accurate or complete. Since 1976, several duplicates of some models and new variations of others have been found, usually selling in the $3,000 to $7,000 price range, depending on condition. Several models have also been found *without* the "M.I. Hummel" signature; these would have much less value to most collectors. Author/collector Miller says,"I feel certain that there are still more rare finds to be made in the future, maybe even some Russian models! Happy Hunting!"

HUM 809   HUM 807   HUM 832   HUM 854

HUM 904   HUM 806   HUM 841   HUM 851

HUM 806 *Bulgarian* **A. Moeller, 1940**

HUM 808 *Bulgarian* **A. Moeller, 1940**

HUM 811 *Bulgarian* **R. Unger, 1940**

HUM 809 *Bulgarian* **A. Moeller, 1940**

HUM 810   **Bulgarian**   **R. Unger, 1940**

HUM 810   **Bulgarian**   **R. Unger, 1940**

HUM 812   **Serbian**   **R. Unger, 1940**

HUM 812   **Serbian**   **R. Unger, 1940**

HUM 813 **Serbian** *R. Unger, 1940*

HUM 824 **Swedish** *A. Moeller, 1940*

HUM 824 **Swedish** *A. Moeller, 1940*

HUM 825 **Swedish** *A. Moeller, 1940*

HUM 825   **Swedish**   **A. Moeller, 1940**

HUM 831   **Slovak**   **R. Unger, 1940**

HUM 832   **Slovak**   **R. Unger, 1940**

HUM 833   **Slovak**   **R. Unger, 1940**

HUM 841   **Czech**   **R. Unger, 1940**   **HUM 842**   **Czech**   **R. Unger, 1940**

HUM 851   **Hungarian**   **A. Moeller, 1940**   **HUM 852**   **Hungarian**   **A. Moeller, 1940**

HUM 852   *Hungarian*   *A. Moeller, 1940*

HUM 853   *Hungarian*   *A. Moeller, 1940*

HUM 853   *Hungarian*   *A. Moeller, 1940*

HUM 854   *Hungarian*   *A. Moeller, 1940*

HUM 904   *Serbian*   **R. Unger, 1940**

HUM 913   *Serbian*   **R. Unger, 1940**

HUM 947   *Serbian*   **A. Moeller, 1940**

HUM 968   *Serbian*   **R. Unger, 1940**

Other Hummel Related Items

Factory Workers Plate

This anniversary plate was produced by the W. Goebel Company, by and for the workers at the factory where the Goebel annual plates are manufactured. Probably as few as 100 were produced and were not made available to the general public. The "M.I. Hummel" signature is on each of the ten individual plates.

Bust of Sister M.I. Hummel

HU 1

This white bisque bust in the likeness of Sister Maria Innocentia Hummel was created by master sculptor Gerhard Skrobek in 1965. It was originally used as a display piece for showrooms or dealer displays featuring Hummel items. It has the signature of "Skrobek 1965" in addition to "HU 1" incised on the back. In recent years it has become a collector's item and is sought after by many avid "M.I. Hummel" lovers. They were originally given to dealers at no cost; but we did, however, purchase two of these large busts in the early 1970's from a store in New York at a cost of $30 each. A smaller version of the same bust with the "M.I. Hummel" signature incised on the front of the base was put on the market in 1967 with the incised number "HU 2" and the 4 trademark. These originally sold for $6 each. This same small-size bust was again put on the market in 1977 for a brief time, retailing for $15 to $17 each, but has once again been discontinued from current production. A third variation of the Sister Hummel bust was issued in 1979 as: "EXCLUSIVE SPECIAL EDITION No. 3 FOR MEMBERS OF THE GOEBEL COLLECTORS' CLUB" only. This piece has an incised "HU 3" as well as 1978 incised copyright date on the bottom. It is in full color with the "M.I. Hummel" signature painted in white on the front. While these busts are not officially classified as true Hummel figurines, they do make a nice addition to any Hummel collection.

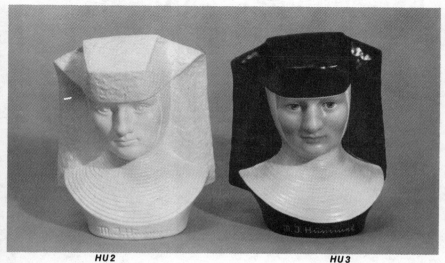

HU2   **HU3**

☐ HU1 .... 13" .... (CE).... ❹ $500-1,000
☐ HU2 .... 5½" .... (CE).... ❹ $50-100
☐ HU2 .... 5½" .... (CE).... ❺ $25-50
☐ HU3 .... 5½" .... (CE).... ❺ $75

Unnumbered "M.I. Hummel" Figurine
"Madonna With Wings"

This very rare, unusual, signed "M.I. Hummel" figurine is truly a collector's item. Found several years ago in Munich, Germany, this beautiful "Madonna with Wings" figurine had been in the possession of a German family for many years, but they could not remember its background or from where it came. The figurine is not numbered nor does it have a trademark—only an incised "X" on the bottom, in addition to the "M.I. Hummel" signature on the back. Research reveals that this piece was in all probability modeled by master sculptor Reinhold Unger in the late 1930's or early 1940's. For some unknown reason it was not approved for production by the Siessen Convent or possibly by Sister Hummel herself. This piece, however, is found pictured in an old 1950 Goebel catalogue listed as "Mel 08" and priced at 11 DM. It is not known whether it was actually produced and marketed at that time. If they were produced, they would not have the "M.I. Hummel" signature. It is the signature that makes this figurine unique, rare and fascinating.

International "M.I. Hummel" Festival Commemorative Bisque Plaques

These white bisque plaques are produced by W. Goebel Porzellanfabrik, Rodental, West Germany, and have all been designed by master modeler Gerhard Skrobek. Each plaque is designed in bas-relief, depicting a Hummel figurine on the front, signed with the familiar "M.I. Hummel" signature on the base. The back commemorates the date and location of each Festival. This is the first and only time that Goebel and the Siessen Convent have been willing to use the "M.I. Hummel" signature in this fashion to commemorate a special event. The community of Eaton, Ohio, feels highly honored that W. Goebel and Siessen Convent would see fit to commemorate the International Festival in this manner.

Actual size: 3" diameter.
Original issue price $10.

☐ 1979	..... 3"	.... (CE)	.... $25-30
☐ 1980	..... 3"	.... (CE)	.... $20-25
☐ 1981	..... 3"	.... (CE)	.... $15-20
☐ 1982	..... 3"	.... (CE)	.... $10-15

The "Mel" Signature: Hum"mel"

A collector will occasionally happen on to a "Hummel"-like figurine that does not have the usual "M.I. Hummel" signature on it. The figurine will have all of the general appearances of an older genuine "M.I. Hummel" figurine, including the Goebel factory trademark, in addition to the letters "Mel" (the last part of "Hummel") incised on it.

To the best of my knowledge, these items have been designed from original drawings by Sister M.I. Hummel, but for some undetermined reasons were not approved by the Siessen Convent for inclusion in the "M.I. Hummel" line of figurines. The Convent of Siessen, near Salgau in West Germany, was the home of Sister Hummel for many years, and now owns or controls much of her artwork. To this day, the Convent must give approval to the Goebel factory for any designs bearing the "M.I. Hummel" name.

Notice the photo of the "Child in Bed" candy dish and the original Hummel drawing upon which it is based. Goebel master sculptor Arthur Moeller modeled this piece in 1945. Since it did not win convent approval, it was later marketed with "Mel 6" incised on the bottom of it. Several other "Mel" items have appeared through the years. The most common of these are the Mel 1, Mel 2, and Mel 3 candlestick holders, modeled by former master sculptor Reinhold Unger in 1939. In the mid-1950's, these items were remodeled by master sculptor Gerhard Skrobek and assigned the model numbers Hum 115 "Girl with Nosegay," Hum 116 "Girl with Fir Tree" and Hum 117 "Boy with Horse" candlesticks with the "M.I. Hummel" signature.

Also modeled by master sculptor Arthur Moeller were Mel 4 "Box with Boy on Top" in 1942, Mel 5 "Box with Girl on Top" in 1942, Mel 6 "Box with Child in Bed on Top" in 1945 and Mel 7 "Box with Sitting Child on Top" in 1946. All "Mel" items were discontinued in 1962, according to Goebel factory information.

Also pictured here is the "Mel 7" candy box and the probable Hummel drawing which inspired it. Another recent discovery came, unexpectedly, from an old 1950 catalogue, apparently distributed only in Germany, containing a photograph of the "Madonna with Wings" designated as "Mel 08." This is the same beautiful "Madonna with Wings" we added to our collection last year when some very good German friends of ours located it in Munich. Our "Madonna," however, has an incised "M.I. Hummel" signature on the back base and an incised "X" on the bottom rather than a model number, indicating that it was an un-numbered factory prototype. This catalogue listing as a "Mel" would tend to confirm that it was, indeed, a Hummel design that was rejected for some unknown reason by the Sisters of Siessen Convent.

Apparently, the "Mel" designation must have been a "catch-all" label intended as a way of marketing these rejected items. I am of the opinion, however, that it was also used to designate *experimental* items. In our years of research, we have accidentally "stumbled" on two other figurine models with the "Mel" label. Both of them were "International" designs. The first was an unsigned figurine of a girl in Bulgarian costume with "Mel 9" on the bottom. The other item is in our personal collection—a boy in Swedish costume. It has the usual incised "M.I. Hummel" signature along with "Mel 24" incised on the bottom.

How many more "Mel" designs will show up in the future is anyone's guess. At least the collectors and readers of this article now have all the information we possess. We will continue our research and pass on any new facts we may find. We ask that readers also share with us any knowledge they may have.

Two original drawings and the "Mel" pieces they inspired: top, "Child in Bed" and above, "Box with Sitting Child on Top."

This article originally appeared in *Collector Editions*, Fall 1982.

Copies From Around the World

It has been said that one of the most sincere compliments that can be given to an artist is to have his work copied. I think this holds true when it comes to the "M.I. Hummel" figurines. W. Goebel Porzellanfabrik of Rodental, West Germany, has had the exclusive rights to produce Hummel figurines, based upon the artwork of Sister Maria Innocentia Hummel, since 1935. The figurines have become so popular over the years that many countries around the world have tried to copy these designs. Korea, Taiwan, Japan, Germany, England and even the United States have all made copies. Most of these are quite inferior in quality when compared to the originals made by Goebel. But a few of the copies are better than others—namely, the Japanese and the English—and we've chosen to show you some of these better copies here.

The Japanese have probably succeeded in making the best copies, with the English running a close second. The Japanese finish and colors are more like the originals and sometimes, at first glance, they may fool even an experienced collector. The Japanese have copied the designs but, to my knowledge, have never gone so far as to copy the familiar "M.I. Hummel" signature. On the other hand, the English finish is quite shiny and they did copy the signature on their early production models. The English figurines were made by "Beswick" during the war years of 1940 and 1941.

It is, of course, most unethical, if not always illegal, to make copies of the Hummel figurines. The question of copies, look-alikes, fakes and their legality is a lengthy and complicated subject and it is not our intention here to delve into that issue. We want only to show readers a few of the better examples of copies that have been done, so as to show how closely they may resemble the originals.

Top photo: HUM 97 (far left) beside English copy #903; HUM 5 (far right) beside English copy #906. Middle photo at left, HUM 71 (far left) with English copy #908; photo at right, HUM 184 (far right) with Japanese copy. HUM 201 with Japanese copy at left.

This article originally appeared in *Collector Editions*, Winter 1982.

Goebel Camels:
Traditionally Used With "M.I. Hummel" Nativity Sets

These three Goebel camels were designed to be used with the "M.I. Hummel" Nativity Sets, either HUM 214 or HUM 260. The standing camel HX 306/O has an incised 1960 copyright date and has been on the market since the early 1960's. The kneeling camel (dromedary) and the lying camel (Bactrian) were both released in 1980 for the first time. All three have been produced both in full color and white overglaze (unpainted) finishes. All models are in current production and are usually found wherever the "M.I. Hummel" figurines are sold.

☐ HX 306/0	8½"	(OE)	Standing	(color)	$110
☐ HX 306/0	8½"	(OE)	Standing	(white)	$60
☐ 46 820-12	5½"	(OE)	Kneeling	(color)	$110
☐ 46 820-12	5½"	(OE)	Kneeling	(white)	$60
☐ 46 821-11	4½"	(OE)	Lying	(color)	$110
☐ 46 821-11	4½"	(OE)	Lying	(white)	$60